The **Rough** Gui

The Grand Canyon

written and researched by

Greg Ward

**ROUGH
GUIDES**

www.roughguides.com

Contents

Hiking the Grand Canyon colour section
following p.112

◄◄ View from Mather Point in winter ◄ Mooney Falls, Havasupai Indian Reservation

Introduction to

the Grand Canyon

Although almost five million people come to see the Grand Canyon of the Colorado every year, it seems to remain beyond the grasp of the human imagination. No photograph, no set of statistics, can prepare you for such overwhelming vastness. At more than one mile deep, it's an inconceivable abyss; varying in its central stretch from four to eighteen miles wide, it's an endless expanse of bewildering shapes and colours, glaring desert brightness and impenetrable shadow, stark promontories and soaring never-to-be-climbed sandstone pinnacles.

While no one is disappointed with their first stunning sight of the chasm, visitors often find themselves struggling to understand what can appear as a remote and impassive spectacle. They race frantically from viewpoint to viewpoint, forever imagining that the next one will be the "best", the place from which the whole thing finally makes sense. This book is an attempt to guide you beyond that initial anxiety. More than anything, it's aimed at encouraging you to slow down, to appreciate whatever small portion of the canyon may be displayed in front of you at any one moment, and to allow enough time for the bigger picture to develop. You don't have to learn the names of all those buttes and mesas – dubbed Shiva Temple, Wotans Throne and so on in a spate of late-Victorian fervour – and you may not ever be able to identify all the different rock strata or desert plants. The longer you linger at the canyon, however, the greater the chance that you will start to hear it speak.

Back in the 1920s, the average visitor would stay at the Grand Canyon for two or three weeks. These days, two or three hours is more typical,

INTRODUCTION | WHERE TO GO | WHEN TO GO

The Grand Canyon in figures

• The total length of the Colorado River is 1450 miles; within the Grand Canyon it measures 277 miles, from Lees Ferry to the Grand Wash Cliffs.

• The river is on average 300ft wide and 40ft deep, and its temperature remains at 48°F year-round.

• Grand Canyon National Park measures 1904 square miles or 1.2 million acres; that's roughly half the size of Yellowstone National Park, a third the size of Death Valley National Park and a tenth the size of the largest US park, Wrangell-St Elias in Alaska.

• The canyon averages ten miles across and one mile deep. Its narrowest point is in Marble Canyon, at 600ft wide, while the maximum width from rim to rim is eighteen miles.

• The highest point on the North Rim, Point Imperial, is 8803ft high; on the South Rim it's Navajo Point, at 7498ft. The elevation at Phantom Ranch, on the central canyon floor, is 2400ft, while at the west end of the canyon, at Lake Mead, it's 1200 feet.

of which perhaps forty minutes are spent actually looking at the canyon. That's partly because most people now arrive by car. As the only part you can reach in a car is the **rim**, seeing the canyon has thus come to mean seeing it from above, from a distance. If you really want to engage with it, however, you need literally to get into it – to **hike** or ride a **mule** down the many inner-canyon trails, to sleep in the backcountry campgrounds or in the cabins at **Phantom Ranch** down beside the river, to **raft** through the whitewater rapids of the river itself.

Mapping and defining precisely what constitutes the "Grand Canyon" has always been controversial; **Grand Canyon National Park**

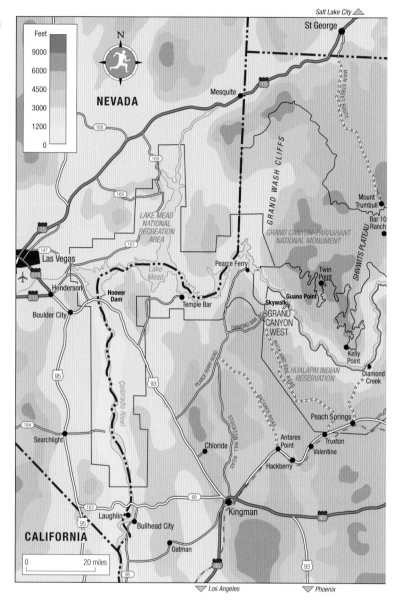

covers a relatively small proportion of the greater Grand Canyon area. Only since 1975 has the park included the full 277-mile length of the Colorado River from Lees Ferry in the east to Grand Wash Cliffs near Lake Mead in the west, and even now for most of that distance it's restricted to the narrow strip of the inner gorge. Ranchers whose animals graze in the federal forests

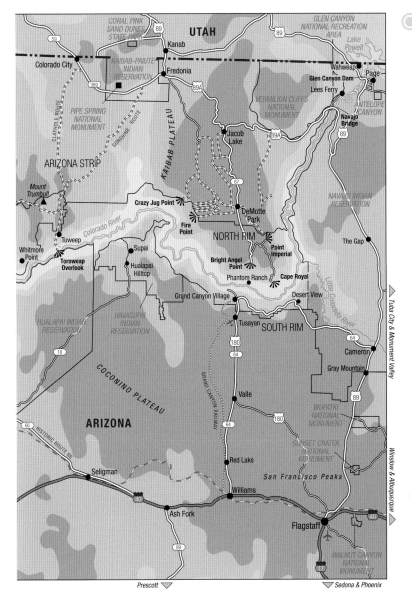

to either side, mining companies eager to exploit the mineral wealth hidden in the ancient rocks, engineers seeking to divert the river to feed the deserts of southern Arizona, and Native Americans who have lived in the canyon since long before the first Europeans reached North America, have all combined to minimize the size of the park.

Where to go

The vast majority of visitors arrive at the **South Rim** – it's much easier to get to, there are far more facilities (mainly at **Grand Canyon Village**, inside the park), and it's open year-round. Another lodge and campground sit atop the **North Rim**, which by virtue of its isolation feels more like a wilderness destination, but at a thousand feet higher this entire area is usually closed by snow from late October until mid-May. On both rims, the main activity for most visitors consists of gazing over the gorge from overlooks placed at strategic intervals along the canyon-edge roads. Both also serve as the starting points for countless **hiking** trails down into the canyon, and it's even possible to hike all the way from one to the other, along the so-called Corridor Trails, a trek that requires a minimum of two days from rim to rim.

Simply to drive from one rim to the other takes 215 miles, while to complete a loop around the entire national park would require you to drive almost eight hundred miles, and pass as far west as Las Vegas, Nevada. Even that long haul would bypass several of the most interesting detours in the greater Grand Canyon region, into the baffling chequerboard of federal, state, Indian and private lands that lies beyond the park. These include several **national monuments**, including two huge ones, **Vermilion Cliffs** and **Grand Canyon–Parashant**, created in 2000, a couple of **national recreation areas** at either end, **Glen Canyon** and **Lake Mead**; two sections of the **Kaibab National Forest**, north and south of the river; and four neighbouring **Indian reservations**, belonging to the **Havasupai**, the **Hualapai**, the **Kaibab Paiute** and the **Navajo**. While most (though not quite all) provide recreational possibilities for visitors, detailed throughout this book, few offer any kind of

▼ Angels Window at Cape Royal

What to bring

Whatever time of year you visit, expect to need **warm clothing**, especially for the evenings, and something **waterproof** to keep off sudden rains. Temperatures vary so much, and so rapidly, that it makes sense to dress in layers. Detailed advice on what to bring if you're **hiking** appears on p.91, and if you're **rafting** on p.193. Otherwise, if you're touring by car, and just sightseeing without strenuous physical activity, no specialist equipment is necessary. Be sure, however, that you have adequate protection from the **sun**, including a broad-brimmed hat, sunblock and sunglasses.

accommodation or other facilities. For that, you need to call in instead at the many busy, commercialized gateway towns on all sides of the canyon, from **Flagstaff** and **Williams** in the south, to **Kanab** in the north.

When to go

There's no definitive answer as to which is the **best season to visit**. Summer on the South Rim can be murderously crowded and, for hikers especially, uncomfortably hot, so if you have the choice, and you plan to spend a lot of time out on the trails, spring and autumn are preferable. That's less of an issue on the North Rim, which receives far fewer visitors, and stays significantly cooler. In winter, the scope for outdoor activities is greatly reduced, and the North Rim is closed altogether, but the South Rim is transformed into a haven of peace and tranquillity. In terms of aesthetics, the canyon can look radiant, flecked with snow, on a crisp winter's day; alive with colour when the cactuses and wildflowers blossom in the spring; and suffused with a golden glow in autumn, as the trees close to rim level start to turn.

The **climate** varies with both the **season** and the **altitude**. Although most people picture the canyon as being in barren desert, in fact both the north and south rims are set in cool, high forests. The **North Rim**, the higher of the two at 8000ft, receives so much snow that it's completely cut off all winter. Nights there remain distinctly chilly at the start and end of each season, and only between June and August do normal daytime temperatures rise above 70°F (21°C).

The **South Rim** is a thousand feet lower, which makes enough of a difference for the visitor facilities to remain open year-round. However, temperatures still drop well below freezing at night between late October and April, so driving conditions can be treacherous, with occasional road closures, and the upper portions of hiking trails may be dangerously icy. Only between May and September can you expect daytime highs above 70°F (21°C).

▼ Kaibab Suspension Bridge, near Phantom Ranch

The **Inner Canyon** is a very different proposition. At river level, almost 5000ft below the South Rim, thermometer readings in excess of 100°F (38°C) are recorded on most days between late May and early September, and it's unlikely to drop below 70°F (21°C) even at night. Winter temperatures are a little cooler than you might expect, because so little direct sun manages to reach the bottom of the canyon, but it very seldom freezes down there, and December highs remain well over 50°F (10°C).

Precipitation is seldom severe enough to spoil a visit; the greatest risk of heavy rain comes in August, when afternoon thunderstorms sweep in (and can create localized flash floods), but they're spectacular to watch and normally blow over fast. However, it has to be said that at any time of year you may turn up and find the canyon invisible beneath a layer of cloud or fog; on average around four times per year, it remains totally obscured all day.

Average daily temperatures and rainfall

	Jan	Feb	Mar	Apr	May	Jun	Jul	Aug	Sep	Oct	Nov	Dec
South Rim												
Max/min (°F)	41/18	45/21	51/25	60/32	70/39	81/47	84/54	82/53	76/47	65/36	52/27	43/20
Precipitation (inches)	1.32	1.55	1.38	0.93	0.66	1.81	1.81	2.25	1.56	1.10	0.94	1.64
Inner canyon												
Max/min (°F)	56/36	62/42	71/48	82/56	92/63	101/72	106/78	103/75	97/69	84/58	68/46	57/37
Precipitation (inches)	0.68	0.75	0.79	0.47	0.36	0.84	0.84	1.40	0.97	0.65	0.43	0.87
North Rim												
Max/min (°F)	37/16	39/18	44/21	53/29	62/34	73/40	77/46	75/45	69/39	59/31	46/24	40/20
Precipitation (inches)	3.17	3.22	2.65	1.73	1.17	1.93	1.93	2.85	1.99	1.38	1.48	2.83

16

things not to miss

With so many things to see and do in the Grand Canyon area, it takes careful planning to make the most of each day. The list below highlights several of the most popular and rewarding attractions in the region. They're arranged in four colour-coded categories to help you find the best to do, see and experience. All have a page reference to take you straight into the Guide, where you can find out more.

01 **Toroweap Point** Page **143** • The remotest major overlook within the national park, perched above sheer 3000ft-high cliffs at the far west end of the North Rim, Toroweap offers unique and extraordinary views into the Inner Gorge.

02 **El Tovar Hotel** Page **53** • The jewel of Grand Canyon Village, this historic hotel provides the South Rim's finest food and lodging.

03 **The Skywalk** Page **182** • Grand Canyon West's much-vaunted glass walkway may not quite live up to the hype, but it's still an undeniable thrill.

04 **Condors at the South Rim** Page **40** • The majestic silhouette of a Californian condor, soaring on its 9ft wings above the canyon, makes an unforgettable spectacle.

06 **Lees Ferry** Page **126** • This scenic little outpost, the launching point for all Grand Canyon rafting trips, has a fascinating and romantic history of its own.

07 **Phantom Ranch** Page **96** • Unless you're on a major backpacking expedition, by far the best way to see the Colorado River close up is by spending a night at Phantom Ranch.

05 **The Bright Angel Trail** Page **54** • It's the most popular hiking trail within the park precisely because it provides such a superb introduction to life below the rim.

08 **Flagstaff** Page **149** • Much the liveliest and most appealing of the gateway towns, this high-desert crossroads remains redolent of the Wild West.

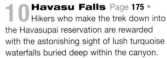

10 **Havasu Falls** Page **175** • Hikers who make the trek down into the Havasupai reservation are rewarded with the astonishing sight of lush turquoise waterfalls buried deep within the canyon.

09 **The South Kaibab Trail** Page **100** • Even if you don't make the entire hair-raising descent to the Colorado, this trail offers perhaps the finest day hikes into the canyon.

11 **Shoshone Point** Page **60** • Accessible only on foot, this little-known South Rim viewpoint provides a rare opportunity to have your very own one-on-one encounter with the Grand Canyon.

12 **Mule Ride to Phantom Ranch** Page **56** • If you fancy yourself as the star of a real-life Western movie, what better place could there be to saddle up?

13 **Antelope Canyon** Page **120** •
Irresistible if often all too crowded slot canyon, just outside Page, that's a magnet for photographers.

14 **Rafting** Page **187** • A rafting expedition through the Grand Canyon, which can take from three days to three weeks, ranks among the world's greatest outdoor experiences.

15 **Bright Angel Point** Page **72** • This superb North Rim overlook is located at the tip of a slender rocky outcrop just a short walk from Grand Canyon Lodge.

16 **Desert View Watchtower** Page **63** • Circular mock-Puebloan tower, blending into the rocks at the east end of the South Rim, which harks back to the golden years of western tourism while still providing stunning views.

Basics

Basics

Getting there

Almost all independent travellers who visit the Grand Canyon, including those who have flown to the US from overseas, drive there. Public transport to the South Rim is minimal, while to the North Rim it's virtually nonexistent. You can only arrive by plane or train at the canyon itself if you're prepared to pay an expensive excursion fare, from Las Vegas or Williams respectively, and while there is limited bus service up from both Flagstaff and Williams to the South Rim, you can't tour the park as a whole unless you have your own vehicle.

By air

For international travellers, as well as US and Canadian citizens who live beyond reasonable driving distance, the most cost-effective way to visit the canyon is to fly to **Las Vegas** or **Phoenix**, rent a car there, make a loop tour and fly home from the same airport. Not that the Grand Canyon is particularly close to either city – Phoenix is 220 miles from the South Rim, by way of Flagstaff, and 345 miles from the North Rim, via Flagstaff and Navajo Bridge; Las Vegas is 285 miles from the North Rim, via St George, and 290 miles from the South Rim, via Kingman and Williams. Las Vegas is the better bet, as it offers low airfares and car rental rates and welcomes more direct flights from overseas, but Phoenix's Sky Harbor International Airport is equally well served by major domestic carriers.

Note that while there is a small airport at **Tusayan**, near the South Rim, it's served almost exclusively by sightseeing flights from Las Vegas (see p.25). None of the national airlines serves the airport.

Flying from elsewhere in the US and Canada

Flights to the Southwest are at their most expensive in summer, which despite soaring temperatures is the peak season for travel. Prices drop from September to shortly before Christmas, and from March through to May, and are cheapest from January to February. Flying on weekends, to Las Vegas in particular, can add a hefty premium to fares; price ranges quoted below assume midweek travel.

In general, the best bargains tend to be on flights to Las Vegas. Every major US airline flies to the city, with the largest operator apart from the national carriers, being Southwest Airlines, which offers nonstop flights from more than sixty cities, ranging from Virginia Beach to Spokane. In addition, Midwest flies from Denver and Milwaukee; JetBlue has direct flights from New York (JFK) and Boston, and also from Burbank in California; SkyWest connects with Salt Lake City; and WestJet serves

Airlines

Aer Lingus Ⓦ www.aerlingus.com
Air Canada Ⓦ www.aircanada.com
Alaska Airlines Ⓦ www.alaskaair.com
American Airlines Ⓦ www.aa.com
British Airways Ⓦ www.ba.com
Continental Airlines Ⓦ www .continental.com
Delta Airlines Ⓦ www.delta.com
Hawaiian Airlines Ⓦ www .hawaiianair.com
JetBlue Ⓦ www.jetblue.com
Midwest Airlines Ⓦ www .midwestairlines.com
Qantas Airways Ⓦ www.qantas.com
Scenic Airlines Ⓦ www.scenic.com
SkyWest Ⓦ www.skywest.com
Southwest Ⓦ www.southwest.com
United Airlines Ⓦ www.united.com
US Airways Ⓦ www.usair.com
Virgin Atlantic Ⓦ www.virgin-atlantic .com
WestJet Ⓦ www.westjet.com

many Canadian destinations. It's usually possible to find return fares to Las Vegas for little more than $100 from Los Angeles, $250 from Seattle, $350 from New York and Can$350 from Toronto.

A return from New York to Phoenix should also cost from $350; equivalent figures for Chicago might be $250–300 and for Los Angeles, less than $150. Sample fares from Montréal to Phoenix start from Can$600, and from Vancouver Can$350.

Flying from Great Britain and Ireland

The only direct, nonstop flights from Britain or Ireland to Las Vegas are the Virgin Atlantic services from London Gatwick (daily) and from Manchester (Thurs & Sun). British Airways provide the only nonstop service to Phoenix, flying from London Heathrow daily except Wednesdays. With their convenient departure times and ten-hour journey duration these are by far the most appealing options, but typical return fares on both range from around £500 in winter up to around £750 in summer. Most other transatlantic carriers fly to Phoenix or Las Vegas for similar or lower fares, but all require at least one stop en route. From Britain, you can either fly nonstop to the West Coast, then double back towards the Southwest, or touch down on the East Coast and then fly west; time-wise, it makes little difference. If you'd rather keep

your flying time to a minimum, consider flying nonstop to California and driving to the Southwest from there, taking advantage of that state's low car rental rates.

From Ireland's Dublin and Shannon airports, Aer Lingus flies to Boston, Chicago, New York and Orlando; American Airlines services Chicago; Continental flies to New York; and Delta to Atlanta. Alternatively, you can fly to London and take your pick of transatlantic routes.

Flying from Australia and New Zealand

There are no direct flights to the Southwest from Australia or New Zealand, so you'll have to fly to one of the main US gateways and pick up a connecting flight or a rental car.

The cheapest route to the US, and the one offering the most flights from Australia and New Zealand, services Los Angeles, which provides plenty of onward flights to Las Vegas and Phoenix. Qantas, American Airlines and Air New Zealand fly to LA at least twice daily, while United flies once a day.

Driving to the Grand Canyon

Most drivers approach the Grand Canyon by means of the **I-40** interstate, which on its east–west route between New Mexico and southern California passes south of the canyon through both **Flagstaff** and **Williams**.

US entry regulations for travellers from overseas

Under the **Visa Waiver Program**, passport-holders from Britain, Ireland, Australia, New Zealand and most European countries do not require visas for trips to the US, so long as they stay less than ninety days and have an onward or return ticket. However, anyone planning to use the Visa Waiver Program is required to apply for **travel authorization** in advance, online. It's a very quick and straightforward process, via the website ⓦ https://esta.cbp.dhs.gov/. Fail to do so, however, and you may well be denied entry. Once you have authorization, you can simply fill in the visa waiver form that's handed out on incoming planes. Immigration control takes place at your point of arrival on US soil.

In addition, your passport must be **machine-readable**, with a barcode-style number. All children need to have their own individual passports. Holders of older non-readable passports should either obtain new ones or apply for visas prior to travel.

Prospective visitors from parts of the world not mentioned above need a valid passport and a non-immigrant visitor's visa. How you'll obtain a visa depends on what country you're in and your status when you apply, so call the nearest US embassy or consulate. For full details visit ⓦ travel.state.gov.

Further details and travel advice are available on the government websites listed on p.24.

Package tours

Although many national and international **tour companies** include the Grand Canyon on their Western-US itineraries, almost all simply stop for an hour or two on one rim or the other, with most preferring the South Rim. For anyone interested enough in exploring the canyon to have bought this book, no such company or tour is worth recommending.

Local tour companies that operate tours to and around the Grand Canyon from nearby towns are listed on p.26.

From Flagstaff, **US-180** takes around eighty miles to wind through the San Francisco Peaks and up to the **South Rim**; **AZ-64** meets it at Valle en route, to make a total drive of sixty miles between Williams and the South Rim. Drivers from southern Arizona can reach Flagstaff by taking I-17 north from Phoenix.

It's also possible to get to the South Rim from the east, by taking AZ-64 for fifty miles west from **US-89** at **Cameron**. That's the obvious way to come if you've been exploring southern Utah or the Four Corners region, and it's also the most direct route from the North Rim.

The North Rim is much more isolated. The only way to get there is via **Jacob Lake**, which stands on **US-89A** 92 miles southeast of the I-15 interstate between Las Vegas and Salt Lake City – **St George**, Utah, is the nearest town on the interstate – or roughly eighty miles southwest of **Page**, Arizona. The final 44 miles south from Jacob Lake to the North Rim are on AZ-67; when that's closed by snow, which it usually is from sometime between October and December until early May each winter, all facilities at the North Rim shut down.

By rail

The nearest that **Amtrak** trains (✆amtrak .com) come to the South Rim are the stations at **Flagstaff** and **Williams** (see p.151 & p.160 for full details). Bus connections are detailed below.

From a separate station in the heart of Williams, the historic **Grand Canyon Railway** (✆928/773-1976 or 1-800/843-8724, ✆thetrain.com), which is hauled by a steam **locomotive** in summer, runs a daily service up to the South Rim. Though it's more of a themed Western attraction than an efficient means of public transport – and thus charges return fares that range from $70 up to $190 – you don't have to travel both ways on the same day, so you can use it to enable a multi-night stay at the canyon. For full details, see p.40.

By bus

Regularly scheduled **Greyhound** buses ply the I-40 corridor south of the canyon, heading east from Las Vegas, Los Angeles and San Francisco and west from Albuquerque and beyond (✆1-800/231-2222, ✆greyhound.com). The closest stops to the canyon are at **Williams** and **Flagstaff**.

Operated by **Arizona Shuttle** (✆928/226-8060 or 1-877/226-8060, ✆arizonashuttle .com), daily buses in each direction connect Flagstaff (three times daily in summer, twice in winter) and Williams (twice daily) with the **South Rim** – for full fares and schedules, see p.41. Departing from Flagstaff's Amtrak station, the route stops at the Grand Canyon Railway's Williams Depot and the Grand Canyon IMAX Theater in Tusayan and winds up at the *Maswik Lodge* in Grand Canyon Village. Arizona Shuttle also runs frequent buses between Flagstaff and **Phoenix**.

The only scheduled bus service – or, indeed, public transport of any kind – to the **North Rim** is the Transcanyon Shuttle (✆928/638-2820, ✆trans-canyonshuttle.com), a daily van service along the 215-mile route between the North and South rims. For more details, see p.115.

Six steps to a better kind of travel

At Rough Guides we are passionately committed to travel. We feel strongly that only through travelling do we truly come to understand the world we live in and the people we share it with – plus tourism has brought a great deal of **benefit** to developing economies around the world over the last few decades. But the extraordinary growth in tourism has also damaged some places irreparably, and of course **climate change** is exacerbated by most forms of transport, especially flying. This means that now more than ever it's important to **travel thoughtfully** and **responsibly**, with respect for the cultures you're visiting – not only to derive the most benefit from your trip but also to preserve the best bits of the planet for everyone to enjoy. At Rough Guides we feel there are six main areas in which you can make a difference:

- Consider what you're contributing to the **local economy**, and how much the services you use do the same, whether it's through employing local workers and guides or sourcing locally grown produce and local services.

- Consider the **environment** on holiday as well as at home. Water is scarce in many developing destinations, and the biodiversity of local flora and fauna can be adversely affected by tourism. Try to patronize businesses that take account of this.

- Travel with a purpose, not just to tick off experiences. Consider **spending longer** in a place, and getting to know it and its people.

- Give thought to how often you **fly**. Try to avoid short hops by air and more harmful night flights.

- Consider **alternatives to flying**, travelling instead by bus, train, boat and even by bike or on foot where possible.

- Make your trips "**climate neutral**" via a reputable carbon offset scheme. All Rough Guide flights are offset, and every year we donate money to a variety of charities devoted to combating the effects of climate change.

Information, websites and maps

There's no single perfect source for information on the entire Grand Canyon region; that's the point of this book, after all. In addition to the national park itself, the area includes assorted other federally managed national monuments, national forests and the like; several Indian reservations; and four separate counties of Arizona.

Park information

The best place to find advance information about **Grand Canyon National Park** is the Park Service website (⊕nps.gov/grca), which provides information about park fees, facilities, activities and programmes. However, **accommodation** within the park is operated· on the South Rim by Xanterra Parks & Resorts

(⊕303/297-2757 or 1-888/297-2757, ⊛grand canyonlodges.com; see p.45), and on the North Rim by Forever Resorts (⊕480/337-1320 or 1-877/386-4383, ⊛grandcanyon lodgenorth.com; see p.70).

Once you arrive, the single most important source of information available is the free park newspaper, *The Guide*, handed out by rangers at the various highway entrance stations. Published in separate editions for the North and South rims, it provides current operating hours for all park facilities, detailed hiking advice, schedules of ranger talks and background on park geology, natural history and other issues. You'll also be given a glossy **park brochure** that holds some useful maps, and, if you specifically ask for them, the **Backcountry Trip Planner**, which carries full details on backpacking and camping in the park, and the **Accessibility Guide** (see p.31).

Although *The Guide* probably contains most of what you need to know, you may well want to call in as well at one of the **visitor centres** within the park, detailed throughout this book. The main ones are at **Canyon View Information Plaza** on the South Rim (daily: May to mid-Oct 8am–6pm; mid-Oct to April till 5pm; ☎928/638-7888; see p.42) and **North Rim Visitor Center** on the North Rim (daily May to mid-Oct 8am–6pm; ☎928/638-7864; see p.68). To prevent wastage, rangers don't display all their leaflets, but if you have a specific query they can often supply you with extra printed information, for example on rafting or flight-seeing operators; the Havasupai reservation; or backcountry hiking and driving routes. They also have up-to-date information on current trail or road conditions,

so be sure to ask if you're planning some specific adventure. All park brochures and publications can also be downloaded from the website.

The official park-service information can be complemented by the much wider range of books, brochures and maps sold in the Grand Canyon Association **bookstores**, at Canyon View, Desert View and several other locations along the South Rim, and at *Grand Canyon Lodge* on the North Rim.

Maps

The best general-purpose **road map** for the total area covered by this book is the *Guide to Indian Country*, available free to members of the American Automobile Association, and sold throughout the Southwest at $4.95. However, it's not reliable for dirt roads and backcountry routes. If you plan to do any exploring on the isolated plateaus that lie north of the Colorado, either on the North Rim or the Arizona Strip, be sure to pick up either the *North Kaibab Ranger District*, published by the Kaibab National Forest, or the BLM Arizona Strip Field Office's *Visitor Map*, from the visitor centres at Jacob Lake (see p.131) or the North Rim.

For hiking, it's important to have an accurate **topographical** map. The best ones for the canyon as a whole are the waterproof

---

Useful websites

Arizona Daily Sun ⓦazdailysun.com. Flagstaff's daily newspaper is the best source for up-to-the-minute news about issues that affect the entire Grand Canyon region; its website includes a searchable archive of past issues.

Arizona Office of Tourism ⓦarizonaguide.com. Comprehensive statewide travel information.

Grand Canyon Association ⓦgrandcanyon.org. This non-profit organization runs the in-park bookstores; its website is a good source for Grand Canyon books and souvenirs.

Grand Canyon Historical Society ⓦgrandcanyonhistory.org. This group of Grand Canyon enthusiasts organizes outings and activities in the region and posts members' latest historical research online.

Grand Canyon National Park South Rim ☎928/638-7888, North Rim ☎928/638-7864, ⓦnps.gov/grca. The Park Service maintains a regularly updated online database of everything you might need to know, with links to rafting operators, tour companies and the like.

High Country News ⓦwww.hcn.org. Biweekly newspaper devoted to Western US environmental issues, with special reference to national parks and public lands. Its searchable online archive covers all the latest Grand Canyon news.

and tearproof maps published by National Geographic–Trails Illustrated, costing $11.95 each (ⓦmaps.nationalgeographic.com). No. 261 focuses specifically on Bright Angel Canyon and the Corridor Trails, at 1:35000, while nos. 262 and 263 cover the eastern and western portions of the canyon respectively, at 1:90000.

Government websites

General travel and visa advice is available at the following websites:

Australian Department of Foreign Affairs ⓦwww.dfat.gov.au, www.smartraveller.gov.au.
British Foreign & Commonwealth Office ⓦwww.fco.gov.uk.
Canadian Department of Foreign Affairs ⓦwww.dfait-maeci.gc.ca.
Irish Department of Foreign Affairs ⓦwww.foreignaffairs.gov.ie.
New Zealand Ministry of Foreign Affairs ⓦwww.mft.govt.nz.
US State Department ⓦtravel.state.gov.

Transport and tours

The only part of the Grand Canyon that it is possible to visit using public transport is the South Rim. In fact, the Park Service would prefer you not to bring a car, and hikers in particular can happily stay several days on the South Rim without feeling the need of one.

As detailed on p.43, **free shuttle buses** link the various lodges and other facilities in Grand Canyon Village; running west to several viewpoints along Hermit Road; and also heading east to Yaki Point, the trailhead for the South Kaibab Trail. In addition, commercial tour buses operate the 52-mile round trip out to **Desert View**.

Driving

To explore anywhere apart from the South Rim, there's little choice but to **drive**. That's the only way to take in various sights on the "road between the rims", detailed in Chapter 4; to admire the views from the North Rim overlooks, in Chapter 2; to visit the stunning overlook at Toroweap, in Chapter 5; or to reach the remote Havasupai Indian Reservation, in Chapter 7.

While the main roads up to the South Rim from I-40 are busy and well maintained, there may be times when you find yourself driving in very empty **desert**. Be sure to have two gallons of water per person in the car, and also carry flares, matches, a first-aid kit and a compass, plus a shovel, air pump and extra gas. Take care driving at **night**; much of the country around the Grand Canyon is open range land, and livestock can wander onto unlit roads. If the car's engine **overheats**, don't turn it off; instead, try to cool it quickly by switching off the air conditioning and turning the heating up full blast. If you do have car problems, it's best to stay with your vehicle, as you'll be harder to find wandering around alone. Note that most roads in the vicinity of the canyon are too remote for **mobile phones** to pick up a signal.

Grand Canyon weather information

For a recorded message about road and weather conditions in the Grand Canyon region, call ☎928/638-7888; for conditions statewide, call ☎1-888/411-7623, or access ⓦaz511.com.

Advice on specific roads is given in the relevant chapters throughout this book.

Cycling

Cycling can make an enjoyable complement to driving, especially as the South Rim roads that are closed to private vehicles remain open to cyclists, but the logistical problems of touring solely by bike in desert conditions, where it can be sixty miles between even the tiniest settlements, defeat all the but the very hardiest of adventurers. Many visitors bring bicycles as well as cars, and use them for exploring park roads, but all hiking trails in the national park are closed to bikes. For details of **bike rental** at the South Rim, see p.44.

Flight-seeing tours

Air tours of the Grand Canyon operate from two main bases – **Tusayan**, close to the South Rim, where, despite its small size, the airport ranks as the second busiest in Arizona, and **Las Vegas**, Nevada. A total of just under 100,000 sightseeing flights, carrying almost a million passengers, take off each year.

Controversy has long surrounded the "flight-seeing" industry. Flying conditions in the vicinity of the canyon are unusually difficult, in that light aircraft especially can struggle with a take-off altitude at Tusayan of 7000ft, followed by fierce and unpredictable air currents over the canyon itself. The **safety record** is, to say the least, alarming. In 1956, a total of 128 people died in what was then the worst crash in US aviation history, when two commercial passenger planes collided above the confluence of the Colorado and Little Colorado rivers. Since then, more than sixty crashes have claimed over 230 more lives.

Both for safety reasons, and to diminish the barrage of **noise** within the park, strict **regulations** surround flights above the national park. Airplanes and helicopters must fly at different altitudes; no one is allowed to fly below rim level; and three quarters of the park, including airspace over the South Rim overlooks and central rim-to-rim corridor, is completely off-limits. The total number of overflights has also been restricted, though that amounts simply to saying the number can't increase above its current, already high level.

Only you can judge whether a flight is worth either the risk or the expense. Yes, in a sense you'll see more of the canyon, but from an even more remote, and potentially alienating, distance than from the rim overlooks. For many visitors, the issue at the Grand Canyon is to find a way to engage with, and understand, this vast, incomprehensible landscape. Taking a scenic flight is unlikely to help. On the other hand, it is undeniably an exciting adventure, and, after all, you are on holiday.

From Tusayan

Helicopter companies based in Tusayan include **Papillon** (☎702/736-7243 or 1-888/635-7272, ⓦpapillon.com) and **Maverick** (☎928/638-2622 or 1-888/261-4414, ⓦwww.maverickhelicopter.com). Each typically flies three standard routes: a half-hour western tour, straight across the canyon and back a few miles west of the village, for around $130 per adult ($115 per child); a forty-minute eastern tour, flying along the rim as far as the confluence of the Colorado and Little Colorado rivers, for roughly $160 ($140); and a fifty-minute loop trip that combines the two by flying across the forest of the North Rim, for perhaps $230 ($200).

The main **aeroplane** or "fixed-wing" tour operators at Tusayan are **Air Grand Canyon** (☎928/638-3300 or 1-800/634-6801, ⓦairgrandcanyon.com) and **Grand Canyon Airlines** (☎928/638-2359 or 1-866/235-9422, ⓦwww.grandcanyonairlines.com). Such tours can cover much greater distances than helicopter companies, but they're obliged to fly at least 1000ft above rim level, and thus don't offer quite such good views. Prices range upwards from $100 for half an hour to as long as you like for as much as you've got.

From Las Vegas

Aeroplane tours from **Las Vegas** to the South Rim are operated by both **Scenic Airlines** (☎ 702/638-3200 or 1-800/634-6801, ⓦwww.scenic.com) and **Grand Canyon Airlines** (see above). Prices for a return flight plus bus tour start at $190.

Several Las Vegas-based companies also fly to **Grand Canyon West** (see p.181), which because it's on the Hualapai reservation is not governed by the same regulations as the rest of the canyon. That enables helicopters to fly down from the rim and land beside the Colorado River. **Helicopter** operators include **Papillon** (☎702/736-7243 or 1-888/635-7272, ⓦwww.papillon.com), **Maverick** (☎702/261-0007 or 1-888/261-4414, ⓦwww.maverickhelicopter.com) and **Sundance** (☎702/736-0606 or 1-800/653-1881, ⓦwww.helicoptour.com). Prices tend to start at almost $300 per person for a trip that includes perhaps just a brief landing beside the Colorado; approach $400 for a flight that doesn't land at all but provides a longer air tour of the canyon; and cost roughly $500 for a package featuring a visit to the Skywalk.

Aeroplane tours to **Grand Canyon West**, with operators like **Scenic Airlines** (☎702/638-3200 or 1-800/634-6801, ⓦwww.scenic.com), start at around $170 for a basic package including a ground tour.

Ground tours

Bus tours along the South Rim, run by Xanterra under the old Fred Harvey banner, are detailed on p.44. However, outfitters in several nearby towns offer guided day-trips and longer excursions to other parts of the canyon. Operators detailed in relevant chapters throughout the book include Dreamland Safari Tours in **Kanab** (☎435/644-5506, ⓦdreamlandtours.net; see p.138); Marvelous Marv's Tours in **Williams** (☎928/707-0291, ⓦmarvelousmarv.com; see p.161); and several operators in **Flagstaff**, including the *DuBeau* and *Grand Canyon* hostels (☎928/774-6731 or 1-800/398-7112, ⓦdubeauhostel.com; see p.153) as well as other companies listed on p.151.

For true expert guidance and an introduction to the canyon backcountry, consider a guided hiking trip with the **Grand Canyon Field Institute** (☎928/638-2485 or 1-866/471-4435, ⓦgrandcanyon.org/fieldinstitute; see p.92), or one of the multitude of educational programmes arranged by Flagstaff's **Museum of Northern Arizona** (☎928/774-5213, ⓦmusnaz.org).

It's also possible to do a day-trip by bus from **Las Vegas** to the South Rim, with operators including Papillon (☎702/736-7243 or 1-888/635-7272, ⓦwww.papillon.com), Prices start at $79, but as trips involve a fifteen-hour day and 550 miles of driving, with little more than an hour at the canyon itself, they're not recommended.

Accommodation

Not surprisingly, most visitors to the Grand Canyon who stay longer than a few hours hope to find accommodation within the national park. Both the South and North rims host comfortable, attractive hotels, known in traditional park parlance as lodges. Each lodge is reviewed in detail in the relevant chapter of this book; demand far exceeds supply, so make your reservations as far in advance as possible. Note that very few rooms indeed – to be specific, around half a dozen rooms on the South Rim and four on the North – offer direct canyon views.

Lodges and motels

The six **lodges** along the **South Rim** collectively offer about a thousand rooms, the best of them being in the venerable *El Tovar* and *Bright Angel Lodge*. Reservations for them all, as well as at Phantom Ranch on the canyon floor (see p.99) and the RV campground in Grand Canyon Village (see p.47), are handled by **Xanterra** (same day ☎928/638-2631, advance ☎303/297-2757

Accommodation price codes

All accommodation rates in this book have been coded using the symbols below. These indicate the **least expensive double room** in each establishment, **excluding taxes**, which are 6.73 percent inside the park, and from five to fifteen percent outside. Significant seasonal variations are noted, as are establishments that hold rooms at widely differing prices. The cheapest price code, ❶, is also used to indicate hostels which offer individual dorm beds, in which cases specific rates are also included.

❶ $35 and under ❹ $76–100 ❼ $161–200
❷ $36–50 ❺ $101–130 ❽ $201–250
❸ $51–75 ❻ $131–160 ❾ $251 and over

or 1-888/297-2757, ⓦgrandcanyonlodges .com). **Room rates** are set by the Park Service; a typical double, en-suite room ranges from $80 to $170 between mid-March and mid-November, and perhaps $10–20 less in winter.

The similarly appealing *Grand Canyon Lodge*, the only option on the North Rim, provides another two hundred rooms, at rates ranging from $113 to $172. It's managed by **Forever Resorts** (same day ☎928/638-2611, advance 480/337-1320 or 1-877/386-4383, ⓦgrandcanyonlodgenorth.com), and is closed in winter.

Close to the **South Rim**, there's alternative accommodation in the gateway community of **Tusayan**, just outside the park, which is only worth considering if the in-park options are fully booked. Several large chain motels there – reviewed on p.46 – hold another thousand rooms between them. The rates tend to be much the same as in the park, but the facilities are often much more modern. Further congregations of motels can be found in the towns of **Flagstaff** (see p.153) and **Williams** (see p.161) on the I-40 interstate, though at eighty and sixty miles respectively from the canyon these are too far away to make convenient bases for multi-day stays.

At the **North Rim**, if there's no room at *Grand Canyon Lodge* your choices are very restricted. **DeMotte Park**, seventeen miles north of the canyon (see p.132), and **Jacob Lake**, 44 miles north (see p.131), hold one small motel each, and there are several more in both **Fredonia**, Arizona (see p.137) and

Kanab, Utah (see p.139), close neighbours another thirty miles north.

Finally, there are also a number of atmospheric roadside lodges and motels scattered along the 215-mile road that connects the North and South rims, for example at **Cameron** (see p.118) and **Marble Canyon** (see p.126).

Camping

The National Park Service maintains appealing, well-equipped **campgrounds** on both sides of the canyon, charging fees of between $15 and $18 per night per vehicle, and as little as $5 for individual backpackers. Spaces at both **Mather Campground** in Grand Canyon Village on the South Rim (see p.47), and **North Rim Campground**, a mile north of *Grand Canyon Lodge* on the North Rim (see p.71), can be reserved in advance (☎1-877/444-6777, ⓦwww .recreation.gov), while the summer-only **Desert View Campground** on the South Rim (see p.47) is first-come, first-served. There's also **RV camping** at Grand Canyon Village in the **Trailer Village** (see p.47), run by Xanterra (☎303/297-2757 or ⓦwww .grandcanyonlodges.com).

Backcountry camping within the park, particularly below the canyon rim, is by permit only under tight Park Service restrictions (for full details, see p.90).

Camping possibilities **outside the park** are detailed wherever relevant in this book; see p.47 for options close to the South Rim, p.132 for the North Rim and p.175 for the Havasupai Indian Reservation.

Travel essentials

Costs and money

This book lists detailed price information for lodging and dining throughout the Grand Canyon region. Generally, prices are broadly similar to those found elsewhere in the US. Food and lodging tend to be cheaper than in major US cities and tourist regions, while gas and groceries, especially in remote places, are a bit more expensive. Most visitors from Europe and Australasia feel their money goes further in the US than it does at home.

Accommodation rates are coded according to the system explained on p.27, which excludes local taxes, while **restaurant** prices only account for food, not drinks or tip. For museums and similar attractions, the entrance fees quoted are for adults; unless otherwise specified, assume that children get in half-price.

Most visitors drive to the park. If you can't bring your own vehicle, **car rental** will cost you around $200/£125/€147. Lodging costs are more flexible. For most of the year in towns away from the canyon, you should have no problem finding a motel room for under $70/£44/€51, though even the cheapest peak-season rates in or near the park are more like $90/£56/€66. Although a few **hostels** in the region offer dorm beds for around $20/£12/€15 per person per night, they're by no means common and really don't save that much money for two or more travel companions. **Camping** is not only cheap (federal and state park campgrounds range from free to perhaps $18/£11/€13 per

Grand Canyon National Park: admission charges and fees

The **entrance fee** to Grand Canyon National Park is payable when you cross the park boundary, which is almost certain to be at one of the three main entry stations. Of the two South Rim stations, one is not far north of **Tusayan** on US-180 coming from Williams and Flagstaff, and the other is just east of **Desert View**, on AZ-64 west of Cameron. The North Rim equivalent is five miles south of **DeMotte Park** on AZ-67, south from Jacob Lake. Admission is valid for seven days, and currently costs **$25** for one private, non-commercial vehicle and all its passengers, or, if you arrive on foot, bicycle or motorcycle, **$12** for each individual.

It's also possible to buy various **passes** at the entrance stations, which supersede the usual admission fee. The **Grand Canyon Pass** ($50) entitles the bearer and any passengers in the same vehicle, or any accompanying family members if you arrive by some other means, to unlimited admission over the following year.

If you plan to visit any other national parks or monuments in coming months, it makes more sense to buy the **Inter-agency Annual Pass** ($80). Also known as the "America the Beautiful Pass", and available at all federal parks and monuments, or online at Ⓦstore.usgs.gov/pass, this grants the bearer and fellow passengers unrestricted access to all such parks and monuments for a year.

None of the passes or fees mentioned above covers or reduces charges for such activities as camping (see p.47), backcountry hiking (see p.90) or private rafting trips (see p.196).

Two further passes, obtainable at any park but not online, grant **free access** for life to all national parks and monuments, again to the holder and any accompanying passengers, and also provide a fifty percent discount on camping fees. The **Senior Pass** is available to any US citizen or permanent resident aged 62 or older for a one-time fee of $10, while the **Access Pass** is issued free to blind or permanently disabled US citizens or permanent residents.

Rough Guides travel insurance

Rough Guides has teamed up with WorldNomads.com to offer great **travel insurance** deals. Policies are available to residents of over 150 countries, with cover for a wide range of **adventure sports**, 24hr emergency assistance, high levels of medical and evacuation cover and a stream of **travel safety information**. Roughguides.com users can take advantage of their policies online 24/7, from anywhere in the world – even if you're already travelling. And since plans often change when you're on the road, you can extend your policy and even claim online. Roughguides.com users who buy travel insurance with WorldNomads.com can also leave a positive footprint and donate to a community development project. For more information go to ⓦ**www .roughguides.com/shop**.

night), but also the only option in many wilderness areas.

As for **food**, $25/£16/€18 per day is enough to support an adequate diet, comprising perhaps one full meal at a local diner supplemented by a stash of groceries, while for $35/£22/€26 per day one can eat pretty well.

The most economical possible holiday, therefore, with two people sharing a rental car, camping in state and federal parks most nights, and eating one restaurant meal per day, will cost a minimum of $400/£249/€294 per person per week.

Expect to pay most of your major expenses by **credit** or **debit card**; hotels and car rental agencies ask for a credit card imprint as security, even if you intend to settle the bill in cash. If you have a Master-Card or Visa, or a cash-dispensing card linked to an international network such as Cirrus or Plus (check with your home bank in advance), you can withdraw cash from appropriate **ATMs**. Also consider carrying US dollar **travellers' cheques**, which offer the security of knowing that lost or stolen cheques will be replaced. Cheques issued by American Express, Visa and Thomas Cook are universally accepted as cash in shops, restaurants and gas stations, and any change from your transactions will be rendered in hard currency. Carry plenty of $10 and $20 denominations, and don't be put off by "no checks" signs, which only refer to personal cheques. Foreign travellers should *not* bring travellers' cheques issued in their own currency, as banks may not exchange them, and few businesses are likely to accept them.

Electricity

The US electricity supply is 110 volts AC, with standard two-pin plugs – foreign visitors will need an adapter and voltage converter to use their electrical appliances.

Emergencies

Dial ⓣ 911.

Health and safety

By far the most important health and safety issues facing visitors to the Grand Canyon relate to hiking and backcountry survival, particularly below the rim. Chapter 3 addresses such concerns in depth, including water and food, wildlife, what to carry and security precautions.

If you're planning any form of backcountry adventure, whether driving, hiking or rafting, be sure to supplement the advice in this book with information on current road or trail conditions from rangers at the park visitor centres.

Insurance

Because medical care in the US is expensive, all travellers visiting from overseas should be sure to buy some form of **travel insurance**.

American and Canadian citizens should check they're not already covered by their homeowners, or – in some cases – credit card policies. Most Canadians are covered for medical mishaps by their provincial health plans.

Phones

Unless you can organize to do all your calling online via **Skype** (ⓦ www.skype.com),

International telephone calls

To make calls **to the US** from the outside world (excluding Canada), first dial 1.
To make international calls **from the US**, dial 011 followed by the country code:

Australia 61   **Ireland** 353
New Zealand 64   **UK** 44

the cheapest way to make long-distance and international calls is to buy a **prepaid phonecard**, available in various denominations from gas stations, supermarkets and other outlets. These offer sizeable savings on conventional phone rates, charging only a few cents per minute to call from the USA to most European and other western countries.

It's still generally easy to find a public phone in the Southwest. As a rule, local calls cost 50¢, but you may have to feed in nine or ten quarters just to call the next town down the highway, and long-distance calls can cost far more. Some budget motels offer guests free local calls, but in general calls from motel rooms are even more expensive.

If you plan to take your **mobile** or **cell phone**, be warned that reception in the Grand Canyon region is not at all dependable. You can usually get a signal in and around Grand Canyon Village on the South Rim; the North Rim varies day by day; and you certainly won't be able to use your phone as soon as you drop below the rim. In addition, travellers from overseas will need a tri-band or quad-band phone that's enabled for international calls, and are liable to incur hefty roaming charges.

Senior travellers

Anyone aged over 62 (with appropriate ID) can enjoy a vast range of discounts in the US. Both Amtrak and Greyhound offer (smallish) percentage reductions on fares to older passengers, while the Senior Pass, detailed on p.28, offers free admission to all national parks.

For discounts on accommodation, group tours and vehicle rental, US residents aged 50 or over can join the AARP (American Association of Retired Persons; ☎1-888/687-2277; ⊛aarp.org) for an annual $16

fee; the website also offers travel tips and features. Road Scholar (☎1-800/454-5768, ⊛roadscholar.org), runs an extensive network of educational and activity programmes for people over 60 throughout the US.

Tax

Though added to virtually everything you buy in a shop, sales tax isn't included in the marked price. While local sales taxes vary, Arizona's base rate is 6.6 percent – except on Indian reservations, which do not levy a sales tax. Most towns also charge lodging taxes of between five and fifteen percent.

Temperature

Always given in Fahrenheit; to convert to Celsius, subtract 32, multiply by 5 and divide by 9.

Time zones

Arizona is on **Mountain Time**, two hours behind Eastern Time and seven hours behind Greenwich Mean Time. When it is 2pm at the Grand Canyon, it is 4pm in New York and 9pm in London. In winter, the time at the canyon is the same as in New Mexico, Utah and Colorado, while Nevada and California are on Pacific Time, another hour behind.

Between the first Sunday in April and the last Sunday in October, New Mexico, Utah, Colorado and Nevada switch to daylight saving time and advance their clocks by one hour. Arizona, however, does not, so in summer the time is an hour behind New Mexico and Utah and the same as in Nevada. Confusingly, the Navajo Nation in northeast Arizona does shift to daylight saving time, putting it an hour ahead of the rest of Arizona in summer.

Tipping

Restaurant waiting staff depend on tips for the bulk (and sometimes all) of their earnings; fifteen to twenty percent is the standard rate. Ten percent is acceptable for bar staff.

Travelling in Indian country

The region covered by this book includes several distinct Indian reservations. As well as the Havasupai and Hualapai reservations, described in chapters 7 and 8 respectively, it also extends in the east to reach the vast Navajo reservation, or "Navajo Nation".

Many outsiders – Americans and non-Americans alike – feel uncomfortable about entering Native American land, but so long as you behave with due cultural sensitivity you will almost always be made to feel welcome. In particular, travellers in "Indian Country" should respect the laws that bar the sale, possession and consumption of alcohol on the reservations. Always request permission before photographing (or even drawing) people or personal property, and accept that you may be asked for a fee. As well as obeying explicit signs that ask you not to enter specific areas, you should also be aware that off-road driving and off-trail hiking or climbing is forbidden. If you have to drive up to someone's home or hogan stay in your car and wait to be approached, rather than blundering in.

On a more general note, attempts to make friends may run contrary to what Native Americans regard as good manners. In the words of a leaflet issued by the Navajo, "the general exuberance many cultures define as friendliness is not considered such by the American Indians". Most Southwestern Indians regard eye contact as rude and will avoid meeting your eye; they may also prefer not to shake hands. Your clothing may also be an issue; the Hopi, for example, request that visitors not wear shorts or hats, or use umbrellas. Persistent, intrusive questioning is obviously liable to offend.

If you're keen to buy **Indian crafts**, museums and galleries throughout the region sell beautiful Pueblo pots, Navajo rugs, and silver and turquoise jewellery of all kinds. Recommended sources at the South Rim include Hopi House and the gift store in the *El Tovar* hotel, while the Museum of Northern Arizona in Flagstaff also stocks an excellent range.

If you want to be sure that whatever you're buying was individually crafted by a Southwestern Indian, you're entitled to ask for a written Certificate of Authenticity. Only the phrase "Authentic Indian handmade" has any legal force. "Indian handmade" means the object was designed and assembled by American Indians; "Indian crafted" means that American Indians had a hand in the process; and words such as "real" and "genuine" mean nothing.

Travelling with children

The canyon is a demanding place, so if you're travelling with young children, pay constant attention to their safety. For kids old enough to be trusted near the drop-offs, however, the national park makes a wonderful destination. Rangers at the South Rim in particular offer a wide range of activities for kids, from daily talks and walks (see p.42) to the Junior Ranger programme, in which children aged 4 to 14 can complete activity books to attain the coveted title and badge. Be especially cautious when hiking with children; it's difficult and dangerous enough for adults without having to carry exhausted little ones. When in doubt, stick to the above-rim trails recommended on p.85. Finally, don't underestimate the sheer amount of driving involved if you plan to visit both rims; consider interrupting your journey with an overnight stay in either Marble Canyon or Page.

Travellers with disabilities

For travellers with disabilities, the South Rim of the Grand Canyon is a much more convenient destination than the North Rim, offering a wider range of accessible overlooks, accommodation and other facilities.

The park *Accessibility Guide*, available at all visitor centres, includes maps and information about wheelchair-accessible buildings and rim trails; such details are also available online via ◉nps.gov/grca/. Broadly speaking, all in-park lodgings on both rims, except *Yavapai Lodge* on the South Rim, are accessible, while some of the older, historic structures along the South Rim, such as Hopi House and Kolb Studio, are not.

When you first arrive at the South Rim, an electric cart service is available for travel between Mather Point and Canyon View Information Plaza, on request either in the car park or at the visitor centre. Wheelchairs are usually available for (free) loan at the visitor centre.

Although most of the South Rim's free **shuttle buses** (see p.43) are not wheelchair-accessible, visitors can call ☎928/638-0591 (TTD ☎928/638-7705) two days in advance to arrange transport in an accessible vehicle. Alternatively, stop by the entrance station, Canyon View Information Plaza, Yavapai Geology Museum or Kolb Studio to obtain a temporary **accessibility permit**, which allows private vehicle access to shuttle-only areas, notably Hermit Road (see p.55). The *Accessibility Guide* includes a map of "windshield views", where you can see the canyon without leaving your vehicle.

On the South Rim, the park **bus tours** (see p.44) and **mule rides** (see p.56) can accom-modate travellers with disabilities; call ☎928/638-2631 for full details. So, too, can several of the **rafting** operators listed on p.193 onward.

As for the **North Rim**, *Grand Canyon Lodge* is accessible and has wheelchairs for loan. The viewpoints at Point Imperial and Cape Royal are accessible along level paved paths, but the undulating, uneven trail out to Bright Angel Point is not recommended.

US mail

You'll find **post offices** in the national park at both the South Rim (in Market Plaza; see p.49) and North Rim (in the *Grand Canyon Lodge*; see p.72), as well as in towns throughout the region; blue mailboxes stand at many street corners. Typical hours at post offices outside the park are Mon–Fri 9am–5pm and Sat 9am–noon. Ordinary mail within the US costs 44¢ for a letter weighing up to an ounce. Airmail between the US and Europe or Australia costs 98¢ for postcards or letters weighing up to half an ounce (a single thin sheet), and delivery generally takes about a week.

Wi-fi and internet access

Almost all hotels, including all the South Rim park lodges, offer free wi-fi. Many also provide a computer or two for the use of guests, sometimes for a fee. Other South Rim hotspots are listed on p.49. On the road, however, it's not so easy to stay in touch; look out for public libraries, which offer free access, and cafés.

Guide

Guide

1

The South Rim

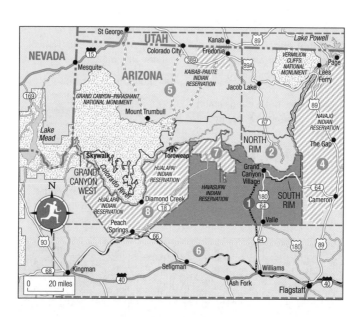

CHAPTER 1 # Highlights

* **Grand Canyon Railway** For families in particular, a ride on the steam train up from Williams makes the perfect introduction to the canyon. See p.40

* **Condors** To see North America's largest bird swooping over the Grand Canyon is an unforgettable experience. See p.40

* **Bright Angel Lodge** The atmospheric, well-priced rim-edge cabins here tend to be reserved way in advance, but a cancellation could give you a real treat. See p.45

* **Mather Point** The overlook closest to the park visitor centre is an ideal spot to get your first view of the abyss. See p.50

* **El Tovar** The jewel of Grand Canyon Village, this rustic, century-old lodge provides the South Rim's best food and accommodation. See p.53

* **Hopi Point** Magnificent canyon views, albeit often crowded at sunset. See p.58

* **Hermits Rest** Architect Mary Jane Colter was responsible for this inviting little rest-stop, right on the canyon's rim. See p.59

* **Shoshone Point** Only accessible on foot, this beautiful viewpoint offers a unique chance to be alone with the canyon. See p.60

* **The Watchtower** This mock-Puebloan tower blends into the rocks at the east end of the South Rim, with stunning canyon views. See p.63

▲ Mather Point

The South Rim

When people casually mention visiting "the Grand Canyon", it's almost certainly the **South Rim** to which they're referring. To be more precise, it's the thirty-mile stretch of the South Rim served by a paved road, and most specifically of all it's **Grand Canyon Village**, the small community sandwiched between the pine forest and the rim that holds a **visitor centre** and most of the park's **lodges** and **restaurants**. In fact, of the almost five million people who visit the national park each year, nine out of ten head for this same tiny spot along the rim. Even an area as vast as the Grand Canyon can find it hard to handle that human influx.

While the South Rim as a whole offers a succession of magnificent, **panoramic views**, Grand Canyon Village itself is not an exceptional spot from which to admire the canyon – it just happens to be where the tourist facilities are concentrated. That said, every visit begins with an eager rush to catch a first breathtaking glimpse of the abyss, and whether you do so from Mather Point near the main visitor centre, or from the heart of the village, the sheer splendour is guaranteed to shock you to a standstill.

To appreciate the full majesty of the spectacle, however – the towering, multi-hued mesas and buttes dubbed "Temples", "Pyramids" and so on; the awesome chasm of the innermost Granite Gorge; the foaming Colorado River battering its way through the depths – you need to allow time to explore along the South Rim in either direction. To the west, the seven-mile **Hermit Road**, closed to private vehicles for most of the year, leads to isolated promontories that command sweeping views in every direction; to the east, overlooks along the 23-mile **Desert View Drive** enable visitors to watch the canyon as it grows and changes, while at spots like **Shoshone Point**, hikers can escape the crowds altogether. Several magnificent trails also drop down into the canyon itself from various points along the South Rim; see Chapter 3 for full details.

Tourism to the South Rim took off towards the end of the nineteenth century, when miners prospecting at various points along the rim began to put up paying guests in simple cabins and inns. Then, in 1901, a railroad was constructed north from Williams to the site that became Grand Canyon Village, and lodges, campsites and other amenities swiftly sprang up around the station. Even after visitors began to arrive by car rather than by train, the convenience of having everything in one place continued to outweigh the problems of overcrowding. And thus things remained for a hundred years, until, as the millennium

---

The first half of this chapter covers South Rim practicalities; jump to "Exploring the South Rim" (p.50) for descriptions of the sights, overlooks and scenic drives.

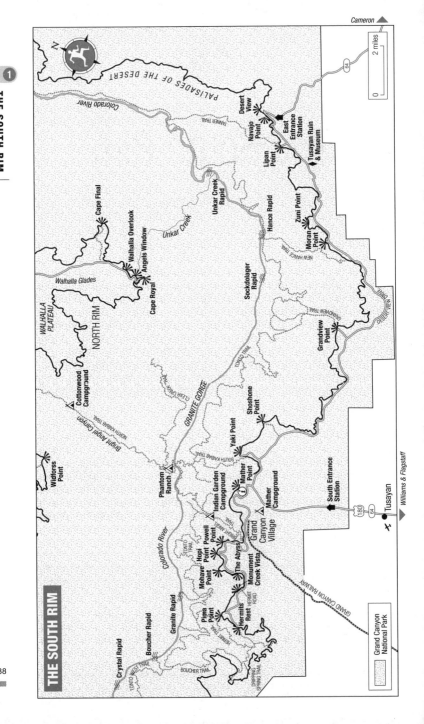

THE SOUTH RIM

38

approached, it was looking as though the village could no longer take the strain, despite the emergence of nearby **Tusayan** as a rival lodging hub.

An ambitious scheme, under which visitors would only be able to access and explore the South Rim using a light rail system, was soon abandoned when for no obvious reason visitor numbers began to fall rather than rise. The brand-new **Canyon View Information Plaza**, built as the hub of the rail network a mile or so east of the village, was kitted out with a new visitor centre and plentiful car parking space, and became the centre instead of a network of free seasonal **shuttle buses**.

While certain canyon overlooks are no longer accessible by car year-round, it remains perfectly possible to visit the South Rim using your own vehicle. Grand Canyon Village still gets clogged with traffic in summer, but it rarely comes to a standstill, and in general it's a nicer and more attractive place to spend time than you might imagine. The major drawback, or rather the price for keeping things bearable, is that all its **accommodation** tends to be booked up way in advance. Assuming you've planned ahead and are able to stay, the various options are of a pretty high standard – especially if you get to stay in historic properties like *El Tovar Hotel* or *Bright Angel Lodge* – and generally well priced.

Arrival

The vast majority of visitors make their way to the South Rim via either **Williams** (58 miles south; see p.160) or **Flagstaff** (81 miles southeast; see p.149). Both towns straddle I-40 and are served by cross-country Amtrak **trains**. In the absence of direct Amtrak service to the canyon, a separate **excursion train** runs from Williams up to the rim, while **buses** also run between Flagstaff and the canyon, calling at Williams en route. A small number of direct **flights** to Tusayan's small airport are available from Las Vegas and other points in the Southwest.

By car

The two main roads up to the South Rim – **AZ-64** from Williams, also known as the Bushmaster Memorial Highway, and **US-180** from Flagstaff – meet at **Valle**. That tiny community lies 25 miles south of **Tusayan**, which is itself just south of the park boundary. En route from Flagstaff, US-180 threads its way through the dramatic San Francisco Peaks, making it the more scenic drive of the two. Both roads, however, run for most of their length over the **Coconino Plateau**, which is covered by the largest **ponderosa pine forest** in the world. Crossing this flat and undramatic landscape, you get no sense of the impending abyss until you reach the very edge of the canyon, close to Mather Point.

You can also get to Grand Canyon Village from the **east**, by driving the fifty-mile section of AZ-64 that sets off from US-89 at **Cameron** (see p.117). Coming this way, you enter the park close to Desert View, and can stop off at the East Rim overlooks before you reach the village. The obvious route to follow if you're coming in from the north, it also makes an alternative approach from Flagstaff to the south, and is useful if you're interested in seeing Sunset Crater and Wupatki national monuments along the way (see p.158).

Current **admission fees** to Grand Canyon National Park, payable at the entrance stations just north of Tusayan and just east of Desert View, are detailed on p.28.

Parking

While there's usually plenty of **parking** available in the three large car parks at the Canyon View Information Plaza, parking in Grand Canyon Village itself can be more problematic. Guests staying at the various lodges – especially *Bright Angel*, *Maswik* and *Yavapai* – should have no trouble parking near their rooms overnight, but finding a space in the middle of the day can be murder. Of the five free public car parks in and around the village, your best bets are unpaved Lot D, across the tracks from the railway station (take the first left after crossing the tracks near the Hermit Road shuttle stop), and Lot A, outside the Park Headquarters building across the main road from Market Plaza.

By train

Amtrak **trains** (ⓦamtrak.com) come no closer to the South Rim than the stations at **Flagstaff** and **Williams**. Schedules vary slightly year to year, but according to the latest summer timetable, westbound trains from Chicago via Albuquerque stop at Flagstaff at 8.51pm and Williams Junction at 9.33pm daily, while eastbound trains from Los Angeles are due at Williams Junction at 4.30am and Flagstaff at 5.16am daily. Winter services run one hour later. Bus connections are detailed below.

Grand Canyon Railway

The **Grand Canyon Railway** (ⓣ303/843-8724 or 1-800/843-8724, ⓦthetrain .com) runs for 65 miles from **Williams** to a picturesque wooden station in the heart of Grand Canyon Village. When the line first opened in 1901, it heralded the start of mass tourism to the canyon, but by 1968 it had been driven out of business by the growth of private car travel. Restored in 1989, the railway is now a tourist attraction in its own right. Passengers in its vintage carriages are entertained throughout the day by Wild West shoot-outs, hold-ups, pistol-packing marshals, singing conductors

The return of the condor

Of all the awesome spectacles on display along the South Rim, few can match the sight of a fully grown **California condor** soaring on the canyon updrafts. These magnificent birds, whose wingspan measures over nine feet, and which live for up to sixty years, were reintroduced to Arizona in 1996. They can now frequently be seen hovering above Grand Canyon Village, or perching just below the rim.

The birds were native to the canyon, and indeed to most of North America, for thousands of years, but their population was dwindling long before the first Europeans arrived. The last condor in the Grand Canyon area was recorded as nesting near Lees Ferry in the 1890s, while a solitary bird was seen circling Williams in 1924. During the 1980s, the last remaining 22 individuals of the species were trapped in California. A captive breeding programme was instigated, with birds being reintroduced first in California, and subsequently in northern Arizona.

At the Arizona release site, located on the Vermilion Cliffs fifty miles northeast of the South Rim – see p.131 – scientists take great pains to keep contact between condors and humans to a minimum, so the birds don't learn to associate humans with food. Condors are very inquisitive creatures, however, and to the delight of tourists almost all the Arizona birds spend much of their time in the vicinity of the village. Project workers and park rangers attempt to discourage them from approaching too close, and leave animal carcasses out for them in remote places. These natural scavengers also manage to find carrion by themselves. Progress has been slow but definite. Over seventy free-flying, but tagged and monitored condors now live in the Grand Canyon, and fledglings have started to hatch in the wild. For the latest news, call in at park visitor centres, or visit the Peregrine Fund website at ⓦperegrinefund.org.

Horseback riding

Just outside the South Entrance at Moqui Lodge (itself permanently closed), **Apache Stables** (☎928/638-2891, ⓦapachestables.com) charges $48.50 for a one-hour trail ride through the Kaibab National Forest or $88.50 for two hours. Evening offerings include campfire rides on horseback for $58.50 or by wagon for $25.50.

and the like. The scenery en route – part desert scrubland, part pine forest – is far from spectacular, and you never actually see the canyon from the train, but it's still a fun and memorable way to visit the park without having to drive.

The train operates daily all year except for Christmas Eve and Christmas Day, leaving central Williams (not the Amtrak station) at 9.30am and arriving at the Grand Canyon at 11.45pm, then setting off back again at 3.30pm and reaching Williams at 5.45pm. Sadly, it's only pulled by a **steam locomotive** during the summer, from late May until the end of September; for the rest of year, diesels are used. Five different kinds of passenger car are in service, offering extra facilities such as larger and more comfortable seats, and complimentary food and beverages. Return fares range from $70 plus tax in Coach Class ($40 for ages 2–15) up to $190 in the Luxury Parlor Car (no under-16s). No Amtrak passes are accepted, and unless you have a National Parks Pass, you'll face an additional $8 park admission fee. Various package deals are available that include discounts on lodging and dining in Williams and/or Grand Canyon Village if you would like to stay overnight, while around Christmas each year the train also offers special hour-long evening trips to meet Santa Claus at the North Pole (which, incidentally, is not located at the Grand Canyon).

By bus

Arizona Shuttle (☎928/226-8060 or 1-877/226-8060, ⓦarizonashuttle.com) runs two **bus services** each day from the Amtrak station in **Flagstaff**, via the Grand Canyon Railway depot in **Williams** and the Grand Canyon IMAX Theater in **Tusayan**, to the **Maswik Lodge** in Grand Canyon Village. Tickets cost $28 each way from Flagstaff for adults, or $22 from Williams and $20/$17 for accompanied children under 12; there's a $4 discount for booking online. The first bus leaves Flagstaff at 8am daily, calling at Williams at 8.30am and reaching Maswik at 9.45am; the second leaves Flagstaff at 3.45pm and Williams at 4.30pm, reaching Maswik at 5.45pm. Return services leave Maswik at 10.15am and 6.15pm, arriving at Williams at 11.30am and 7.30pm, and Flagstaff at 12.15pm and 8.15pm, respectively. Between March and October, a third bus leaves Flagstaff at 2pm daily, and doesn't stop at Williams en route to reaching Maswik at 3.45pm; the return journey leaves Maswik at 4.15pm and gets to Flagstaff at 5.45pm. Guided **bus tours** to the park from Flagstaff and Williams are detailed on p.151 and p.161, respectively.

By air

The small **airport** (ⓦgrandcanyonairport.org) at Tusayan, six miles from the South Rim, just outside the park boundary, is used primarily by "flight-seeing" tour companies (see p.25). The only airlines that currently fly here offer excursions from **Las Vegas**; almost all passengers come on day-trips, but it is possible to arrange a one-way flight. The major operators are **Scenic Airlines** (☎702/638-3200 or 1-800/634-6801, ⓦscenic.com), and **Grand Canyon Airlines** (☎928/638-2359 or 1-866/235-9422, ⓦwww.grandcanyonairlines.com).

Most Tusayan hotels offer courtesy pick-up for guests. There is no **car rental** outlet at the airport.

Information

Although the **Canyon View Information Plaza** makes an obvious first stop at the South Rim, unless you have specific questions you should find all the information you need in the park's **free newspaper**. Handed out at the two **entrance stations** on AZ-64, when you pay the admission fees detailed on p.28 – one's just north of Tusayan, the other a mile east of Desert View – *The Guide* is also available in all the **lodges**.

As well as listing current opening hours and shuttle-bus schedules, *The Guide* carries a full programme of **park activities** such as ranger talks and guided hikes. On a typical day in high season, more than a dozen such talks or hikes are likely to be taking place, at venues ranging from shuttle bus stops and overlooks to the visitor centre, or simply the canyon rim in the village. All are free of charge, and it's well worth trying to time your tour of the various viewpoints and facilities to coincide with whatever's going on.

In addition to the plaza, further **information desks** can be found at Verkamp's Visitor Center (see p.53), Yavapai Geology Museum (see p.52), Tusayan Museum (see p.62) and Desert View (see p.63). For details of the **Backcountry Office**, which issues permits for backpacking and camping in the canyon, see p.91.

Canyon View Information Plaza

Surrounded by large car parks, immediately north of the spur road that heads west into the village from AZ-64, the **Canyon View Information Plaza** is both the main source of information for the South Rim, and the hub of its free shuttle-bus system. Despite its name, however, the plaza offers no canyon views; for those, you have to walk a few hundred yards north, to Mather Point.

In the centre of the plaza, extensive well-illustrated open-air displays explain different aspects of the canyon, and detail its various hiking trails. This whole complex was originally intended as the terminus of a **light rail** system that would ferry visitors up from Tusayan, and the outdoor panels erected to give passengers something to read while they waited for the shuttle buses.

Now, however, it's also home to the official **Grand Canyon Visitor Center** (daily: May to mid-Oct 8am–6pm, mid-Oct to April till 5pm; ☎928/638-7888, ⓦ www.nps.gov/grca), which holds very little information you can't find elsewhere, but is staffed by helpful rangers eager to advise on any topic you care to mention. Across the plaza, an excellent separate bookstore, Books and More, is run by the Grand Canyon Association.

Finally be warned that while the plaza is accessible on foot from *Yavapai Lodge*, it's a solid mile; most official park maps are not drawn to scale.

Getting around

The ongoing failure to implement an efficient and user-friendly **public transport** system on the South Rim, and thereby persuade visitors not to use their own vehicles, means that getting around Grand Canyon Village can still be a frustrating experience. Almost all new arrivals still start by driving into the centre of Grand Canyon Village, where they swiftly discover that the village **shuttle bus** is too slow and awkward to make a convenient alternative, and remain as dependent on their cars as ever. If visitors stayed long enough to get used to the shuttles, it might help, but as it is, only the **Hermits Rest Route** service, carrying sightseers to the overlooks west of the village, is an unqualified success.

Driving

Grand Canyon Village is always accessible to private vehicles – though as noted on p.40 **parking** can be a major problem in high season – and so too is the road **east** from the village to **Desert View**. Both the road **west** from the village to **Hermits Rest**, however, and the short access road to **Yaki Point**, which is the first overlook east of Mather Point and the trailhead for the popular **South Kaibab Trail**, are only open to private vehicles during December, January and February.

Park shuttle buses

The Guide lists current schedules for the four main Park Service shuttle routes, which interconnect but do not overlap. The busiest, the **Village Route**, coded **blue** on official park maps, loops between Grand Canyon Village and Canyon View Information Plaza, stopping at *Bright Angel*, *Maswik* and *Yavapai* lodges and Mather Campground, as well as Yavapai Point. Starting an hour before sunrise, buses run at half-hourly intervals until 6.30am, and then at fifteen-minute intervals till 7.30pm (May & Sept) or 9pm (June–Aug), after which they revert to half-hourly intervals until either 10pm (May & Sept) or 11pm (June–Aug).

The whole circuit is without canyon views, and follows a roundabout route that takes up to an hour to complete, which is ridiculous considering the short distances involved; you have to suspect that it's designed as much to deter visitors from travelling around the village at all as it is to make their journeys easier.

The shuttle is most useful for getting between the campsite or *Yavapai Lodge* and the *Bright Angel Lodge* area, but it still remains far quicker to drive. Wherever you're staying, you'd do better to visit the information plaza when you first drive in rather than to make your way back there by bus.

The **Kaibab Trail Route**, coded **green**, connects Canyon View Information Plaza with **Yaki Point**, off Desert View Drive a couple of miles east of the village. Buses start running at half-hourly intervals an hour before sunrise, then from either 6.30am (May–Aug) or 7.30am (Sept) they run at fifteen-minute intervals until an hour after sunset. In order to use this route, you have first to catch a village bus to the information plaza, so for anyone planning to hike along the **South Kaibab Trail** from the Yaki Point trailhead, as described on p.100, it's a lot quicker to catch the early-morning **Hikers' Express**. This runs direct to the trailhead at Yaki Point from *Bright Angel Lodge*, via the Backcountry Information Center and the information plaza (daily June–Aug 4am, 5am & 6am; March & Nov 7am, 8am & 9am; April & Oct 6am, 7am & 8am; May & Sept 5am, 6am & 7am; Dec–Feb 8am & 9am). Note that you can also use a **taxi** on this route; see p.44.

Buses on the **Hermits Rest Route**, coded **red**, operate between March and November. They follow Hermit Road, a scenic seven-mile drive west of the village that holds eight canyon overlooks; all are described, together with advice on making the best use of the shuttle, from p.55 onwards. The whole point of the trip is to take your time and enjoy the views; allow at least two hours. Buses run from an hour before sunrise until an hour after sunset, at fifteen-minute intervals between 7.30am and sunset and at half-hourly intervals otherwise. Demand is always high for buses out from the village to see the sunset, so be sure to get to the stop at least an hour in advance, and for buses back to the village once the sun has gone down.

Finally, the **Tusayan Route**, coded **purple**, makes regular twenty-minute runs between Tusayan, where there are four separate stops, and Canyon View Information-tion Plaza. The first bus leaves Tusayan at 8am daily, and the information plaza at 8.40am; the last service from both is at 9.30pm. All passengers entering the park must already have permits.

Park bus tours

As well as managing the park lodges, Xanterra also operates guided **bus tours** along the South Rim. To make a reservation or check schedules, which vary according to the times of sunrise and sunset, contact the transport desk in any lodge, or call ☎928/638-2631. Accompanied children under the age of 17 travel free on all the in-park tours.

Short Sunrise and Sunset tours head east and west of the village, respectively, and cost $20. West of the village, the Hermits Rest Tour is a two-hour jaunt along Hermit Road that costs $25. As it follows the same route, with some but not all of the same stops, as the free Hermits Rest shuttle bus – see above – you're basically paying for the rather banal commentary.

The **Desert View Tour** skirts the East Rim along Desert View Drive – a route open to private vehicles but not served by park shuttle buses. Stops include Yavapai Geology Museum, Lipan Point, and Desert View at road's end. The 52-mile round trip takes just under four hours and costs $44; you can combine it with any of the tours above, not necessarily on the same day, for $57. The evening run coincides with sunset at Desert View.

It's also possible to take a tour down to Williams, travelling there by bus and back on the **Grand Canyon Railway** ($70, under-17s $40; see p.40).

Taxis

If you're pressed for time, consider taking advantage of the local 24-hour **taxi** service (☎928/638-2631, ext 6563). In particular, a taxi can spare you the lengthy wait for a shuttle bus to the South Kaibab trailhead at Yaki Point; expect to pay around $8.

Cycling

Cycling is permitted on any paved road in the park, including Hermit Road when it's closed to private vehicles. You can also ride on the Greenway network of paths, which includes a stretch of the Rim Trail on either side of Mather Point, a trail that links the information plaza with the village and a newer segment that starts at Monument Creek Vista (see p.59), four miles west of the village on Hermit Road, and runs another three miles west to Hermits Rest.

Bright Angel Bicycle Rentals, based in a kiosk at the information plaza (daily 8am–6pm; ☎928/814-8704, ⓦbikegrandcanyon.com), rent bikes for $10 per hour, $25 for four hours, $35 for a full day and $30 per day for multi-day rentals, with slightly reduced rates for under-18s. Trailers to pull children behind are also available.

Bright Angel also run an hourly **cyclists' shuttle** to Hopi Point and two other stops on Hermit Road, for $6 one-way or $9 return, and offer 2 hour 30 minute **cycle tours** for $40.

Accommodation

Roughly two thousand guest **rooms** are available in the immediate vicinity of the South Rim: half of them in and around **Grand Canyon Village** within the park, of which under three hundred are close to the rim, and a further thousand can be found seven miles south, just outside the park in the dull gateway community of **Tusayan**. Given the choice – and with demand far exceeding supply in high season, you probably won't be – the best place to stay has to be on the very lip of the canyon, but only a handful of rooms have canyon views.

While the more basic in-park lodges, away from the rim, still make more convenient bases than Tusayan, the hotels in Tusayan do tend to be more modern and better equipped. On the other hand, some of the rates available inside the park represent extraordinarily good value.

Grand Canyon Village

Xanterra Parks & Resorts (advance reservations ☎303/297-2757 or 1-888/297-2757 same-day reservations, or to contact a guest, ☎928/638-2631, ⓦgrandcanyonlodges .com) handles **reservations** for all accommodation within Grand Canyon Village and down at Phantom Ranch (see p.99), though not those on the North Rim.

Most of the nicest lodgings are available in two venerable Fred Harvey properties right on the rim at Grand Canyon Village – the magnificent **El Tovar Hotel**, and the almost as attractive **Bright Angel Lodge**. As rates are set by the National Park Service, and depend on hotel facilities rather than whether there's a canyon view, it's no more expensive to stay in a characterful rim-side cabin than in a room in a charmless motel block a mile from the edge. There are, however, far more of the latter than the former; in fact the number of rooms with significant canyon views barely reaches double figures. In any case, during busy periods – pretty much from early May until late September – the best rooms are likely to be booked up to thirteen months in advance, and by June it would be very unusual for any same-day bookings to be available at all.

The rates shown here apply during high season; in the depths of winter, prices along the rim drop by around $20 per night, while *Maswik* and *Yavapai* lodges can be as much as $40 cheaper. Bear in mind that even once you've made your booking, it's well worth making repeated follow-up calls to see if any cancellations have become available; you can easily end up getting a nicer room at *Bright Angel Lodge*, for example, for half the asking price of *Yavapai Lodge*.

Lodges

Bright Angel Lodge Designed by Mary Jane Colter and built in 1935, the *Bright Angel* complex consists of an imposing central lodge and a westward sprawl of rustic but comfortable detached log cabins. Staying in a cabin makes for a delightful experience, whether you're in a Rim Cabin with a tremendous view or one of the cheaper Historic Cabins, set back closer to the mule corral. Though reasonably sized, appealingly furnished, well priced and equipped with phones, many of the lodge rooms share bathrooms and/or toilets; a few do offer private showers. All have phones, but only the cabins have TVs. Best of all is the Buckey O'Neill Suite, which boasts a large living room with working fireplace and two front doors that open on the rim. Lodge rooms ❹, Historic Cabins ❺, Rim Cabins ❻, Buckey O'Neill Suite ❾

El Tovar Named for an early Spanish explorer, this log-construction rim-side hotel remains the centrepiece of Grand Canyon Village. Extensively refurbished to celebrate its centennial in 2005, it continues to exude the same combination of rough-hewn charm and elegant sophistication that made it the very peak of fashion when it first opened. Only three suites offer extensive canyon views; the rest of the 78 tastefully furnished guest rooms come in two different sizes, but are otherwise very similar, with no extra charge for those offering partial glimpses of the abyss. Almost all provide just one bed. Standard ❼, larger ❽, suites ❾

Kachina Lodge Anonymous but perfectly adequate motel-style rooms, each with two queen-size beds, TV, phone and full bath, set in a low and utterly undistinguished two-storey block separated by just twenty yards of grass from the rim. Although the lodge makes no formal claim of canyon views, in fact the upper-floor rooms on the canyon side – which cost $10 extra – provide great panoramas. Registration is handled in the lobby of the adjoining *El Tovar*. **❼**

Maswik Lodge Set a few hundred yards back from the rim at the southwest end of the village, the large *Maswik* complex includes two distinct blocks of motel-style rooms, which are often booked by tour groups, as well as a cluster of basic summer-only cabins, each of which holds two double beds. When split among four travellers, the cabins are the closest the village comes to budget lodgings. Rooms in the Maswik North building are considerably nicer than those in the smaller, cramped Maswik South. Cabins and Maswik South **❹**, Maswik North **❼**

Thunderbird Lodge Both the *Thunderbird* and the identical *Kachina Lodge* next door were built of grey brick in the 1960s and intended to last only ten years. Both are still going strong without being in any way distinctive. Run from the front desk of *Bright Angel Lodge*, the *Thunderbird* offers 55 rooms with twin beds, TV, phone and full bath, 37 of which are on the canyon side of the building and cost $10 extra. **❼**

Yavapai Lodge With 358 rooms, *Yavapai* is the largest of the in-park lodges and the last to fill up, so it's the most likely to be available if you try to book on short notice. The main drawback is that it's half a mile from the rim, and twice that – further than you'd want to walk, especially at night – from the heart of Grand Canyon Village, which leaves guests without vehicles all too dependent on the slow park shuttles. In late autumn and early spring, either of the lodge's two similar sections, the air-conditioned *Yavapai East* or the smaller *Yavapai West*, which has ceiling fans only, may be closed, while the whole lodge shuts down in winter. Despite the lacklustre complex, the rooms themselves are perfectly decent motel-style accommodation, most with twin beds. As they're set back in the woods in smallish blocks, they're also fairly quiet. Yavapai West **❺**, Yavapai East **❻**

Outside the park: Tusayan

Sprawling along the highway just over a mile south of the park entrance, and thus seven miles from Grand Canyon Village, **TUSAYAN** is an unattractive strip-mall of a town that holds nothing beyond an IMAX cinema (reviewed on p.49), a few stores and restaurants and half a dozen large **hotel/motels**. Although it has traditionally functioned as an overspill when all the in-park accommodation is full, large tour operators have in recent years come to prefer its hotels as offering a higher standard of amenities and a greater ease in feeding, entertaining and generally managing their groups. No independent visitor, however, would or should choose to stay in Tusayan rather than the village. Note that the prices below are for high season; all are liable to drop significantly in low season.

Hotels and motels

Best Western Grand Canyon Squire Inn 100 AZ-64 ☎928/638-2681 or 1-800/622-6966, ⓦgrandcanyonsquire.com. While Tusayan's most lavish option bills itself as the canyon's "only resort hotel", with an outdoor pool, indoor spa and even its own four-lane bowling alley, its rates compare favourably with those of its neighbours. Most rooms are spacious and very comfortable, if unremarkable; paying a little extra gets you an enormous deluxe room with oval bath. **❼**

Canyon Plaza Resort 406 Canyon Plaza Lane ☎928/638-2673 or 1-800/995-2521, ⓦgrandcanyonplaza.com. Though it's not very conspicuous from the highway, tucked behind the IMAX theatre and the *Red Feather Lodge*, the *Canyon Plaza* is actually huge, with 176 rooms and 56 suites, plus an outdoor pool, an indoor spa and a large but uninspiring restaurant in its central atrium. **❻**

The Grand Hotel 149 AZ-64 ☎928/638-3333, ⓦgrandcanyongrandhotel.com. The overall look of this modern hotel is a nod towards traditional park lodges. Once you get past the smart public spaces, however – designed with tour groups in mind – the rooms themselves are no better than those at its cheaper neighbours or lesser in-park options, although there is a nice figure-of-eight indoor pool, and it's also home to the *Canyon Star* restaurant (see p.49). **❽**

Holiday Inn Express AZ-64 ☎928/638-3000 or 1-888/473-2269, ⓦwww.hiexpress.com.

Unexciting, expensive but otherwise acceptable chain motel on the highway, with no pool or restaurant. ❼

Red Feather Lodge AZ-64 ℡928/638-2414 or 1-800/538-2345, ⓦredfeatherlodge.com. This long-established motel was joined a few years back by a large new hotel block; they share a pool, the rates aren't bad and the newer rooms offer a reasonably high standard. Motel ❻, hotel ❼

Seven Mile Lodge AZ-64 ℡928/638-2291. The last remaining little roadside motel in Tusayan, this twenty-room place is very plain beyond its Pueblo-style doorway and hanging flowers, but it's the least expensive option around. Reservations are not accepted; rooms are simply doled out from 9am daily. Despite the slight premium charged for housing three or four guests in the same room, it's still great value for groups of (close) friends. ❹

Further afield

If even Tusayan is booked up, it's worth considering the large *Grand Canyon Inn* (℡928/635-9203 or 1-800/635-9203, ⓦgrandcanyoninn.com; ❺), beside the Chevron station at the intersection of AZ-64 and US-180 in **VALLE**, another twenty miles south. This may be a bit of a godforsaken spot, with only the Flintstones for company (see below), but the inn has modern rooms at reasonable prices, a heated outdoor pool and a standard restaurant that's open for all meals. The more rudimentary *Grand Canyon Motel*, across the highway and open in summer only (❹), is booked through the same office.

Failing either of these, your closest options are in Flagstaff, Williams and Cameron.

Camping

Tent and RV camping (without hook-ups) is available at the Park Service's year-round **Mather Campground**, south of the main road through Grand Canyon Village, not far from Market Plaza. Sites for up to two vehicles and six people cost $18 per night between March and mid-November, when reservations (strongly recommended) can be made up to six months in advance (℡1-877/444-6777, ⓦwww.recreation.gov). If you're running late on the day of your reservation, you can contact the campsite directly on ℡928/638-7851 to confirm your arrival. Between December and February sites are first-come, first-served and the fee drops to $15 per night. They also have walk-in sites for hikers and bikers year round ($6).

Trailer Village, adjacent to Mather Campground and open between May and mid-October only, offers exclusively RV sites with hook-ups, which cost $34 per site per night for two people, plus $3 for each additional adult. Reserve through Xanterra (℡303/297-2757 or 1-888/297-2757, ⓦgrandcanyonlodges.com).

In summer, additional first-come, first-served sites without hook-ups, are available 25 miles east of Grand Canyon Village at the NPS-run **Desert View Campground** (May to mid-Oct; no reservations; $12).

Outside the park, **Tusayan** holds a commercial campsite, *Camper Village* (℡928/638-2887, ⓦgrandcanyoncampervillage.com; some RV hook-ups; $25–50), while two miles further south the Kaibab National Forest runs the minimally equipped, first-come, first-served *Ten-X Campground* (℡928/638-2443; May–Sept; no hook-ups or showers; $10). Twenty miles further south, in Valle, *Flintstone's Bedrock City* (mid-March to Oct; ℡928/635-2600; $20 tents, $25 RV hook-ups) is a run-down commercial campsite with a simple store, snack bar and its own prehistoric theme park based on the cartoon series.

For regulations governing **backcountry camping** in the park, see p.90.

Eating and drinking

Although only the gorgeous canyon-rim dining room at *El Tovar* is noteworthy, you'll find a reasonable selection of places to **eat** in Grand Canyon Village, and you certainly won't gain anything by opting for Tusayan instead. It's also possible to buy basic **groceries** at the Canyon Village General Store, near *Yavapai Lodge*, or in Tusayan. If you're out exploring, you'll find **snack bars** at Hermits Rest (daily: summer 9am–5pm, otherwise till 4pm) and Desert View (same hours).

Grand Canyon Village

Both *El Tovar* and *Bright Angel Lodge* offer proper **restaurants**, but since their capacity is far too low to meet demand, you'll probably end up eating in the large *Maswik* or *Yavapai* **cafeterias**. For an even quicker meal, the Canyon Village General Store runs a pretty good **deli counter** (daily: summer 7am–6pm, otherwise 8am–5pm).

As for **drinking**, *El Tovar* provides a cosy, wood-panelled **cocktail lounge** (daily 11am–11pm), which serves a small menu of appetizers and desserts; at sunset, retreat with your goodies to the lovely and strangely underused outdoor terrace, on the lawn within a few feet of the rim. The lounge at *Bright Angel* (daily 11am–11pm) often features live country music and doubles as a **coffee bar** from 5.30am daily. In *Maswik Lodge*, the *Pizza Pub* is a **sports bar** with big-screen TV.

Arizona Room *Bright Angel Lodge.* Informal, plain but good-quality restaurant, just a few yards from the rim; no views to speak of, but you do get a strong sense of the vast space nearby. The open kitchen serves conventional meat and seafood meals, with sandwiches, salads and simple main dishes costing $8–11 at lunchtime, and typical dinner prices including a slab of baby back ribs for $26, a 10oz steak for $25 or a blue corn-crusted chicken breast for $16. No reservations accepted; nip in a little before sunset, or you may have to wait in the bar by the entrance for up to two hours. Daily 11.30am–3pm (March to mid-Sept only) & 4.30–10pm. Closed early Jan to mid-Feb.

Bright Angel Restaurant *Bright Angel Lodge.* Straightforward, windowless diner open for every meal and serving pretty much anything you might want, from snacks, burgers, sandwiches and salads for under $10 to steaks at around $20. Daily 6.30am–10pm; no reservations.

Canyon Cafe *Yavapai Lodge.* Locals prefer the *Yavapai*'s large cafeteria to the *Maswik*'s for its salad bar and fried chicken, and slightly lower prices, but if you're not staying here, it's not worth a special trip. All main dishes cost under $10, with daily specials at $9 and a two-piece chicken dinner for $6.20. The lines are often long, but it's possible to skip straight to the chicken counter. Beyond the central dining area, which has a dull canteen-like feel, there's a nicer glassed-in annexe. Summer daily 6am–10pm,

spring and autumn daily 7am–8pm; shorter hours and closures in low season.

Canyon Coffee House *Bright Angel Lodge.* Early-morning organic coffees and scones, served in the *Bright Angel's* bar. Daily 5.30–11am.

El Tovar *El Tovar* ☎ 928/638-2631, ext 6432. Very grand, very classy dark-wood dining room, with subdued lighting and lovely big windows that focus all attention outwards, especially at sunset – though only the front tier of tables have actual canyon views. Reservations are accepted for dinner only, and tend to be grabbed days or weeks in advance. The food itself is rich and expensive, especially at dinner, when main dishes such as roast duck or salmon tostada cost around $25, and steaks more like $35. Appetizers are a bit more imaginative, with devilled crab cakes at $13 and French onion soup at $7. Lunchtime sandwiches, tacos and so on cost more like $10–15. Daily 6.30am–11am, 11.30am–2pm & 5–10pm.

Maswik Cafeteria *Maswik Lodge.* Self-service fast food, aimed especially at tour groups, with separate Mexican and Italian sections, as well as burgers and standard plate lunches. Breakfast can come in under $5, but main dishes at lunch and dinner are closer to $10. Offers two spacious seating areas plus an adjoining "Pizza Pub", with sports TV and a substantial menu of pizzas. Daily 6am–10pm; pub Mon–Fri 5–11pm, Sat & Sun 3–11pm.

Tusayan

Tusayan's two finest restaurants are, no surprise, in its two fanciest hotels. All other sizable hotels have run-of-the-mill dining rooms, while the town hosts such self-explanatory family restaurants as *We Cook Pizza & Pasta* (☎928/638-2278), and *Yippe-Ei-O!*, plus fast-food chains including *McDonald's* and *Pizza Hut*, and a couple of small coffee-and-wi-fi places (see below).

Canyon Star *The Grand Hotel* ☎928/638-3333. Large, attractive hotel restaurant, where dinner is a choice between "hardy ranch fare", like $30 steaks or $18 barbecue ribs, or lighter salads and fish dishes. Lunchtime salads, sandwiches and Mexican staples mostly cost around $10. The food's nothing special, but the central dancefloor hosts "Native American Experience" dances (6.30pm & 8pm nightly), scheduled primarily for tour groups and often featuring hoop dancers, and live country music. The adjoining saloon has big-screen live sports. Daily 7–10am, 11am–2pm & 5–9pm.

Coronado Room *Best Western Grand Canyon Squire Inn* ☎928/638-2681. The *Squire Inn*'s smart dinner-only dining room serves reasonable-quality all-American main dishes like prime rib or filet mignon for around $28, as well as such Southwestern fare as chimichangas and fajitas for around $20. Its trademark dessert is a white chocolate piano filled with chocolate mousse. Daily 5–10pm.

Listings

Bank Chase Bank in Market Plaza is open Mon–Thurs 9am–5pm & Fri till 6pm, and has a 24hr ATM.

Camping equipment For sale or rent at the Canyon Village General Store in Market Plaza (daily: summer 7am–9pm, spring & autumn 8am–8pm, winter till 7pm; ☎928/638-2262).

Garage The auto repair garage in the heart of Grand Canyon Village is open daily 8am–noon & 1–5pm; 24hr emergency service also available (☎928/638-2631).

Gas The closest gas stations to the South Rim are in Tusayan and at Desert View.

IMAX Grand Canyon IMAX Theater is in the National Geographic Visitor Center in Tusayan (☎928/638-2203, ◍explorethecanyon.com; March–Oct daily 8.30am–8.30pm, Nov–Feb daily 10.30am–6.30pm; $12.50 adults, under 11s $9.50). The hourly showings, on the half-hour, of its 34min big-screen movie are mildly entertaining, but far from essential viewing.

Laundromat A large and inexpensive coin-operated laundry is located just outside the entrance to *Mather Campground*. Summer daily 6am–11pm, last load 9.45pm; spring and autumn daily 7am–9pm, last load 7.45pm; winter daily 8am–6pm, last load 4.45pm.

Medical help Call ☎911 for emergencies; ☎928/638-2551 for the village clinic (daily 8am–6pm; emergencies only at other times); and ☎928/638-2395 for dental services.

Post office In Market Plaza, near *Yavapai Lodge* (Mon–Fri 9am–4.30pm, Sat 11am–1pm; lobby, with stamp machines, daily 5am–10pm).

Showers Coin-op showers, starting at $2 and open to all visitors, are in the laundry building at the entrance to *Mather Campground* (daily: summer 6am–11pm, spring and autumn 7am–9pm, winter 8am–6pm).

Travellers with disabilities The park's comprehensive *Accessibility Guide* is available at all visitor centres and lodges, or online at ◍nps.gov/grca. For more information, see p.31.

Weddings Between May and mid-October, the Park Service allows visitors to rent the lovely isolated overlook at Shoshone Point (see p.60) for weddings and other special occasions (☎928/638-7761).

Wi-fi and internet access Although in theory all the lodges in Grand Canyon Village offer free wi-fi access, it's not very reliable. Your best bet is the lobby and courtyard of the park headquarters, across the road from Market Plaza. There are also two internet cafés in Tusayan, *Canyon Coffee* and *RP's Stage Stop*.

Exploring the South Rim

Naturally enough, the first thing that every visitor wants to do is to see the canyon. Where you see it for the first time doesn't actually matter all that much; of the twenty or so major, named viewpoints along the South Rim, plus any number of others in between, no single one can be said to be the "best". In any case, you don't have to move from place to place to obtain radically different views of the canyon; staying in one spot, and watching the colours and shadows change as the day progresses, achieves much the same end.

However, contrary to what you might expect, the views from **Grand Canyon Village** itself are not exceptionally good. To enjoy long-range panoramas, you have to head at least as far from the central village as **Maricopa** or **Yavapai** points. Both of those, as well as the majority of the overlooks along the two rim-edge sightseeing routes – **Hermit Road** to the west, and **Desert View Drive** to the east – make ideal vantage points from which to see an unforgettable canyon **sunrise** or **sunset**.

Grand Canyon Village and around

For almost a century after the *El Tovar* opened in 1905, at the centre of what was to become **Grand Canyon Village**, most South Rim visitors got their first glimpse of the canyon from the rim-edge footpath alongside the hotel. These days, however, your initiation may well come at **Mather Point**, more than a mile to the east, which is the closest overlook to the information plaza. That's no cause for regret; the sweeping canyonscape visible from there is far more comprehensive than any obtainable from the village.

Mather Point

An easy walk of just a few hundred yards from the information plaza, busy **Mather Point** centres on a pair of rocky outcrops that jut out just below the rim. When the crowds prove too much, there's always space somewhere along the railed rim trail nearby, with subtly changing views at every step.

For prospective hikers in particular, Mather Point makes a perfect introduction to the canyon. Its basic orientation being northeastwards, you find yourself looking straight up Bright Angel Canyon on the far side, as it skewers its way down from the North Rim. This is the route followed by the **North Kaibab Trail**, which starts its descent not far east of *Grand Canyon Lodge* (see p.102); a glint of metal halfway along betrays the presence of the footbridge that spans Bright Angel Creek. Two other rim-to-river trails can be spotted closer at hand. To the east, the **South Kaibab Trail** zigzags down from Yaki Point, while the further west of the two visible stretches of the Colorado River marks the point where it's reached by the **Bright Angel Trail**. And you can even see what all the trails are heading for: nestling close to the other tiny patch of river are the cabins of **Phantom Ranch**.

Yavapai Point

If you walk west for around ten minutes from Mather Point – that is, turn left along the rim as you come from the information plaza – you'll come to **Yavapai Point**. This is also the easternmost point served by shuttle buses on the blue Village Route, and offers parking for private vehicles as well, though not enough to meet demand at busy periods. Long-range views from here are similar to those from Mather, meaning that the full range of pyramid-shaped buttes known as "temples" line up in front of the North Rim. From left to right, the sequence runs Osiris, Shiva, Isis, Buddha, Manu, Deva, Brahma, Zoroaster and Vishnu. Two

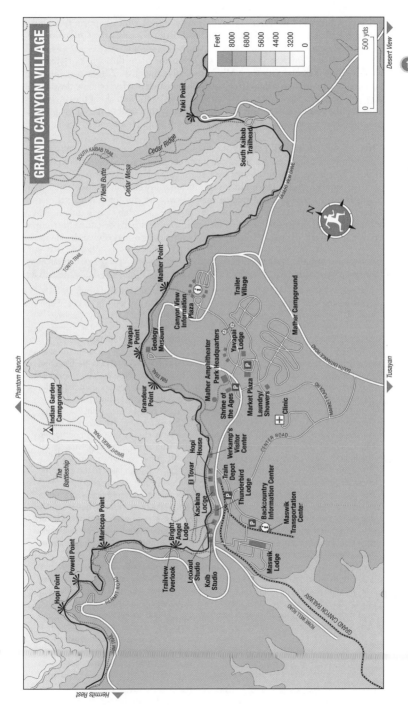

GRAND CANYON VILLAGE

different segments of the river are now on view, one of which happens to include both the Kaibab Suspension Bridge, or "Black Bridge", across the Colorado, and Phantom Ranch.

Nearby, if you can tear your eyes away from the view through its tinted bay windows, the **Yavapai Geology Museum** (daily: hours vary from 8am–8pm in summer to 8am–5pm in winter; free) holds illuminating displays on how the canyon may have been formed. It takes another ten minutes' walk west along the rim before rounding the corner of Grandeur Point brings you within sight of the village proper, and a good ten minutes more beyond that to reach Hopi House and *El Tovar*.

The view from El Tovar

Grand Canyon Village ranges along the inner curve of a recess that cuts well back into the South Rim. Such features are known to geologists as "**arenas**"; this one is also a "**swale**", in that the middle is significantly lower than the two sides. As a result, from the paved, railed terrace that follows the rim for the length of the village you can only see straight across the canyon – though by any standards that's still a stupendous prospect. The long promontories to either side end at **Maricopa Point** to the west, the ridge beneath which stretches into a sturdy sandstone mesa

---

Sunset and sunrise

Perhaps the single question Grand Canyon park rangers most tire of being asked is, "Where's the best place to watch the sunset?" The answer is, there is no best place, neither for sunset nor for sunrise. How could there be? Each rim of the canyon is almost three hundred miles long, and every yard of the way along, the views are different. The weather, cloud cover and visibility too are in constant flux.

That said, the canyon *does* look especially dramatic at the start and end of each day. When the sun is high in the sky, the colours of the rocks tend to be bleached out, and heat and dust can diminish visibility. By contrast, when the sun is low, the rich reds and oranges of the sandstone formations emerge, in stark contrast to the sharp black shadows, and the whole spectacle can be simply stunning.

It's well worth ensuring that you're at a major canyon viewpoint as sunset approaches, and, to a lesser extent, at dawn. On the South Rim, that basically means getting away from the village itself, which because it stands at a low spot on an indentation in the canyon wall does not command long-range canyon views to either the east or west. Ideally, it's best to have both, which means somewhere like Hopi, Mohave or Pima points to the west, or Yavapai, Yaki or Desert View to the east. The most popular spots of all tend to be Hopi Point for the sunset and Yavapai for sunrise; the down side of that, however, is that often a thousand or more people attempt to cram into those single small areas at the relevant moment. It's always better to play things by ear, and simply hope to find a relatively quiet area where you can wander at will, rather than jostle for position. A strong recommendation would be Shoshone Point, which because it's a twenty-minute walk from the nearest road rarely sees more than a handful of visitors.

Finally, bear in mind that it's not the sunset that's the spectacle, it's the canyon; if you aim to arrive five minutes before the precise time the sun goes down, you'll see very little. To illuminate anything within the canyon itself, the sun has to be significantly above the horizon, so the finest viewing comes in the final hour or so before sunset, and it comes from looking east, away from the sun and towards those buttes and temples that continue to catch direct sunlight, not west into the shadows. Similarly, it doesn't matter if you miss the moment of dawn; it's the ensuing hour, in which the rising sun picks out the canyon's pinnacles one by one, that will live in your memory.

The actual time the sun rises over the Grand Canyon varies from 5.11am in midsummer to 7.40am in midwinter; sunset ranges from 7.49pm down to 5.13pm.

known picturesquely as the Battleship, and **Grandeur Point** to the east. Straight down below, the **Bright Angel Trail** threads through the oasis of **Indian Gardens** before disappearing into a deep crevice, while another long trail leads across the flat, pale-green Tonto Platform to its dead end at **Plateau Point**.

The defining absence in the view from *El Tovar* is the **Colorado River** itself. Although the mighty walls of the Granite Gorge – the chasm in the centre of the canyon that holds the actual river – are visible on the far side, you can't see their full 1300ft depth, and the river remains out of sight at the bottom. Thanks to the Bright Angel geological fault, however, there is a gap in the gorge, where Bright Angel Canyon slices into the **North Rim**. Just to the left at the top is *Grand Canyon Lodge*, though you're only likely to spot it after dark, when the lights come on.

A village walking tour

Grand Canyon Village stretches a lot farther back into the woods than you might imagine and includes a well-hidden residential district for park employees. While those parts hold no interest for sightseers, the rim itself is lined by an attractive assortment of historic buildings, marred only by the very plain *Thunderbird* and *Kachina* lodges.

El Tovar

Designed by Charles F. Whittlesey, the *El Tovar Hotel* opened in 1905, two years after the *Old Faithful Inn* in Yellowstone National Park had established a taste for this kind of overgrown log cabin. It took its name from Pedro El Tovar, a member of Coronado's expedition who was the first European to hear about the canyon, but was not among the party who actually came here in 1540 (see p.200).

According to the hotel's original brochure, *El Tovar* "combined in admirable proportions the Swiss châlet and the Norway villa", and guests were invited to come in search of "freedom from ultra-fashionable restrictions". At that time, each of its four floors held one single bathroom to serve 25 rooms. While you won't find any historical exhibits or displays, you can get the old-time, unhurried flavour of the place by wandering through the lobby, with its impressive displays of stuffed animal heads, and both its dining room and cocktail lounge are highly recommended (see p.48). There's also a high-quality gift store. Accommodation at *El Tovar* is reviewed on p.45.

Hopi House

Grand Canyon Village's most distinctive structure, the triple-tiered **Hopi House**, opened on January 1, 1905, just two weeks before its close neighbour the *El Tovar*. Modelled on an actual Hopi dwelling in the village of Oraibi, a hundred miles east, it was designed – by **Mary Jane Colter** (see p.54) – as a place where "the most primitive Indians in America" could both live and display their skills. Early residents included the now venerated Pueblo potter Nampeyo. These days it's neither so overtly educational nor so patronizing; instead it's a high-class gift store showcasing such Native American crafts as silver jewellery, Navajo rugs and ceramics. The main store on the ground floor is open daily from 8am until 8pm (9am–5pm in winter), while the more exclusive upstairs gallery is always open between 9am and 5pm only.

Verkamp's Visitor Center

The easternmost building on the rim, the small two-storey **Verkamp's Visitor Center** (summer daily 9am–8pm, autumn and spring daily 9am–7.30pm, winter daily till 5pm), clashes with the prevailing log-cabin style elsewhere in the village. Trader John G. Verkamp, who first appeared on the South Rim selling souvenirs from a tent in 1898, erected it as a gift store in 1905, and it remained in his family as Verkamp's Curios for a full century. The Park Service finally took it over in 2005, and it now holds displays on the history of Grand Canyon Village, including a reconstruction of Verkamp's tent, as well as a bookstore.

Bright Angel Lodge

Bright Angel Lodge, a few hundred yards west of *El Tovar* beyond the nondescript *Thunderbird* and *Kachina* lodges, was Mary Jane Colter's last major

Mary Jane Colter

No one has done more to shape and enhance visitors' experiences of the Grand Canyon than the remarkable architect **Mary Jane Colter** (1869–1958). Not only was she largely responsible for crafting the look of Grand Canyon Village, but her hand can be seen along the full length of the South Rim, from Hermits Rest in the west to the Desert View Watchtower in the east, and down by the river at Phantom Ranch. Indeed her influence extended all the way from Chicago to LA; she designed the interiors of Union Station in the former and La Grande Station in the latter, as well as numerous hotels and restaurants in between.

Colter spent fifty years working for both the Santa Fe Railroad and the Fred Harvey Company, in an era when women architects were few and far between. That Fred Harvey, the concessionaire responsible for lodging, dining and entertaining tourists on the transcontinental railroad, is often said to have "invented the Southwest" is due in large part to her vision.

Born in Pittsburgh in 1869, Mary Colter was raised in St Paul, Minnesota. Trained at the California School of Design in San Francisco, she was heavily influenced by the nascent Arts and Crafts movement, which argued that American architects should seek their inspiration at home, using local materials and looking to indigenous examples, rather than feeling obliged to work in traditional European styles. Colter herself, above all, had a lifelong passion for Native American design.

Colter's first Grand Canyon commission produced the Pueblo-influenced **Hopi House**, a showcase for Hopi craft workers, in 1905. Both **Hermits Rest** and **Lookout Studio** followed in 1914, with **Phantom Ranch** appearing in 1922. Her best-loved masterpiece, the **Watchtower** at Desert View, was completed in 1932, and **Bright Angel Lodge** came along three years later. Meanwhile she also created such signature Harvey hotels as **El Navajo** in Gallup and the wonderful **La Posada** in Wilmslow.

Her role went far beyond producing the overall design. She'd supervise every step of construction, choosing individual rocks and timbers for both authenticity and inherent beauty, and tearing apart anything that failed to meet her exacting standards. Her attention to detail was legendary, with the interior design seen as every bit as important as the overall edifice. Thus she was responsible for the china service used on the *Super Chief* train, which incorporated motifs taken from ancient Mimbres pottery.

Even as Colter was completing her final job in 1949, a cocktail lounge at *La Fonda* hotel in Santa Fe, her various Route 66 landmarks were starting to close down. Having sadly observed "there's such a thing as living too long," she died in January 1958, bequeathing her extensive collection of Native American jewellery and ceramics to the museum at Mesa Verde National Park. Since her death, however, her unique contribution to the American West has been increasingly recognized, and much of her finest work has been lovingly restored.

Author Frank Waters conjured up a beautifully romantic portrait of Colter in his 1950 book, *Masked Gods*: "For years an incomprehensible woman in pants, she rode horseback through the Four Corners, making sketches of prehistoric Pueblo ruins, studying details of construction…She could teach masons how to lay adobe bricks, plasterers how to mix washes, carpenters how to fix viga joints."

work at the canyon. Completed in 1935, as tourist numbers began to pick up after the worst of the Depression, it replaced *Bright Angel Camp*, a ramshackle assortment of cabins and tents. The idea was to provide several cheaper grades of accommodation in a complex of differing but homogenous buildings that looked more like a genuine village. Two historic structures were incorporated in their entirety: the gable-roofed pioneer **Buckey O'Neill Cabin**, attached to the main lodge, and the separate **Cameron Hotel**, also known as Red Horse Station, which has at various times been a stagecoach station, a hotel and a US post office.

To the left of the lobby, the lodge's **History Room** features a ten-foot-tall fireplace that displays all the principal types of rock found in the Grand Canyon, in the correct chronological sequence. It also hosts displays on varying aspects of the canyon's past, focusing especially on the heyday of the Fred Harvey Company (see p.202). Lodging at *Bright Angel Lodge* is reviewed on p.45, and its restaurant on p.48.

Lookout Studio

Lookout Studio, which appears to grow organically from a narrow rocky protuberance just west of *Bright Angel Lodge*, was built by Mary Jane Colter for the Fred Harvey Company in 1914 as a "tiny rustic club". The idea was that tourists would shelter here rather than the rival Kolb Studio during bad weather, or simply while away their afternoons in solitude. Both the building itself, with its Pueblo stylings, and the view from its open-air terrace, are as appealing as ever, but it now holds just another hectic gift store (summer daily 8am–sunset, otherwise 9am–5pm).

Kolb Studio

At the head of the Bright Angel Trail, the **Kolb Studio** (daily: spring and autumn 8am–7pm; summer till 8pm; winter till 5pm) spills over the edge of the canyon, with its entrance at rim level and another storey down below. This was originally the home and workplace of Emery and Ellsworth Kolb, two brothers who opened a photographic studio here in 1902. They'd take pictures of each day's contingent of departing mule riders, run down the trail to do their developing using the water at Indian Gardens and then run back to have the prints ready when the riders returned. In 1911 and 1912, they also shot the first-ever film of a boating expedition along the entire canyon. This became the longest-running movie of all time; Emery presented it here daily from 1915 until soon before his death, aged 95, in 1976.

Its photographic days long over, the studio is now divided between a well-stocked bookstore upstairs, where there's also a nice little bay window offering superb views, and a very nice gallery whose single room takes up the whole of the downstairs floor and hosts changing exhibitions.

Hermit Road

The seven-mile, dead-end scenic drive officially known as **Hermit Road**, but familiar to many returning visitors as **West Rim Drive**, starts a hundred yards west of *Bright Angel Lodge*, just as Grand Canyon Village peters out. Offering a succession of very different but consistently impressive canyon panoramas, it's the most obvious, and most enjoyable, half-day sightseeing trip from the village. In summer it offers a welcome escape from the crowds and traffic elsewhere along the rim, as the only vehicles allowed access are the Hermits Rest Route **shuttle buses**,

All hiking trails that descend into the canyon from the South Rim are described in **Chapter 3**, and shown, along with the rim trails described in this chapter, on the map on p.86.

Mule rides

Joining a **mule train** from Grand Canyon Village is a fine old canyon tradition. These days, however, you can only ride down into the canyon itself as part of an overnight excursion; the shorter day-trips stay above, and indeed largely away from, the rim.

All rides set off from Grand Canyon Village; precise timings vary. The **overnight** trips spend the morning descending the Bright Angel Trail to the riverside **Phantom Ranch**, where you'll spend the day exploring and sleep in two-person cabins. Soon after sunrise the next morning, the mules set off back up the Bright Angel Trail (though it's anticipated that they'll return to their former route, ascending the South Kaibab Trail, at some point in the future). You should be back at *Bright Angel Lodge* in time for lunch. Trip costs, including lodgings and all meals, are $482 for one person or $850 for two. **Two-night** rides, available between November and March only, follow the same route but stay another night down at the ranch, at a cost of $674 for one or $1121 for two.

The only **day-trip** available is a three-hour round trip, which heads through the woods as far as the **Abyss Overlook**, west of Mohave Point. The ride takes 75 minutes each way, and the half-hour at the overlook is the only time you get any canyon views. Offered twice daily from March to mid-October, and once daily otherwise, it costs $117.

Riders must be at least four feet seven inches tall (1.38m), speak fluent English and weigh not more than 200 pounds (91kg) for the overnight rides, or 225 pounds (102kg) for the day-trips. It's not unusual to see would-be mule riders jogging in a desperate attempt to sweat off those last few pounds. While prior experience is unnecessary, take seriously the warnings that you should be afraid neither of large animals nor of great heights.

Places are limited, so make a reservation as early as possible (℡928/638-3283, 1-888/297-2757 or 303-297-2757); they're accepted up to thirteen months in advance. If you arrive without a reservation, put yourself on the waiting list at the *Bright Angel Lodge* Transportation Desk and turn up there at 6am on the morning you want to ride; there are usually a few last-minute cancellations each day.

the Xanterra tour buses and those displaying disabled permits. Private cars are otherwise permitted only between December and February.

What was then called the **Hermit Rim Road** was constructed by the Santa Fe Railroad between 1910 and 1912 in order to provide stagecoach excursions for their rail passengers. At that time, the Bright Angel Trail was privately owned, so the Santa Fe laid out their own Hermit Trail, at the far end of the road, which they used for mule rides and overnight trips. It's still there; see p.107. The **"Hermit"** name, incidentally, was a piece of harmless myth-making centred around one Louis Boucher, a white-bearded old prospector who made his home for twenty years at Dripping Springs, just below the trailhead.

While for most of its length the road runs within a few yards of the canyon, it's parallelled, as ever, by the **Rim Trail** (T1), even closer to the edge. No one ever bothers to walk the trail's entire seven miles, but the ideal way to explore is to combine judicious use of the shuttle buses with stretches of **walking**. Paved for the first 1.4 miles, as far as Maricopa Point, the trail later becomes an unmarked, and not always very conspicuous, dirt path. It's not an utterly straightforward hike, as it can be very uneven underfoot and occasionally teeters along alarming drop-offs – in which case you can always retreat to the road – but it's not nearly as tiring as the inner canyon trails. So long as you bring a bottle of water, you should have no problems.

It's important to realize that although the buses make eight stops, they do so only on their **outward** journey. You can only pick up a bus heading back to the village from four places: Hermits Rest, Pima Point, Mohave Point or Powell Point. That means you can't simply walk or take a bus to either of the first two overlooks and then ride straight back again. You can ride to one of those overlooks and hike back, but if you want to catch a bus home you must first get at least as far as Powell Point.

Travelling the full length of Hermit Road, out and back, without ever getting off the bus takes about 75 minutes. To allow time for a couple of short hikes, and a stop at Hermits Rest, give yourself perhaps three hours. Alternatively, you need never get on a bus at all; the four-mile round trip hike from the village to Hopi Point and back, for example, takes under two hours.

Finally, **cycling** is permitted on Hermit Road year-round, though you're expected to dismount every time a shuttle goes past. For details of cycle rental and shuttle services, see p.44.

Trailview Overlook

The first shuttle stop, **Trailview Overlook**, is in fact a large car park that serves two distinct viewpoints, known as **Trailview I** and **II**. Although the road initially makes an extravagant loop inland, this spot is less than three-quarters of a mile from the village, thus the views are similar, albeit from a slightly higher elevation. However, you will find a sweeping prospect of the village itself, staggered along the canyon rim.

As the name suggests, the viewpoints also offer a fine overview of the **Bright Angel Trail**. Prospective hikers can see exactly what they're in for, as every cruel red-dirt switchback is clearly etched against the canyon walls below.

Maricopa Point

A little over a mile along, the Rim Trail, thus far fully paved, rounds a corner and passes out of sight of Grand Canyon Village. Views now finally open up to the west as well as to the east, so the railed, rocky overlook at **Maricopa Point** commands a sweeping canyon panorama. The second shuttle stop, 1.4 miles out from the village, this is a prime spot for identifying the majestic buttes on the far side of the river, such as the Brahma and Zoroaster "temples", each with its capping layer of hard red sandstone.

The monumental parade stretches from Vishnu Temple in the east, isolated beyond Cape Royal – the last point visible on the North Rim – to Isis Temple far to the west. Lower in the foreground stands Cheops Pyramid, with beneath it what geologists call the "Grand Canyon Series" of tilted silt, shale and sandstone, and below that the harsh twisted schist of the Granite Gorge. To the south of the unseen river, the Battleship promontory, so stark and conspicuous from the village, can now be seen, if not as readily recognized, from above.

Powell Point

West of Maricopa Point, both the road and the trail (now unpaved) detour inland around a high fence festooned with solemn radiation warnings. In the heart of this enclosure lurks what remains of the **Orphan Mine**. Having started out mining copper a thousand feet below the rim in 1893, it became America's largest uranium producer in the 1950s. Amazingly, the company that owned it also ran an on-site hotel, the *Grand Canyon Inn*, which it threatened to expand in terraces far beneath the rim. Both hotel and mine went out of business in the late 1960s, however, and the land here was acquired by the park in 1988. A clean-up effort is slowly continuing, and the mine's hulking headframe was finally dismantled in 2009. There are still significant uranium deposits in the vicinity, located by no coincidence at all in areas that remain outside the protection of the park.

The headland immediately west of the mine is **Powell Point**, where a short walk from the next shuttle stop leads to the spot where the park was officially dedicated on April 30, 1920. This was known as Sentinel Point until 1916, when a small Maya-style stepped pyramid was erected as a memorial to John Wesley Powell, who had recently died, and the crews of his two Colorado expeditions. From the paved but rail-less viewing area on its far side, you can look across the river to the curious semicircular cliff wall of the "temple" known as the **Tower of Set**; shaped like an opening bracket, it's mirrored by a similar wall on **Isis Temple** to the east.

Hopi Point

Two miles out from Grand Canyon Village, **Hopi Point** is the busiest of the western viewpoints. Its reputation as the perfect place from which to admire the **sunset** rests on the fact that this promontory thrusts further north than any of its neighbours, with the vast panoply that spreads to the west forming just part of what's virtually a 360-degree canyon prospect. As described in the box on p.52, however, literally thousands of visitors flock to Hopi Point on summer evenings, which can make it feel uncomfortably crowded.

The shuttle buses don't go right to the tip of the large car park here, so you can take a short loop stroll around its tiered perimeter, catching assorted glimpses of the Colorado along the way. The most dramatic segment of the river lies immediately below Plateau Point (see p.95), the last few yards of the trail to which are also visible. It's hard to believe that the river is 350ft wide down there, lying at the foot of gnarled and impossibly ancient walls of black schist streaked through with vertical pink faults. To the west, the Colorado threads its tortuous way towards the ocean between interleaved spurs of red rock, and a maze of lesser canyons twists among the mighty buttes.

A plaque at Hopi Point commemorates the Civilian Conservation Corps, a Depression-era labour force set up by Franklin Roosevelt. Nicknamed "The President's Tree Army", the corps did much valuable work in the park between 1933 and 1942. Another directs your attention to Birdseye Point on the North Rim, and honours Colonel Claude Hale Birdseye, the Chief Topographic Engineer of the US Geological Survey, who headed a survey expedition through the canyon in 1923.

Mohave Point

Road and trail curve gracefully west of Hopi Point for three-quarters of a mile, tracing the lip of a lesser basin sometimes known as **The Inferno**, to reach **Mohave Point**. The long-range prospect from this large railed promontory (pronounced *mo-harvey*) remains substantially unchanged, though for once there are no placards to tell you what you're seeing.

Views back to the east are comprehensively blocked by the sheer cliffs below Hopi Point – at least now you can appreciate quite how steep it is. These stark sandstone walls glow spectacular shades of red towards dusk, while the equally impressive cliffs to the west acquire creeping impenetrable shadows. Two more stretches of the Colorado can now be seen, including the foaming white turmoil of **Granite Rapid**.

The Abyss

Another huge recess indents the line of the South Rim west of Mohave Point, named **The Abyss** in deference to its immensely steep sides. Shuttle buses make their next stop a mile along, at the far end of the **Great Mohave Wall**, which plummets over three thousand feet straight down.

Though the casual observer might well assume that the peaks now visible on the western horizon lie further along the South Rim, they are in fact across on the far side of the river. They belong to the **Uinkarets** range, and include the 8026ft **Mount Trumbull**, which is almost sixty miles distant. Closer at hand, four successive parallel sandstone ridges stand like stage scenery in front of Pima Point.

The main reason anyone gets off the bus at the Abyss is to hike in either direction along the vertiginous Rim Trail. There's no real danger to the trail, but as ever, if the drop starts to bother you, you can always walk along the road instead.

Monument Creek Vista

Almost a mile west of the Abyss, shuttle buses halt at another overlook, **Monument Creek Vista**, which as the name suggests is set back at the head of the drainage channel cut by Monument Creek. The main reason to dismount at this stop is that from here on west, the paved, three-mile **Greenway Trail**, constructed closer to the canyon edge than the modern highway, along the 1910 route of the Hermit Rim Road, offers superbly peaceful and exhilarating hiking and cycling.

Pima Point

Pima Point lies four miles beyond Mohave Point, along a spur road off Hermit Road, and at the tip of a promontory that separates the basins cut by Monument Creek to the east – responsible for the Abyss – and Hermit Creek to the west. By now, this side of the canyon is so abrupt that the Colorado is less than two horizontal miles distant, and you can look straight down into the maw of the three-quarters of a mile **Granite Rapid**. From the far bank, however, it's another twelve labyrinthine miles to the North Rim. Looking west, a significant stretch of **Boucher Rapid**, named after the "Hermit" Louis Boucher (see below), is also visible. This whole westward prospect is especially stunning in the early morning, with the last headland visible on the South Rim, **Havasupai Point**, separated by only the tiniest notch in the horizon from **Powell Plateau** on the North Rim. Helpful park-service displays near the bus stop illustrate the canyon's geological structure using photos of nearby formations, and explain how the canyon starts to change further to the west, beyond the areas visible from Hermit Road.

In the days when Santa Fe mule rides headed down the Hermit Trail – also conspicuous down on the Tonto Platform below – tourists would stay overnight at **Hermit Camp**. Few traces survive of the camp itself, and none of the aerial tramway that supplied it, from the west side of Pima Point.

Hermits Rest

Hermit Road ends slightly over a mile past Pima Point, at the **Hermits Rest** waystation, laid out by Mary Jane Colter in 1914 as an artful evocation of the dwelling of some imaginary canyon prospector. The path from the car park leads through a deliberately crude archway of stone slabs, decked with a hanging bell found by Colter in an antique store, and then along the canyon rim to what at first glance appears to be no more than a ramshackle pile of rocks stacked against the hillside. Closer inspection reveals a rambling but very inviting structure, centring on a massive domed fireplace, and holding a large gift store that also sells simple snacks, like sandwiches and cookies (daily: summer 8am–7.30pm; rest of year 9am–sunset). Even the soot that blackens the fireplace is fake; as Colter put it, "You can't imagine what it cost to make this place look old". President Obama stopped in to admire it in August 2010.

As Hermits Rest is oriented towards the side canyon shaped by Hermit Creek, it doesn't offer quite the same extensive views as Pima or Maricopa points. Only a tiny patch of the Colorado is now visible, but you can at least look up the creek towards its source, **Dripping Spring**, where hermit Louis Boucher really did make his home. The **Hermit Trail**, abandoned by the Santa Fe Railroad in 1931 but still popular with inner-canyon hikers (see p.107), starts a little way past the store.

❶ Desert View Drive

Desert View Drive runs for 23 miles east from Mather Point to Desert View itself, just inside the park's eastern entrance station. It was constructed in 1931, as East Rim Drive; more visitors were now arriving by car than by rail, and they wanted to be able to follow the full length of the South Rim. These days it counts as a continuation of AZ-64 up from Williams, which extends all the way east to Cameron, but there are no further canyon overlooks beyond Desert View.

Desert View Drive is the one part of the South Rim that's open year-round for self-guided driving tours; only Yaki Point along the way, the easternmost stop on the shuttle-bus network, is ever closed to private vehicles. Xanterra bus tours make the entire round trip to the end and back, as described on p.44. If you're driving yourself, allow two hours at the very least to complete the round trip. In addition to the formal viewpoints described below, the road occasionally runs very close to the rim; you're not supposed to stop for picnics and sightseeing, but plenty of people do.

Yaki Point

The first of the Desert View Drive lookouts, **Yaki Point**, stands a mile along a spur road that begins a short way east of the start of the drive. Closed to private vehicles between March and November, it's served year-round by free shuttle buses from the village (see p.43).

A mere two miles east of Yavapai Point as the condor flies, Yaki Point commands much the same trans-canyon views as its neighbour. Straight across the river stands Zoroaster Temple with its fluted sides, while thanks to the curve of the Colorado, Vishnu Temple to the right is silhouetted against the eastern horizon. The stark finger of the Watchtower at Desert View can also be seen to the east, almost fifteen miles distant.

Although five different **inner-canyon trails** are visible from Yaki Point – including the Bright Angel, Plateau Point and Tonto trails this side of the river, and the Clear Creek Trail on the far side – the Colorado itself remains stubbornly out of view. The fifth trail, the **South Kaibab Trail** (see p.100), is the main reason people take the turn-off to Yaki Point; it starts its quickfire descent to Phantom Ranch from its own separate car park, just 0.3 miles off Desert View Drive. From the main overlook, you can spot it far below, switchbacking down an exposed scree slope of red rock between two buttes, while scrambling out onto the rocks beyond the viewpoint offers clearer views down to its principal staging post, O'Neill Butte. Unless you're actually hiking the trail, there's no reason to call in at the trailhead car park.

Shoshone Point

A couple of miles east of Yaki Point, **Shoshone Point** is the least-known and least-visited of the South Rim viewpoints, for the simple reason that it's only accessible on **foot**, along the easy one-mile **Shoshone Point Trail** (**T2**) from Desert View Drive. It's an absolute gem of a place, offering beautiful views along with an unparalleled sense of peace and privacy. An hour's round trip hike from the road may well offer your only chance to be alone with the canyon on the South Rim, and in fact it's arguably the finest Grand Canyon viewpoint on either rim.

The trail to Shoshone Point begins from an unpaved car park in the woods on the canyon side of Desert View Drive, 1.4 miles east of the turn-off to Yaki Point. You'll know you're at the right place if you see a grey gate barring a dirt road, and a brown park notice reading "Site Use by Permit Only". The sign is there because the park service deliberately does not publicize Shoshone Point to casual visitors, preferring instead to make it available, between May and mid-October, for weddings and other private gatherings; as mentioned on p.49, it can be reserved by calling ☎928/638-7761. However, rangers at the information plaza keep no record of whether or not the point has been reserved on any particular day, and there's no system for issuing permits to casual hikers. Instead, you're simply asked to respect the privacy of any group that may be out there, and not to hike out at all if there are a lot of vehicles at the car park. Off season, you can always be sure that it hasn't been reserved.

Walking at a fairly brisk pace, it takes around fifteen minutes to follow the meandering trail, with minimal elevation change, through first ponderosa pines and then pinyon and juniper – the shade is welcome in summer – as far as the canyon rim. It's a very pleasant hike, with plenty of bird and animal life along the way to hold your attention.

Beyond a clearing that holds picnic tables, BBQ grills and a couple of portable toilets, the point itself stands in splendid isolation, far from the clamour of the crowds and the noise of traffic on the roads. A solitary pale hoodoo, or rock column, marks the tip of its slender neck, which can feel a little precarious in the absence of the usual railings. The sublime views range along the full panoply of the North Rim, culminating to the east with Cape Royal at the southern tip of the Walhalla Plateau, and the crest of Vishnu Temple out in the canyon. All but straight ahead, Zoroaster and Brahma temples stand in line.

Grandview Point

Eight miles east of Yaki Point along Desert View Drive, or 6.4 miles beyond the Shoshone Point car park – making a total of twelve miles out from the village – a spur road leaves the highway to reach the first year-round car park at **Grandview Point**. Among the most dramatic and all-embracing of all canyon viewpoints, this was the place where **tourism** first took off at the Grand Canyon. After discovering rich copper deposits 3000ft below the rim in 1890, prospector Peter Berry forged the **Grandview Trail** down to his **Last Chance** mine in 1892. Five years later, with visitors gravitating to the site, Berry opened the *Grandview Hotel*. It thrived at first, but within ten years the coming of the railroad, over to the west, drove Berry out of business. A few traces of the hotel now remain, amid the forest a mile or so back from the edge.

Railroad or no, Grandview is in terms of **views** unarguably superior to Grand Canyon Village. There's no need to set foot on the precarious Grandview Trail (see p.106) in order to plot the sinuous course of the Colorado, which makes its broad and langorous entrance off to the east before disappearing into the stunning sandstone labyrinth. Down below, the twin prongs of **Horseshoe Mesa**, home to Berry's copper mine, reach out towards the North Rim. The left points to the mesa of **Wotan's Throne**, detached from the rim but still towering a couple of hundred feet taller than Grandview itself; in the centre is **Cape Royal**, at the tip of the Walhalla Plateau (see p.79); and more obvious to the right, **Cape Final** juts out at the far eastern end of the North Rim, above and behind Vishnu Temple,

Grandview Point is also an attractive spot in its own right, nestled in one of the very few stands of pure ponderosa pine to be found on the South Rim, and frequented by roaming elk at both sunset and sunrise. It's a popular haunt of coach parties, but you can always escape the hubbub if you arrive at a busy time by walking a short way down the trail.

Grandview Monocline

Starting three miles beyond Grandview, Desert View Drive abruptly descends the 300ft incline of **Buggeln Hill**, the most visible evidence of the **Grandview Monocline**. In a land of such wonders this inconspicuous geological hitch – a small fold in the rock manifesting itself as an unremarkable little hill – hardly merits a second glance, but it may well be responsible for the greatest wonder of all. As far as this point, the course of the Colorado has been southwards, slicing through softer Moenkopi Formation rock as it skirts the edge of the Kaibab Plateau. Now, however, the Grandview Monocline thrusts into its path, presenting an equally difficult wall of hard Kaibab Limestone. With no easy way out, the river is finally forced to turn west, and cut down into the Kaibab, creating the Grand Canyon as we know it.

Moran Point

Just beyond Buggeln Hill lies **Moran Point**, named after nineteenth-century artist Thomas Moran. This overlook faces west towards the heart of the maelstrom. Close at hand, higher than the lookout, an isolated rock fin known as the **Sinking Ship** juts into the canyon from atop the hill, its stratified sandstone layers bearing witness to the Grandview Monocline's angle of tilt.

Panel displays at the point explain that it was from somewhere in this general vicinity that Spanish adventurers first saw the Grand Canyon, in 1540 (see p.200). It's thought that their Hopi guides deliberately led them to a spot from which no trails were visible, to make the gorge appear an even more impassable obstacle.

Tusayan Ruin and Museum

The next parking lot, four miles on from Moran Point, is unexpectedly located south rather than north of the highway. Set back in the forest a quarter of a mile from the rim, **Tusayan Ruin** – not to be confused with the modern town of Tusayan – is an open-air archeological site that centres on the remains of a typical twelfth-century **pueblo**. Consisting of fifteen separate "rooms", including two circular ceremonial chambers or *kivas* – which suggests it was home to two separate clans – this was built in approximately 1185 AD. It was occupied for perhaps 25 years by a community of around thirty people, whose clear cultural connection with modern Pueblo Indians, and with Arizona's Hopi people in particular, means that these days they're referred to as **Ancestral Puebloans**, in preference to the older and more familiar term **Anasazi**.

Although at that time the Ancestral Puebloans were gradually withdrawing from the Grand Canyon area, the inhabitants of Tusayan, as well as farming the wash close to their homes, trekked regularly into the canyon, using what's now called the Tanner Trail. They seem to have felt some sense of menace or apprehension, as fort-like structures found at various points along the rim nearby date from the same era.

Only low stone walls now survive of the original Tusayan complex, so – much like the other two thousand or so Ancestral Puebloan sites so far identified in and around the Grand Canyon – it's nothing like as spectacular as the relics to be found in such places as Canyon de Chelly and Mesa Verde. Its very existence, however, enabled President Teddy Roosevelt to accord national monument status to the entire Grand Canyon (see p.203). A small **museum** on site (daily 9am–5pm; free) holds displays on the contemporary Navajo and Hopi peoples, as well as 4000-year-old twig figurines and Ancestral Puebloan pottery found nearby. Park rangers lead **tours** of the ruins daily at 11am and 1.30pm.

Lipan Point

Reached by a short but steeply curving access road another couple of miles on from Tusayan Ruin, **Lipan Point** ranks in the very top tier of South Rim overlooks. While the overall prospect is not very different to that from Desert View, less than three miles east, and there are no comparable facilities, Lipan tends to be a lot quieter, and it's even more perfectly poised to appreciate several pivotal events in the life of the Colorado.

Emerging from Marble Canyon to the north, the Colorado becomes visible just after it meets the Little Colorado, which cuts in from the east through the endless, flat Marble Platform. The vertical canyon walls marking the edge of the platform are known as the **Palisades of the Desert**. Immediately below Lipan, at the mouth of Tanner Canyon – a spot accessible via the **Tanner Trail** (see p.104), which starts beside the car park – the river makes its dramatic change of direction, to flow westwards rather than southwards. At first it meanders through the gently sloping eroded formations of the Grand Canyon Series, making an extravagant double curve at the mouth of **Unkar Creek**. The Unkar Delta here once held an extensive Ancestral Puebloan population, who farmed both down by the river and up on the Walhalla Plateau of the North Rim (see p.78). It's a beautiful spot, with distinct sandstone strata that strike maroon, ruby and raspberry notes at sunset. To the west, river runners face their first major whitewater challenge, as the Colorado gouges its way into the Inner Gorge and enters the ferocious mile-long **Hance Rapid**.

Desert View

Desert View, 25 miles east of Grand Canyon Village, is the last canyon viewpoint along Desert View Drive. As AZ-64, however, the road continues another 34 miles to meet US-89 at Cameron (see p.117), so Desert View also provides visitors approaching from the east with their *first* opportunity to see what all the fuss is about. Few will be disappointed: like Lipan Point, Desert View offers two staggering panoramas in one.

To the north, four miles distant, the Colorado River can be seen approaching its sudden westward turn. The stark Palisades of the Desert delineate the South Rim, while above them the pallid plains of the Marble Plateau stretch to the horizon, beneath an overwhelming sky. Ninety miles northeast, beyond the Vermilion and Echo Cliffs, lies the grey bulk of Navajo Mountain. During the Mesozoic era, until 65 million years ago, this entire vast landscape was buried beneath an additional four or five thousand feet of sedimentary sandstone. Thanks to subsequent erosion, all that remains are a few tiny vestiges, such as the reddish mesa of **Cedar Mountain** a mile or two back from the rim.

Over to the west, by contrast, the river disappears deep into the Granite Gorge, engulfed on all sides by buttes and mesas, temples, shrines and tabernacles. During the morning they present an extraordinary panoply of colours and shapes; the rich golds and reds are the first to go, leached out by the midday sun, while as dusk draws on they seem to lose all form as well, turning into mysterious interleaving shadowy screens, devoid of all three-dimensional quality.

Rather than the canyon itself, however, what immediately draws the eye is the remarkable structure perched at its very lip – the **Desert View Watchtower**. Melded almost imperceptibly into the sandstone blocks of the rim, this circular tower counts as the greatest *tour de force* of architect **Mary Jane Colter** (see p.54). Based on her study of Ancestral Puebloan remains throughout the Four Corners region, it was completed in 1932, with its design modelled on the Round Tower in southwest Colorado's Mesa Verde National Park, and the style of its masonry construction on the various towers at Hovenweep National Monument in southeast Utah. Some of the stone used was taken from nearby ruins, while it also incorporated genuine petroglyphs found near Ash Fork and even timbers from the much more recent, abandoned *Grandview Hotel* (see p.61).

Colter's aim was not to replicate an actual Puebloan building; she simply wanted to provide a fitting but not too intrusive landmark at journey's end for Fred Harvey's sightseeing tours, and to educate tourists about Native American culture ancient and modern. The building remains very much a product of its time; while it's arguably culturally intrusive, it's hard to conceive of any new park-service construction displaying even a fraction of its imagination and flair, or attracting such openness and cooperation from Native American groups.

It's no longer obvious that the ground floor of the Watchtower, which is open daily between 8am and sunset, was laid out as a ceremonial *kiva* – it's too cluttered with gifts and souvenirs – but it's still well worth taking the time to climb through its three upper storeys. A mural by Hopi artist Fred Kabotie in the first circular chamber depicts the snake legend of the Hopis, while the second holds reproduction pictographs and petroglyphs painted by a Fred Harvey employee. The uppermost floor, or "Eagle's Nest", is all but bare, but holds large panoramic windows. There's no access to the roof itself, but there is an open-air terrace adjoining the second floor, complete with strange 1930s "reflectoscopes", a sort of upside-down mirror in a box designed to enhance the aesthetic appeal of the views.

Over the years, the Watchtower has acquired a plethora of much less distinguished neighbours, including a **visitor centre** and bookstore (daily 9am–5pm); the Desert View **general store** (daily: May 9am–6pm; June–Aug 8am–6pm; Sept–April 9am–5pm); a **gas station** (daily; 24hr access with credit card); and the Trading Post gift store and **snack bar** (daily; summer 8am–7.30pm; rest of year hours vary), where the ultra-basic menu features a hamburger for $5, a cold sandwich for $4.25 and a slice of pie for $2.75. The **Desert View Campground** (see p.47) is located at the end of a short spur road from the gas station.

Few visitors make a beeline for **Navajo Point**, served by a separate car park a few hundred yards west of Desert View, even though it's the highest spot along the whole South Rim. At 7498 feet, it's still 500 feet lower than **Cape Final**, eight miles away on the North Rim, but at least you get a real sense of the forested plateau on the far side.

2

The North Rim

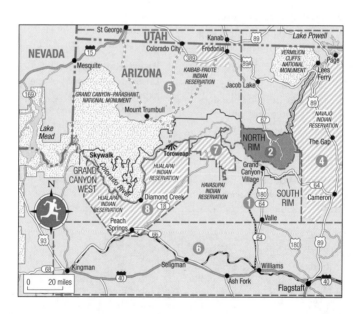

CHAPTER 2 # Highlights

✳ **Western cabins at Grand Canyon Lodge** What could be finer than a rim-edge cabin at one of the great US national park lodges? See p.70

✳ **Dining Room at Grand Canyon Lodge** Good food, friendly service and unbeatable views; just be sure to reserve in advance. See p.71

✳ **North Rim Campground** The most spacious and least crowded of the national park campgrounds. See p.71

✳ **Bright Angel Point** Pick your way beyond the lodge to the end of this perilous-looking little promontory, for magnificent sunrise and sunset views. See p.72

✳ **Point Imperial** The park's highest viewpoint enables you to see the Grand Canyon taking shape as the river cuts through the Marble Platform. See p.75

✳ **Cape Royal** The perfect vantage point from which to appreciate the overall shape of the canyon. See p.79

✳ **Angels Window** Through this natural window in the rock, the Colorado is visible far below; walk across the top for an eagle's-eye view. See p.79

✳ **Kaibab National Forest** Drive the gravel roads off the highway to explore lovely woodlands, at their most majestic in autumn. See p.80

✳ **Monument Point** This remote and little-visited viewpoint abounds in ancient marine fossils. See p.82

▲ View from Cape Royal

2

The North Rim

igher, bleaker, and much more remote than the South Rim, the **North Rim** of the Grand Canyon is only accessible to travellers about half the year. Once the only road in, **AZ–67**, has been blocked by the first major snowfall of each winter, the entire North Rim section of the national park remains closed until the following spring. Although traditionally that first snow has arrived towards the end of October, in several recent years the area has received a mere fraction of its official average annual snowfall of 140 inches, and the road has been known to close as late as December 19. That said, however, the one accommodation option on the North Rim, *Grand Canyon Lodge*, continues to operate to a more rigid schedule, opening during the second week of May and closing on October 15. After it closes, there's a hiatus until the snow comes, during which the park itself remains open, but no food, gas or lodging other than camping is available, and visitors must be prepared to leave at a moment's notice.

Even in peak season, the North Rim offers a sense of splendid isolation, and its annual quota of between 350,000 and 450,000 visitors is less than a tenth of the South Rim's. While that doesn't mean you'll have the place to yourself, it can still make you feel as though you're venturing into unexplored wilderness. The basic principle, however, is the same as at the South Rim, with a cluster of venerable park-service buildings at **Bright Angel Point**, where the main highway reaches the canyon, and another rim-edge road, on the neighbouring **Walhalla Plateau**, to the east, where drivers can take their pick from additional lookouts. **Hiking** possibilities on the North Rim are more restricted than on the South; the one inner-canyon route, the **North Kaibab Trail**, is covered in Chapter 3, while selected **rim-edge trails** are described on p.73 onwards.

Driving to the North Rim, much like the South, entails a long haul across a forested plateau. While it's actually the other half of the south side's Coconino Plateau, having been bisected by the canyon, it's here known as the **Kaibab Plateau**. AZ-67 is a much more attractive road than its South Rim counterpart, however, sweeping past majestic stands of spruce, aspen and fir, and repeatedly emerging into appealing, often flower-filled, natural meadows. The canyon too is significantly different on this side of the Colorado. Erosion is much more active; twice as much rain falls, and it freezes more often. As the Kaibab Plateau slopes south, water here flows towards the rim, which it has cut twice as far back from the river. Thus the North Rim is far more indented with massive side canyons, the largest of which, the little-known **Kanab Canyon**, effectively splits it in two. The area known as the "North Rim", and covered in this chapter, is strictly speaking just the eastern portion of the Grand Canyon's northern rim, and does not extend as far as Kanab Canyon. Its western half, and most notably the superb **Toroweap** viewpoint, can only be reached from the Arizona Strip, and is therefore covered in Chapter 5.

Human occupation of the North Rim has always been minimal. Native Americans would traditionally pass through only in summer, while Mormons and prospectors seldom ventured this way. Apart from the odd trapper and adventurer, the North Rim was hardly explored until geologists, hunters and even a few tourists began turning up at the start of the twentieth century. The first dirt road arrived from Kanab, Utah, in 1919, while driving from the South Rim only became practicable with the opening of Navajo Bridge, near Lees Ferry, in 1929.

Arrival, information and getting around

The only access to the North Rim is via **AZ-67**, which, as described on p.131, runs south for 44 miles from **Jacob Lake** to Bright Angel Point. En route, it climbs one thousand feet, reaching the highest portion of the Kaibab Plateau five miles south of **DeMotte Park**. That barely perceptible 9000ft ridge, around twelve miles short of the North Rim, roughly corresponds to the boundary of the national park. Rangers at the **North Entrance Station** just beyond collect the fees detailed on p.28, and hand out the park newspaper, *The Guide*, which is published in a separate edition for the North Rim.

AZ-67 then drops gradually south for another six miles before it intersects with Fuller Canyon Road, the access road to the Walhalla Plateau overlooks (see p.75), and for another three miles beyond that to its dead end at Bright Angel Point, passing further turn-offs for the backcountry office, the North Kaibab Trailhead and the campground, You never quite see the canyon from the highway, which comes to a halt at a turnaround in front of *Grand Canyon Lodge*, with several large car parks off to the left.

Information

The **North Rim Visitor Center**, the first building on the left as you approach the lodge complex, is the main source of information for visitors (daily May to mid-Oct 8am–6pm; ☎ 928/638-7864, ⓦ nps.gov/grca). Staff drawn from several public-lands agencies can advise on routes and conditions for hiking and backcountry road trips. They also have details of each day's free programme of **ranger talks** – held at both the lodge and the campground, as well as at certain Walhalla Plateau viewpoints – and **guided walks**. An hour-long nature walk starts here daily at 8am. Sharing the same space, the small Grand Canyon Association **bookstore** (ⓦ grandcanyon.org) stocks maps and trail guides.

The **North Rim Backcountry Office**, which issues the backcountry permits required by anyone going on an overnight hiking trip, is housed in a different ranger station, just over a mile back up the highway a quarter of a mile north of the campground (daily: mid-May to mid-Oct 8am–noon & 1–5pm; mid-Oct until winter road closure 9am–noon & 1–4pm; ☎ 928/638-7814). Day hikers do not need permits.

Transport and tours

No organized sightseeing tours are currently available at the North Rim, and there's no equivalent to the shuttle buses that serve the South Rim. The only long-distance

For more information about backcountry permits and trails from the North Rim, turn to Chapter 3, "Hiking the inner canyon".

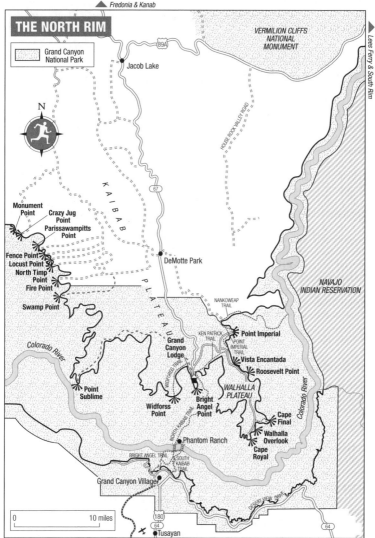

public transport is the **Transcanyon Shuttle** ($80 one-way, $150 return; cash only; ☏928/638-2820, ⓦtrans-canyonshuttle.com), which runs daily van services to the **South Rim**. Leaving from *Grand Canyon Lodge* at 7am, it reaches the South Rim at 11.30am, then departs at 1.30pm for a 6.30pm return to the lodge.

There's also a **hiker shuttle** to the North Kaibab Trailhead, which leaves the lodge at 5.45am and 7.10am daily, and costs $7 per person.

A desk in the lodge lobby handles reservations for North Rim **mule rides** (☏435/679-8665, ⓦcanyonrides.com). A one-hour rim-edge ride costs $40, while two half-day options – either along the rim to Uncle Jim Point or down the North Kaibab as far as the Supai Tunnel – cost $75. There are no full-day rides or overnight trips. The minimum age limit is 7 for the one-hour rides, and 10 for the half-day trip.

② Grand Canyon Lodge and around

The rambling, atmospheric **Grand Canyon Lodge**, a glorified log cabin in the finest national-park tradition, is poised majestically near the tip of the promontory that ends at **Bright Angel Point**. Designed by Gilbert Stanley Underwood, it was built in 1928 for the Union Pacific Railroad. Not that their trains passed anywhere nearby; instead they'd bring excursionists here as part of bus tours that also took in Zion and Bryce. After the lodge (but not its cabins) burned down in 1932, it was rebuilt in 1936 using a bit more stone and a bit less timber. The park service took it over in 1971, when Union Pacific closed down.

The lodge's lovely dining room, reviewed on opposite, is just to the right of the entrance lobby. Straight ahead, however, steps down lead to the building's best feature, a spacious viewing lounge known as the **Sun Room**, where rows of comfortable armchairs face huge picture windows. The foreground view here is of the side canyon known as **The Transept**; the Grand Canyon proper lies beyond, though you don't so much see it as sense its vast empty presence.

Open patios to either side of the Sun Room encourage you to relax and enjoy the spectacle. The one to the left holds ranks of long benches, which makes it an ideal venue for ranger talks – recent seasons have seen daily talks about canyon geology at 3pm, and condors at 5pm – while the smaller one to the right is equipped with individual reading chairs. Short footpaths lead to railed rim-edge overlooks just below, quite as dramatic as those at the point itself, and invariably packed at sunset.

Accommodation

The **guest rooms** at *Grand Canyon Lodge* are located not in the main building, but in a complex of individual cabins and larger motel-style blocks. Most of them are ranged in tiers over the well-wooded hillside beside the approach road; as they're across the road from the car park, they're usually remarkably quiet. Little paved footways thread between them, dimly lit at night beneath a sky filled with stars.

There are three different cabin types. Each of the 51 well-appointed **Western cabins** (❼) holds two queen beds, with a gas fireplace, a full-size bathroom and a porch complete with rocking chairs, and can sleep up to four people. Just four cabins stand close enough to the rim to offer **canyon views**, the only North Rim lodging options to do so; they cost $10 extra per night, which makes them fabulous value, but very difficult to reserve.

The 83 spartan **Frontier cabins** (❺) can accommodate three guests each, with one double bed and one single, and have smaller bathrooms with showers only, while the 22 upgraded **Pioneer cabins** (❻), capable of sleeping six people, comprise two separate bedrooms – with a double bed, twin bunk beds and a pull-out double futon – and a small bathroom.

Furthest from the lodge are a couple of two-storey blocks, each of which holds twenty **hotel rooms** (❺), with queen beds and private bathrooms. All cabins and rooms provide telephones but not TVs or internet access.

Reservations are available up to thirteen months in advance, and are absolutely essential; contact Forever Resorts (same day or to contact guest ☎928/638-2611, advance 480/337-1320 or 1-877/386-4383, ⊛grandcanyonlodgenorth.com). Cancellations are frequently available at short notice, so keep calling if you can't get a room, or the precise kind of room you want.

Eating and drinking

Meals in the main **Dining Room** (daily 6.30–10am, 11.30am–2.30pm & 4.45–9.45pm) are truly memorable. The room itself, with its soaring timber ceiling, is elegant and impressive, and if you're lucky enough to have a window table (assigned at random, not by reservation), you'll enjoy awesome canyon views. The actual food is not quite so exceptional; the menu consists of standard American resort cuisine, with mains such as margarita blackened salmon or five-cheese ravioli, costing around $20, and prime rib and steaks ranging up to $34. Lunch options, at around $10, centre on sandwiches, light grilled specials and salads, though there's also an all-you-can-eat buffet, while breakfast can either be a full buffet for around $12 or à la carte. Service is friendly rather than formal, and the staff seem admirably keen to answer the same old canyon queries from every table.

Reservations (☎928/638-2611) are accepted only for dinner, when they're essential. In fact, you should book your table as early in the season as possible; trying to do so once you arrive at the North Rim is liable to be way too late. Turn up without a reservation, and you'll eat at 9pm at the very best, or more likely not at all.

Two alternative options stand to either side of the lodge driveway, neither within sight of the canyon. The **Deli in the Pines**, a little windowless cafeteria, is open daily from 7am until 9pm, serving very ordinary breakfasts, then deli sandwiches or salads for around $7 and pizza either by the slice or whole pie ($15–20). Across the way, the **Rough Rider Saloon** (daily 5.30–10.30am & 11.30am–11pm) is a suitably rough-hewn **bar**, stocked with a wide range of beers and liquor, which has a separate early-morning incarnation as an **espresso bar** doling out coffee and pastries.

The **Grand Canyon Cookout Experience** is a nightly dinner show, with country music and all-you-can-eat buffet, staged close to the campground; a shuttle bus picks up diners from the *Lodge* around 6pm, and returns them by 8pm ($35, ages 3–12 $22).

Groceries and espresso are available at the general store by the campground, while the Dining Room also sells box lunches.

Camping

At the end of a spur road off AZ-67, just over a mile north of the lodge, the pleasant *North Rim Campground* offers 87 car-camping sites amid the forest; RV hook-ups are not available. All sites cost $18 per night, except for the four that flank the rim of The Transept, which cost $25. While it's important to reserve as far in advance as possible (☎1-877/444-6777 or 518/885-3639, ⊛www.recreation.gov), space is always available for backpackers, bicyclists and others travelling without vehicles ($5 each). No one can stay at the campground for more than seven nights in a calendar year.

The campground reopens each year at the same time as the lodge, but depending on the weather often stays open a little longer at the end of the season, until perhaps late October. A general store, a gas station and a laundromat with coin-operated showers are located just outside the gates.

For details of **backcountry camping** within the park, for which permits are required, see Chapter 3. It's also possible to camp outside the park boundaries in the Kaibab National Forest – contact the North Rim (see p.68) or Kaibab Plateau (see p.131) visitor centres for details – or at the campgrounds at Jacob Lake (see p.131) and DeMotte Park (see p.132).

Listings

ATM machines At the General Store alongside *North Rim Campground*, and the *Rough Rider Saloon* at Grand Canyon Lodge.

Bicycle rental Bikes, tandems and even surrey carriages are available for rent at the Outfitter Station, at the Chevron station near the campground ($17 per 2hr up to $40 per day).

Camping equipment and groceries Available at the General Store (daily 7am–8pm).

Gas Chevron station near the campground; limited hours (daily 7am–7pm).

Laundromat and showers Also near campground (daily 7am–10pm; showers $1.50, washers $1.50).

Medical help There is no health clinic on the North Rim. Call ☏911 for emergencies.

Post office In *Grand Canyon Lodge* (Mon–Fri 8–noon & 1–5pm).

Weather For the latest North Rim weather information, call ☏928/638-7888.

Wi-fi and internet access Free wi-fi inside, and on the porch of, the General Store.

Bright Angel Point

A short paved trail, starting to the left of *Grand Canyon Lodge*, leads to the very tip of **Bright Angel Point**. It's an easy walk, but the path does rise and fall a little, and in places it fills the full width of the slender spit of land, with sheer drops to either side. You're poised here between two relatively minor tributary canyons, with the deep **Transept** to your right and the mighty red wall of **Roaring Springs Canyon** to your left.

After four hundred yards, you reach the sanctuary of a railed viewing area, backed by massive boulders that daredevils climb in search of solitude. Everyone understandably regards the prospect ahead as one of the great Grand Canyon panoramas, but strictly speaking the canyon itself is all but obscured by the long straight gorge of **Bright Angel Canyon**, cutting at an oblique angle across your entire field of vision.

Bright Angel Canyon is so unusually straight because it was formed at least in part by seismic action. It therefore follows the line of the **Bright Angel Fault**, earthquakes along which were responsible for creating both this and corresponding canyons south of the river (see p.207).

Away to the right, you can just about see where it joins the Grand Canyon proper, but none of the Granite Gorge, let alone the Colorado River, is visible. You may hear the sound of rushing water, but it's coming from **Roaring Springs**, much closer to hand at almost 3500ft below, which supplies all the water used by the park on both rims (see p.103).

Mentally extending the line of Bright Angel Canyon across to the far side reveals the fault continuing up to the South Rim, though it's hard to spot a sign of life at Grand Canyon Village, eleven miles away, until the sun goes down and the lights start to flicker. That simple turn of the head also traces the easiest transcanyon hiking route – the **North Kaibab Trail**, which drops down to the Colorado on this side via Roaring Springs and Bright Angel canyons, and climbs up via the matching **Bright Angel Trail** across the river. On foot, that's a 24-mile one-way hike.

On a clear day, looking directly ahead from Bright Angel Point, you can see far beyond the South Rim to the **San Francisco Peaks** near Flagstaff. The highest point on the horizon, **Mount Humphreys**, is 62 miles distant and 12,633ft high. A few major inner-canyon buttes can be identified immediately below it, sandwiched between the far wall of Bright Angel Canyon and the South Rim beyond. The most prominent is the neat-capped **Brahma Temple**, framed between the lesser Deva and Zoroaster temples.

Kaibab Plateau trails

All **inner-canyon** hiking trails, including those that start from the North Rim, are described in Chapter 3, where you'll also find detailed advice on necessary precautions and preparations. Assuming that you're reasonably fit, and that you're not here on a scorching midsummer's day, then at least a brief foray down the **North Kaibab Trail** – see p.102 – has to be the most satisfying day hike for North Rim visitors. However, a number of much less demanding trails remain on top of the **Kaibab Plateau**, offering the chance to experience the silence of the ponderosa forest as well as lesser-known canyon perspectives. No **permits** are necessary for day hikes on any of the trails described below. Please see map on p.86 for location of hikes marked with a (T) symbol.

2

THE NORTH RIM | Kaibab Plateau trails

T3 The Transept Trail

The short **Transept Trail**, measuring 1.5 miles one way, is a backwoods route between **Grand Canyon Lodge** and the **campground**. Rather than walking along the highway, you hike beside the tributary canyon known as **The Transept** instead. Though dwarfed by the Grand Canyon proper, it still plummets an awesome half-mile below the cliff-edge path. Starting from the west side of the lodge, the trail follows the contours of the rim, circling the campground to arrive beside the general store. While it's an enjoyable enough walk, it's not so much a hiking trail in its own right as simply a convenient route from A to B, and almost no one takes it for pleasure alone.

T4 The Uncle Jim Trail

If you're looking for a medium-length day hike on the Kaibab Plateau, the four-mile loop along the **Uncle Jim Trail** is your best option. It sets off from the same car park as the North Kaibab Trail (see p.102), beside the highway 1.5 miles north of *Grand Canyon Lodge*.

Uncle Jim and his lions

The "Uncle Jim" commemorated by the Uncle Jim Trail was **James T. Owens**, a forest service warden credited with shooting 532 **mountain lions** on the North Rim between 1906 and 1918. Theodore Roosevelt wrote approvingly of Owens that "he early hailed with delight the growth of the movement among our people to put a stop to the senseless and wanton destruction of our wild life". The destruction Roosevelt and Owens deplored was of "good" animals, such as deer, by "bad" predators such as lions; their solution, to eliminate the lions, had the bonus of leaving plenty of deer for hunters to kill, which they of course saw as being neither senseless nor wanton. That early attempt at wildlife management resulted in an explosion of the deer population, followed by mass starvation, and led to a change in the policy of the Park Service, which no longer attempts to wipe out predators.

Uncle Jim was also responsible for introducing the **buffalo** herd that inhabits House Rock Valley, near the Vermilion Cliffs, as described on p.130. He and Charles Jesse "Buffalo" Jones drove 56 buffalo into the valley in 1906, where they attempted to cross-breed them with cattle and raise "cattalo". While that venture was not a commercial success, the herd continues to thrive to this day, and its members still carry cattle genes, though that's not obvious to the untrained eye. In recent years they have ventured in ever greater numbers onto the North Rim, and they're now in their turn posing wildlife management problems for the Park Service, wary of introducing non-native species onto the Kaibab Plateau.

From the mule corral at the east end of the car park, the trail heads up into the woods. At first, you get some inspiring views down the full length of **Roaring Springs Canyon**, but before long the path loses touch with the canyon rim. Half a mile along, the Ken Patrick Trail, described below, forks to the left while the Uncle Jim veers right.

Another half-mile further on, a second junction marks the start of its loop segment. Whichever route you choose will take you in the course of the next two miles to two stunning overlooks. One, the closest to **Uncle Jim Point**, faces east across the head of Bright Angel Canyon towards the Walhalla Plateau. The other looks south, to the South Rim and beyond, and also back west towards the trailhead, offering a superb view of the switchbacks via which the North Kaibab Trail insinuates itself into Roaring Springs Canyon.

T5 The Ken Patrick Trail

A much longer plateau day hike can be had by following the **Ken Patrick Trail**, which as mentioned above branches off the Uncle Jim Trail half a mile along. It's a total of ten miles long, meeting **Cape Royal Road** seven miles out from the trailhead, and then continuing to **Point Imperial** (see p.75) three miles after that. Not all that many hikers pass this way, so route-finding can be hard, with the occasional fallen tree and large patches still bearing the scars of the ferocious **Outlet Fire** of 2000, a "prescribed burn", set by the forest service, that rapidly blew out of control to cover 14,500 acres.

The most scenic stretch is the final rim-edge climb from Cape Royal Road to Point Imperial, which offers wonderful prospects of Marble Plateau to the east. If you can arrange to be dropped off along the road and picked up at the point, or vice versa, that section makes a great three-mile hike. It's also possible to continue north from Point Imperial along the **Point Imperial Trail** (T6), which leads a further three miles along the rim, again through a heavily burned area, to Saddle Mountain, where it meets the **Nankoweap Trail** (see p.111) down to the inner canyon.

T7 The Widforss Trail

The only trail to offer access to the North Rim west of the lodge area, the **Widforss Trail** is a five-mile trek to the tip of the next headland along from Bright Angel Point. While it's relatively easy walk, the only way home is to double back on yourself, entailing a ten-mile round trip that's likely to take around five hours. Making it all the way to the end is rewarded with tremendous views, but the second half of the trail runs through dense forest, so most visitors choose instead to hike just a short distance, and settle for enjoying the views close to the start.

To reach the Widforss trailhead, follow the gravel road that heads west from AZ-67 a quarter of a mile south of its junction with Fuller Canyon Road, roughly three miles north of *Grand Canyon Lodge*. Just over half a mile along, you come to the natural clearing of **Harvey Meadow**; with luck, a dispenser here should hold copies of a park-service brochure detailing fourteen numbered points along the first two miles of the trail (note that the gravel road continues for seventeen miles to **Point Sublime**, as described on p.80, but deteriorates enough to be only recommended for 4WD vehicles).

After skirting Harvey Meadow, the trail climbs gently to crest some forested rocky outcrops before serving up its first glimpse of the yawning chasm of **The Transept**. Thereafter, as it meanders and undulates up to the rim and then back into the woods, you get repeated variations on the same theme. The longest-range panorama comes just under two miles along, at the very head of the Transept. By now your trusty brochure will have identified especially fine specimens of ponderosa pine, oak, aspen and maple, as well as a droning sewage treatment facility concealed beneath the lodge.

Pressing on further takes you into the depths of the forest for something over two miles. You finally re-emerge at a stunning overlook that faces due south. Bright Angel Point is now hidden from view, but by way of compensation the core of the Grand Canyon lies right there in front of you. Lift your eyes from the Buddha and Isis temples straight ahead, and the whole of the Grand Canyon Village area of the South Rim, and the Coconino Plateau beyond, spreads out for your delectation.

Strictly speaking, you're not quite at **Widforss Point**, which is the stark headland a few hundred yards to your left, but in the absence of a permanent trail there you'd do best to settle for what you've got. Both trail and point were named for Gunnar Mauritz Widforss, the so-called "Painter of the National Parks", who was born in Sweden in 1879 and was renowned for his vivid Grand Canyon watercolours.

The Walhalla Plateau

Except for those around *Grand Canyon Lodge*, all the North Rim **canyon overlooks** accessible by paved road are ranged along the eastern edge of the **Walhalla Plateau**. This fifteen-mile headland, east of Bright Angel Point, juts far out towards the Colorado as the river makes a colossal sweeping curve, and stops flowing southwards to head northwest instead. As a result, the plateau makes a superb vantage point, affording some of the finest views available anywhere in the national park, and revealing how the Grand Canyon fits into the larger context of the northern Arizona desertscape.

Once you've driven as far as the lodge, it's a real mistake to turn back without exploring the Walhalla Plateau as well. Be warned, however, that barring a few chemical toilets it holds no facilities of any kind. That includes gas stations; make sure your tank is full enough for a round trip of at least fifty miles. It takes perhaps half a day to see the whole area thoroughly, and the views are generally at their best as the afternoon progresses. If you don't mind driving back in the dark, it's worth aiming to be at Cape Royal, the plateau's furthest point, for the hour or so leading up to sunset.

Access is provided by the **Cape Royal Scenic Drive**, reached by turning east from AZ-67 onto **Fuller Canyon Road** three miles north of the lodge. Just over five miles along, you come to a junction where **Point Imperial Road** branches off to the left, while **Cape Royal Road** turns right to cross the neck of the plateau itself and winds its way into the cool dense woods. The area around the junction remains visibly scarred by the Outlet Fire of 2000, though the black soil is partly obscured by an amazing proliferation of young aspens.

Point Imperial

Before or after your exploration of the Walhalla Plateau, it's well worth driving the short detour to **Point Imperial**, a gradual climb of just under three miles along a dead-end road from the intersection described above. At 8803ft, this is the highest spot along either rim of the entire canyon, though to reach the actual overlook you have to descend a very short distance from the car park.

A long, red sandy ridge pokes out just below the viewing area, with a stark butte at the end. Looking down into the dry-as-dust labyrinth below, it's virtually

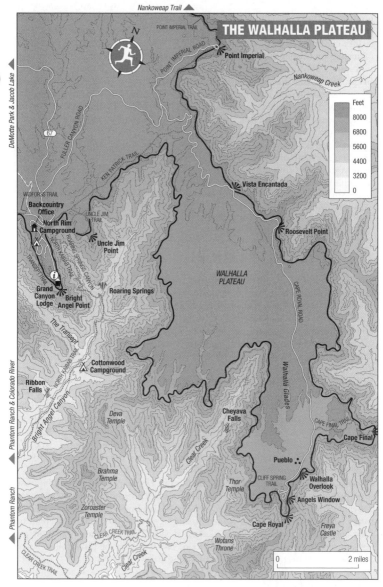

THE WALHALLA PLATEAU

DeMotte Park & Jacob Lake ◄

POINT IMPERIAL TRAIL

POINT IMPERIAL ROAD

Point Imperial

Nankoweap Creek

FULLER CANYON ROAD

67

KEN PATRICK TRAIL

Vista Encantada

WIDFORSS TRAIL

Backcountry
Office

UNCLE JIM
TRAIL

North Rim
Campground

NORTH KAIBAB TRAIL

Uncle Jim
Point

ROARING SPRINGS CANYON

Roosevelt Point

WALHALLA
PLATEAU

CAPE ROYAL ROAD

Roaring Springs

Grand
Canyon
Lodge

Bright
Angel Point

The Transept

Cottonwood
Campground

Walhalla Glades

Phantom Ranch & Colorado River ◄

Ribbon
Falls

NORTH KAIBAB TRAIL

Bright Angel Canyon

Deva
Temple

Clear Creek

Cheyava
Falls

CAPE FINAL TRAIL

Cape Final

Pueblo

Phantom Ranch ◄

Brahma
Temple

Thor
Temple

CLIFF SPRING
TRAIL

Walhalla
Overlook

Angels Window

Zoroaster
Temple

CLEAR CREEK TRAIL

Cape Royal

Freya
Castle

CLEAR CREEK TRAIL

Wotans
Throne

Clear Creek

Feet
8000
6800
5600
4400
3200
0

0   2 miles

impossible to guess which is the main gorge of the Colorado. In fact, the canyon
here is just over nine miles wide, but the river is less than a mile from the sheer wall
of the **Desert Facade** on the far side. Almost everything you can see within the
canyon is on the same side of the river as you.

Nonetheless, the horizon recedes a phenomenal distance beyond the canyon.
The vast spreading **Marble Platform** is almost 3000ft lower than Point
Imperial, so a huge swathe of the Navajo reservation lies flat and bare before you.

Almost the only breaks in the monotony are the slight hump of Navajo Mountain in the far distance, and the crack cut by the Little Colorado River as it meets its elder sibling.

An even better prospect of the Marble Platform can be enjoyed from an overlook closer to the car park, labelled **"Northeast View"**. Through a notch between two minor peaks, you can see Marble Canyon snaking its way through the rock. It's framed by the Vermilion Cliffs to the left and the Echo Cliffs to the right, so the dot where the two seem to meet can only mark Lees Ferry.

Vista Encantada

The Walhalla Plateau is narrowest at its northern end, where it clings to the rest of the North Rim by a slender thread. At some point, it will presumably become a mighty detached mesa; for the moment, however, Cape Royal Road manages to wriggle onto the level plateau top. The first stop comes after just over four miles, where the **Vista Encantada** overlook faces northeast across the canyon. The highway signs don't name the overlook explicitly, but simply point to "picnic area"; tables beside the car park mean it is indeed a popular spot for midday breaks.

The views here are much the same as from Point Imperial; both look down into the basin of **Nankoweap Creek**, which was responsible for the curving rim between the two. Once again, the Colorado is nowhere to be seen, but the pale green flatlands of the Navajo reservation spread away endlessly into the haze.

Roosevelt Point

Until it was renamed during the 1990s in honour of Theodore Roosevelt – an early champion of the Grand Canyon – **Roosevelt Point** was known as the Painted Desert Overlook. It's only two miles on from Vista Encantada, so the short-range views are naturally similar, but that's enough to open up additional panoramas of the Navajo Nation, way off to the east. Navajo Mountain is still there on the northeast horizon, eighty miles distant, but you can now see southeast as well, to catch at least a hint of the **Painted Desert** badlands that extend southeast from Cameron almost to New Mexico. That said, the name change was probably for the best, in that the most spectacular parts of the Painted Desert are much too far away to be seen from here.

Closer at hand, Roosevelt Point provides a unique chance to gaze head-on at the **confluence** of the Colorado and the Little Colorado. Oddly, the rivers meet at right angles, with the Little Colorado emerging from a sheer-sided, half-mile-deep gorge of its own. Geologists puzzle over how that came about, with some suggesting that the Colorado itself once flowed east through the Little Colorado gorge, before being somehow "captured" and set on its present westward course.

An easy ten-minute unpaved trail leads north from the Roosevelt Point car park, heading through fire-ravaged landscape to loop around a small promontory that offers slightly varying views and a much greater sense of isolation.

Cape Final

For the next six miles beyond Roosevelt Point, Cape Royal Road stays within the forest. Your one chance to get a glimpse of the canyon comes towards the end of that stretch, when a **hike** of two miles each way leads to the remote viewpoint of **Cape Final**. By now, you're near enough to Cape Royal that there's no great need to add yet another overlook to your itinerary. The reason to pause here is if you just plain like the idea of spending a couple of hours on an easy trail through the woods, away from the crowds and with the bonus of a couple of little-known perspectives on the inner canyon.

The **Cape Final Trail (T8)**, leads uphill from a little forest clearing, exactly 11.8 miles south of the intersection with Point Imperial Road. The car park itself is a long way from the rim, and offers no views whatsoever. Though you'd never know to look at it, the rudimentary dirt track that meanders away from it through the pines, was once a fully-fledged park road. It soon levels off, then drops gently down until after half an hour it suddenly confronts the lip of the canyon at a big northeastward view. Nearby to the left, colossal monoliths such as **Poston Butte** and **Siegfried Pyre** soar almost to the height of the rim, but the **Chuar Valley** below slopes evenly down towards the river.

Turning right, away from the rim, the trail thins out. As the ponderosas dwindle, to be replaced by oak and piñon, it crosses to the south side of this minor headland, and comes to an end after another half-hour at a south-facing eminence. The Colorado is now very clearly visible, at the point where it's joined by Unkar Creek to create the **Unkar Delta Rapid**, as described below.

Walhalla Overlook

A mile on from the Cape Final trailhead, the **Walhalla Overlook** is a canyon-edge car park that offers another fine view down to the confluence of Unkar Creek and the Colorado, almost exactly a mile below. The **Unkar Delta** there cradles some of the most fertile farming land in the canyon, and was home to a thriving **Ancestral Puebloan** community around a thousand years ago. They grew corn, squash and beans on irrigated fields close to the river, and terraces at higher, drier elevations.

As population pressure increased, the group adopted a sophisticated strategy to exploit resources along the North Rim as well as down in the inner canyon. With its heavy annual snowfall, most of the North Rim is simply too cold to support agriculture, but the Walhalla Plateau is a unique case. It's effectively a peninsula, all but surrounded by the Grand Canyon, and thus warmed by the air that rises from the canyon depths.

Over one hundred ancient farming sites have been identified near the southern tip of the plateau, in the so-called **Walhalla Glades**. After wintering on the canyon floor, the Ancestral Puebloans would climb out in early spring along the line of Unkar Creek – there's no trail now, but back then they managed it as an arduous two-day hike – and plant their crops where they'd be fed by snowmelt. They'd also pack snow into storage jars, to water the seedlings as they grew. Harvest season, in the autumn, would coincide with the best time to hunt deer and other forest mammals.

A very short trail, across the road from the overlook, leads through a hundred yards of fire-blackened forest to end at the foundation walls of a small **pueblo**. The main six-room structure is thought to have been occupied for roughly a century, from 1050 onwards, by a family group of around twenty members. In truth, these crude stone outlines do not make a spectacular sight – certainly not for anyone familiar with ancient ruins elsewhere in the Southwest – but they do provide an emotive reminder of the canyon's long human history.

T9 Cliff Spring Trail

A quarter of a mile past **Walhalla Overlook**, another minor overlook offers views towards Cape Royal, and in particular the Angels Window described below. The same car park serves as the start of the short **Cliff Spring Trail**, which crosses the road and then descends a dry, gravelly streambed towards the west. Shortly after passing a remarkably complete Ancestral Puebloan granary, tucked under a boulder, you reach a damp, mossy alcove hidden beneath the canyon rim. Seepage through the Kaibab limestone above collects in small pools, but the water is not safe to drink.

The round trip hike this far is about a mile, and takes less than half an hour. Continuing as far again, on what becomes a difficult trail that requires a certain amount of scrambling, leads to impressive westward views. Eventually the ledge you're on dwindles to nothing, above a 1000ft drop, and you're forced to turn back.

Cape Royal

By the time you reach **Cape Royal**, where the Walhalla Plateau finally peters out, the promontory extends so far out above the canyon that it's constantly bathed by warm air currents. As a result, the ponderosa disappears, and piñon-juniper woodland predominates.

There's nothing to see from the unremarkable loop car park where the highway turns back, 14.3 miles from the Point Imperial Road junction. Instead, the even, paved **Cape Royal Trail** (T10), laid out as a nature trail identifying the trees and plants along the way, leads to the two principal overlooks. A round trip **hike** of roughly half a mile, it's just long enough to make it worth wearing real shoes and carrying water.

The trail leads first of all to the **Angels Window**, a wedge-shaped natural archway pierced just below the top of a rocky spur. From certain vantage points as you approach, it perfectly frames a small segment of the Colorado River. Unless you're especially afraid of heights, it's well worth taking the brief detour to the left of the main trail that leads across the top of the "window", along a safe but extremely narrow railed pathway, to the precarious and also railed slab at the far end, for views over to the Navajo flatlands. Two broad, green-trimmed stretches of the river are now on show, including once again the foaming Unkar Creek Rapid. This is an extremely dangerous place to be during a thunderstorm; if there's lightning around, keep away.

Views from **Cape Royal** itself, a couple of hundred yards further along the main trail, extend much further west – virtually the full 360 degrees, though the intervening ridge immediately west obscures Bright Angel Point. This is the only Walhalla viewpoint from which you can see the central portion of the Grand Canyon, with major landmarks like **Wotan's Throne** and **Vishnu Temple** straight ahead, and **Brahma** and **Zoroaster** temples off to the right.

As the crow flies, the canyon is now roughly eight miles wide. In theory, most of the best-known **South Rim viewpoints** are visible, including Desert View – with the flat-topped little mesa known as Cedar Mountain just behind it – and Yaki, Yavapai, Hopi and Pima points. Without strong binoculars, it's hard to distinguish one from the next, though the Watchtower at Desert View serves as a landmark if you can work out where to look. It's tempting to leave the path and ledge-hop even closer to the rim, but bear in mind that with its crumbling stone slabs this spot is notorious for fatal falls.

The Western Kaibab Plateau

Many North Rim visitors are frustrated that such a vast area should seem to hold so few roads. You can't help feeling that there must be a whole lot more spectacular scenery nearby that you'll never get to see. In fact, get hold of a good map – ideally the *North Kaibab Ranger District*, published by the Kaibab National Forest, or the BLM Arizona Strip Field Office's *Visitor Map*, and *not* the otherwise reliable

AAA *Indian Country* one – and you'll soon realize there are plenty of minor roads out there. The trouble is, none is paved. All are gravel, dirt or worse, and while the overall picture has considerably improved in recent years, many are still only recommended for **high-clearance 4WD vehicles**.

The most rewarding area to explore lies to the **west** of Bright Angel Point and AZ-67. Most of this belongs to the **Kaibab National Forest**, where the roads tend to be passable in ordinary vehicles – this is after all a "land of many uses", so they're maintained for logging trucks and the like. However, the canyon rim itself remains inside the national park boundaries, and it's liable to be the final section of the drive to any viewpoint, on Park Service roads, that requires 4WD.

The routes described below are the pick of literally dozens of possibilities, leading to exceptional viewpoints and also hiking trailheads. Before taking any of them, it's absolutely essential to **ask for advice** either at the Forest Service information centre in Jacob Lake (see p.131) or at the North Rim Visitor Center. As well as selling the best maps, rangers will be able to tell you which roads are clear, which may well entail following a highly convoluted route rather than what looks the shortest. Road closures can vary from day to day, depending not only on weather conditions but also, for example, whether any prescribed or natural fires are currently burning. Don't follow your own whims, and don't underestimate how much time it will all take, particularly because seeing more than one overlook may well require an hour or more backtracking. While on the better roads it's often possible to drive at around forty miles per hour, as a rule of thumb you should reckon on averaging more like twenty miles per hour. On a more positive note, at least the roads are seldom less than ravishing, with late September and early October, when the autumn colour displays are in full swing, as the best time to come.

Point Sublime

In the estimation of Clarence Dutton, the pioneer surveyor who named it in 1882, **Point Sublime** is perhaps the finest Grand Canyon viewpoint of them all. Sadly for less hardy modern visitors, however, it stands at the end of a seventeen-mile dirt road that's usually restricted to 4WD vehicles. If you have one, drive three miles north of *Grand Canyon Lodge*, then take the gravel road west of AZ-67 that leads to the Widforss Trail, as detailed on p.74. Assuming you follow the curve of the road by turning left half a mile after the trailhead, you can't go wrong.

The views at the far end are absolutely colossal, extending both east and west and incorporating a fifty-mile stretch of the full glory of the inner canyon. Point Sublime is closer to the Colorado than any other North Rim viewpoint, so you even get a glimpse of the river itself, at **Boucher Rapid**. Rhapsodizing that "the infinity of sharply defined detail is amazing", Dutton was especially struck by the isolated butte he called **Shiva Temple**. The American Museum of Natural History sent an expedition to this "lost world" in 1937, hoping that its flat 275-acre summit might hold species unknown to science. All they found was evidence that large mammals somehow manage to visit the mesa-top regularly – and that the Ancestral Puebloans did so too.

Tuna Creek, immediately below Point Sublime to the east, was the scene of a dramatic rescue in June 1944. Three airmen who parachuted from a bomber whose engines had failed during a training run were stranded down there for ten days, before park rangers were able to plot a route to reach them on foot.

Although the magnificent Toroweap Overlook is technically on the North Rim, it's only accessible from the Arizona Strip and is therefore covered in Chapter 5.

Swamp Point

Both the Colorado, and the canyon rim with it, curve northwards to the west of Point Sublime. The next major promontory along, the **Powell Plateau**, comes even closer to the river, to within just two miles. However, despite being higher than the rest of the North Rim at this point, it has become detached from it, so there's no accessible overlook at its far end. The closest viewpoint, **Swamp Point**, is located just above the **Muav Saddle**, the short "neck" of land, dropping a thousand feet below the rim, that leads to the plateau.

As well as providing a view of the plateau itself – which although it holds no permanent water sustained a sizable Ancestral Puebloan population – Swamp Point commands a fine prospect northwest, centring on the **Tapeats Amphitheater**. Even so, almost no one drives here just to enjoy the view. They come because it's also the trailhead for the gruelling, experts-only **North Bass Trail**, as described on p.112, and the shorter **Powell Saddle Trail**, a five-mile dead-end hike onto the Powell Plateau.

Once again, 4WD is essential, and even that won't help you before early June each year, when the previous winter's fallen trees still block the way. Once rangers give the all clear, take Forest Development Road (FDR) 22, which climbs away enticingly due west from AZ-67 just under a mile south of DeMotte Park; the road actually runs all the way to Fredonia, so you could approach from that direction too. Turn south onto FDR 270 after 2.1 miles, then west again on FDR 223 (signed for Fire Point) 2.3 miles beyond that. Another 5.8 miles on, turn left onto FDR 268, and follow the signs, which should point you along another turn, onto FDR 268B, after 0.3 miles. Once you cross the park boundary, 1.2 miles along, the road seriously deteriorates; it's 7.8 more miles to the end.

Fire Point

Little more than a mile north of Swamp Point, but much more likely to be accessible in an ordinary vehicle, **Fire Point** is another spectacular overlook that provides a dramatic side-on prospect of the striated Powell Plateau, and also gazes right across the canyon to **Great Thumb Mesa** on the far side.

To reach it, start by following the directions for Swamp Point above, but simply keep going on FDR 223 rather than turning left onto FDR 268. Six miles after that junction – a total of sixteen miles from AZ-67 – you're there. The whole route is normally passable in summer, though to be on the safe side, if you're driving a non-4WD vehicle, it's worth expecting that you'll have to park up half a mile from the end, by which time you're half a mile within the national park, and tackle the final stretch on foot.

Parissawampitts Point

A cluster of five points on separate finger-like promontories north of Fire Point are connected by the eighteen-mile **Rainbow Rim Trail**. The closest North-Rim equivalent to the South Rim's Rim Trail, this is a demanding and little-used trail that dips repeatedly into steep side canyons in between a succession of differing canyon prospects.

The northernmost of the five, **Parissawampitts Point**, is the easiest to reach by road. Once again, take FDR 22 west from AZ-67, not far south of DeMotte Park. Follow that for 10.9 miles, then turn south along FDR 206 for another 3.7 miles. Now turn right – west – and follow the distinctly worse FDR 214 for eight miles, as it makes its way past some lovely, secluded potential camping sites. Park in the clearing at the end, but as you walk down from there towards the rim, don't go straight ahead, which would seem intuitive, but instead turn left. You'll soon come to clearings that command huge vistas across the **Tapeats Amphitheater** to where the Colorado River – invisible at the bottom of the Granite Gorge – winds its way westwards towards Mount Trumbull.

Each of the four points to the south of Parissawampitts – ordered north to south, they're **Fence, Locust, North Timp** and **Timp** – can be reached by a separate spur road off FDR 206, so it would be possible to leave a vehicle at one of those and hike the Rainbow Rim Trail in one direction only. It strays so far inland between each one, however, that it's probably simplest just to take a day hike out and back from Parissawampitts. That makes for a much more varied forest hike than you'd get on the South Rim, but in all honesty the views aren't in the same league.

Crazy Jug Point

Of the many other western Kaibab Plateau viewpoints, the one most readily accessible in a standard vehicle is usually **Crazy Jug Point**. It stands, however, a full 27 miles of gravel- and dirt-road driving from the highway, a trip that in good conditions takes a little under an hour each way. Your reward if you make it is a colossal panorama of the Granite Gorge, (though once again not the Colorado itself), snaking its way between Powell Plateau and Great Thumb Mesa, with the **Tapeats Amphitheater** spread out below you.

As before, take FDR 22 either west from DeMotte Park, or all the way south from Fredonia. This time, turn north rather than south when you meet FDR 206 after 10.9 miles, and then left (west) onto FDR 425 another 7.4 miles along.

Monument Point

Having driven as far as Crazy Jug Point, it's well worth continuing another 1.5 miles west, despite the steadily deteriorating road surface, to reach the car park for **Monument Point.** You may well be surprised by the number of vehicles parked in such a remote spot; they're here because this also marks the trailhead for the very challenging backcountry **Bill Hall Trail**, which meets the **Thunder River Trail** 3.4 miles along and drops down to the Colorado River via Tapeats Creek.

Monument Point itself stands atop a small hill just under a mile's walk from the car park. If you don't feel you can spare the time to walk even that far, there's an equally impressive viewpoint closer at hand, poised right at the head of the Tapeats Amphitheater. Ancient marine fossils embedded in the limestone at the very rim of the canyon here provide a stark reminder of how this landscape has mutated over the aeons.

Hiking the inner canyon

CHAPTER 3 # Highlights

✳ **The Bright Angel Trail**
Deservedly the park's
most popular hiking trail; a
superb introduction to life
below the rim. See p.94

✳ **Phantom Ranch** Rest your
feet from all that hiking
with an overnight stay at
this rustic lodging on the
canyon floor. See p.99

✳ **The South Kaibab Trail**
This dramatic, exposed
descent to the canyon floor
offers the best day hikes in
the park. See p.100

✳ **The North Kaibab Trail**
The North Rim's finest trail

passes superb waterfalls
and stupendous scenery
on its two-day, fourteen-
mile drop to the Colorado
River. See p.102

✳ **The Grandview Trail**
A great day hike on a
challenging but rewarding
– and skilfully engineered –
trail. See p.106

✳ **Day hike to Santa Maria
Spring** Escape the crowds
with a peaceful and
relatively easy day hike
that abounds in canyon
wildlife and vegetation.
See p.107

▲ Hikers on the North Kaibab Trail

3

Hiking the inner canyon

What seemed to be easy from above was not so, but instead very hard and difficult.
– Don García López de Cárdenas, 1540

Undertaking a **hike** below the rim, into the very maw of the canyon, may well be both the most challenging, and most rewarding, thing you do in Grand Canyon National Park – or, for that matter, in your entire life. It's essential not to underestimate how difficult hiking in the canyon can be. The mere fact that the easier part, the descent, comes before the much harder slog back to the rim is enough to confuse and exhaust the hardiest mountain hikers, while the summer heat, along with the high altitude and thin air of the Colorado Plateau, can turn even the shortest hike into a gruelling trek. You'll find an overview of the issues involved in planning a Grand Canyon expedition, as well as summaries of highly recommended day hikes, in the **colour insert** at the centre of this book.

Above all, park rangers have one simple message for all would-be hikers: **don't try to hike to the river and back in one day**. It's hard to stress quite how important that advice is. It might not look far on the map, but completing a

---

Hiking along the rim

This chapter deals exclusively with hikes that descend **below** the rim. However, there are plenty of good, and much less physically demanding, trails at rim level. Here's a selection of the finest, which are described in detail elsewhere in this book:

T1	Rim Trail	South Rim	8 miles one-way	p.56
T2	Shoshone Point	South Rim	2 miles round trip	p.60
T3	Transept Trail	North Rim	1.5 miles one-way	p.73
T4	Uncle Jim Trail	North Rim	4-mile loop	p.73
T5	Ken Patrick Trail	North Rim	6 miles round trip	p.74
T6	Point Imperial Trail	North Rim	5.5 miles round trip	p.111
T7	Widforss Trail	North Rim	10 miles round trip	p.74
T8	Cape Final Trail	North Rim	4 miles round trip	p.78
T9	Cliff Spring Trail	North Rim	2 miles round trip	p.78
T10	Cape Royal Trail	North Rim	Half-mile round trip	p.79

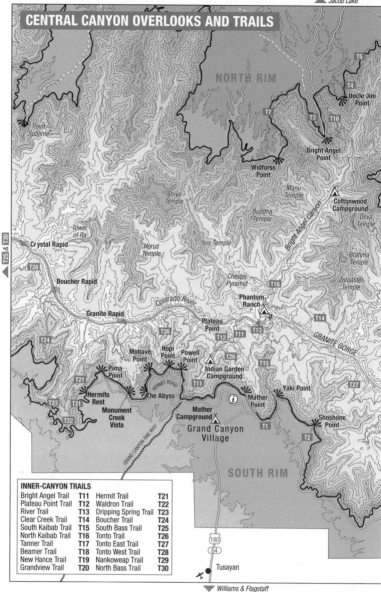

CENTRAL CANYON OVERLOOKS AND TRAILS

INNER-CANYON TRAILS			
Bright Angel Trail	T11	Hermit Trail	T21
Plateau Point Trail	T12	Waldron Trail	T22
River Trail	T13	Dripping Spring Trail	T23
Clear Creek Trail	T14	Boucher Trail	T24
South Kaibab Trail	T15	South Bass Trail	T25
North Kaibab Trail	T16	Tonto Trail	T26
Tanner Trail	T17	Tonto East Trail	T27
Beamer Trail	T18	Tonto West Trail	T28
New Hance Trail	T19	Nankoweap Trail	T29
Grandview Trail	T20	North Bass Trail	T30

round trip day hike to the canyon floor, which involves a total walk of at least fourteen miles and an elevation change of one mile in each direction, is harder than running a marathon. That's the plain, unadorned truth, even though you may well meet people on the trail who are doing it, and there are plenty of canyon obsessives who not only perform greater feats of endurance than that, but also make sure everyone knows about it.

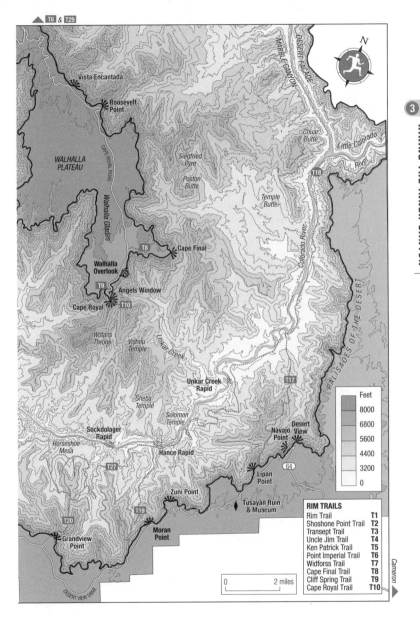

Feet	
	8000
	6800
	5600
	4400
	3200
	0

RIM TRAILS

Rim Trail	**T1**
Shoshone Point Trail	**T2**
Transept Trail	**T3**
Uncle Jim Trail	**T4**
Ken Patrick Trail	**T5**
Point Imperial Trail	**T6**
Widforss Trail	**T7**
Cape Final Trail	**T8**
Cliff Spring Trail	**T9**
Cape Royal Trail	**T10**

0   2 miles

The point is, the Grand Canyon is an extreme arena that attracts extreme athletes; unless you know exactly what you're doing, which means at the very least that you've already hiked extensively in the canyon, it's a mistake to think you can match them. While it won't necessarily be you who dies – if you're lucky, on a cool overcast day in April or October, you might even find it straightforward – several hikers do die each year in the attempt, and several hundred more receive emergency medical treatment. Casualties regularly include fit, healthy young people. For example, a 24-year-old woman died hiking within months of completing the Boston Marathon.

③ Choosing a trail and other practicalities

All hiking should be on designated **trails**. Grand Canyon National Park offers about five hundred miles of such routes, on terrain divided into four official zones of difficulty – not to say that any of it is easy.

First-time hikers are advised to restrict themselves to the **Corridor Zone**, which comprises the 33 miles of trail regularly maintained by park rangers and is, thanks to two footbridges, the only area in which it's possible for hikers to cross the Colorado River. The Bright Angel, South Kaibab and North Kaibab trails here are regularly patrolled and offer facilities such as emergency phones and piped water.

Almost all other trails reviewed in this chapter lie within the **Threshold Zone**, where trails are often rough underfoot, harder to follow and liable to lack water, toilets and formal campgrounds. A few pass wholly or partly through the **Primitive Zone**, where trails are not maintained, facilities are nonexistent, and you may well need route-finding skills to stay on course. Only backcountry experts should venture into the **Wild Zone**, which holds virtually no formal trails or water sources. The Park Service recommends against entering the Primitive or Wild zones in summer.

It's best not to be too ambitious on your first canyon hike. Even if you're sure you want to go as far as the river at some point during your stay, you won't regret having a practise **day hike** before the main event. On the South Rim, most first-timers opt for the **Bright Angel** or **South Kaibab** trails, though both the **Grandview** and **Hermit** also offer good short trips. On the North Rim, the **North Kaibab** is the only sensible option.

Die-hard wilderness enthusiasts often grumble that the sheer mass of hikers in summer, especially on the trails to and from Phantom Ranch, diminishes their enjoyment. If that strikes a chord with you, then you may prefer to hike one of the lesser-known trails, though of course such trails can be brutal in summer. For most casual visitors, however, the traffic on the Corridor Trails is not a problem – it's not *that* bad, and it provides a greater sense of companionship and solidarity.

Hiking safety

The secret to successful hiking is to **plan ahead**. Follow rangers' advice and allow twice as long to climb back out of the canyon as you take to hike down. That takes a bit of getting used to, but basically, if you set off at 8am and want to be back on the rim at 5pm, you should start your ascent at 11am.

Assuming you're adequately equipped with water and other supplies, as outlined below, the best way to guarantee your safety is never to leave the trail. If you imagine you've spotted a shortcut, you're wrong; leaving the trail will make you much harder to find in an emergency. That's especially true for solo hikers, who form a large proportion of canyon casualties. Ideally, you shouldn't hike alone; if you must, stick to the busier trails and, preferably, day hikes.

On a more general note, try to walk slowly, so you're never out of breath. If you're having trouble maintaining an ordinary conversation, you're walking too fast. And take at least one five-minute break every hour, ideally lying down with legs raised above the level of your heart.

Water and food

The sheer quantity of **water** that you have to carry – and drink – while hiking in the Grand Canyon almost defies belief. In typical summer temperatures exceeding 100°F, your body loses a phenomenal four pints of fluid every hour spent on the trail. To keep up with that sort of demand, you should reckon on drinking **one gallon** for each day's hiking in summer, down perhaps to half that in cooler conditions.

Find out whether water will be available on your chosen trail – rangers keep abreast of the latest conditions – and carry at least two pints with you at all times, even if you expect to be able to refill en route. Only the Bright Angel and North Kaibab trails provide piped drinking water, and even that can be unexpectedly cut off if the pipeline breaks. On other trails where water is to be had, you'll have to **treat** it first, either by boiling it for at least five minutes or cleansing it with iodine-based purifying tablets or a Giardia-rated filter, available from any camping or sporting goods store.

Pre-hydrate before a big hike, by drinking large amounts the night before. Once you set off, drink regularly, even if you don't feel thirsty. There's a limit to how much liquid your body can actually absorb at any one time – around one quart per hour – so you need to be drinking steadily; hydration systems such as those made by CamelBak, in which a mouthpiece and tube connects to a water pouch in your backpack, are highly recommended.

Early symptoms of **heat exhaustion** include loss of both appetite and thirst, so it's possible to become seriously dehydrated without feeling thirsty. Other warning signs include nausea, dizziness, headache, cramps and strangely cool skin. The best indicator of whether you're drinking enough is your **urine**; its frequency and quantity should be the same as normal, and it should remain clear rather than discoloured (on that note, incidentally, if there's no restroom nearby, the official line is that you should try to urinate on bare rock or sand, away from water sources, rather than on plants or soil). Just to confuse things, there's also the risk of **hyponatremia**, or **water intoxication**, which in its first stages closely resembles heat exhaustion and happens if you drink too much without eating.

As hikers can burn up to a thousand calories per hour – not just in the actual walking, but also in the energy it takes to keep cool – expect to eat at least twice as much **food** as normal, both before and during your hike. Eat every time you drink. Salty snacks such as cookies, crackers and trail mix are recommended, as are jerky or salami and ready-made dehydrated meals. **Electrolyte replacement** drinks, which you can buy either prepared or in powder form, are a great help; many hikers carry two hydration packs, one filled with water and one with Gatorade or a similar product. Avoid salt tablets, however, as taking salt on its own can do more harm than good.

In addition, whenever you come to a water source within the canyon, **soak yourself** – your head, your hair, your clothing, everything. That will keep you much cooler as you hike on.

Finally, it's easy to forget that at the end of a long hike there may be no facilities at the trailhead. Be sure to leave some food and water in your vehicle as well.

Snakes and creepy crawlies

No one is known to have died in the Grand Canyon from being bitten or stung by a snake, scorpion, or indeed any other form of reptile, insect or spider.

Although the canyon is home to several species of **snake**, including three kinds of rattlesnake, bites are extremely rare and almost invariably the result of misguided attempts at handling. If you do get bitten, current medical thinking rejects the concept of cutting yourself open and attempting to suck out the venom; in most cases, in fact, no venom is injected. You'd do better to stay calm, apply a cold compress to the wound, constrict the area with a tourniquet, drink lots of water, rest in a shady place and send for help.

Scorpion stings, especially from bark scorpions, are more common. Their poison is nasty, but causes nausea rather than serious illness or death. When camping, be sure to shake out your shoes, clothing and bedding before use.

To avoid painful bites from **red ants**, tidy up any crumbs or spillages after you eat and don't sit or sleep on the same spot afterward.

Security precautions

Though it issues permits to all backcountry hikers, the Park Service doesn't formally keep track of what happens to each group. There is no official check-in or checkout, so no one will necessarily notice if you fail to return. It's therefore essential to leave details of your planned itinerary with family, friends or colleagues and arrange to call them when you've emerged safely from the canyon. If you fail to do so, they can raise the alarm by calling the Park Service at ☏928/638-2477. Stick to your itinerary – you'll be held liable for the cost of any search and rescue operation, which can run into the thousands of dollars, especially if helicopter evacuation becomes necessary.

Note that mobile phones are very unlikely to work, as most areas, both along the rim and down in the canyon, are too remote to get a signal. Satellite phones are somewhat more reliable, but often fail in the gorge.

Backcountry camping

To restrict numbers, **backcountry camping** within Grand Canyon National Park – as opposed to camping in the developed *Mather Campground* and *Desert View* sites on the South Rim and the *North Rim Campground* near Bright Angel Point – is by **permit** only. Demand is very high, and more than half of all applications are turned down. Anyone overnighting in the canyon without a permit, other than guests in the cabins or dorms at Phantom Ranch, is subject to a heavy fine.

Permits cost a flat fee of $10, plus an additional $5 per person per night for sites below the rim or $5 per group per night for undeveloped campsites on the rim. Applications are not accepted online, or by email or phone; you can only apply **in person**, by **mail** (Backcountry Information Center, PO Box 129, Grand Canyon, AZ 86023) or by **fax** (℉928/638-2125). Full details, including the relevant form, are available online in the Backcountry Permit section of the park website (ⓦnps.gov/grca), or in the park's free *Trip Planner*, available at all visitor centres. All applications must specify an exact **itinerary**, with precise details of where you'll spend each night; depending on where you're hiking, this will be either named campgrounds or the wide-ranging "Use Areas" indicated on official park maps (also available online). Between March and mid-November, there's a limit on the most popular trails of two nights per party per campsite, whether or not those nights are consecutive. Applicants can suggest up to three alternative dates and routes. You'll also be asked for the number in your group – which can't exceed eleven – and even your vehicle licence plate numbers. The fee is payable in advance, preferably by credit card but also by cheque or money order, and is non-refundable. Frequent Hiker Membership ($25 per year) spares you paying the $10 fee each time, but confers no other benefits.

Mailed or **faxed** applications are accepted for dates until the end of the fourth complete month after they're submitted. Thus in January you can apply for nothing later than the end of May, while if you're planning a trip in the peak month of July, you'd better mail your application on March 1. Both mail and fax applications are responded to by mail.

To apply **in person**, turn up at either the **Backcountry Information Center** (daily 8am–noon & 1–5pm), near *Maswik Lodge* in Grand Canyon Village on the South Rim, or at the **North Rim Backcountry Office** (mid-May to mid-Oct, daily 8am–noon & 1–5pm), a quarter of a mile north of the *North Rim Campground*. They share the same phone number, for information enquiries only (☎928/638-7875, Mon–Fri 1–5pm only).

While both offices accept advance applications, and turning up in person does jump you ahead of all unprocessed applicants, most hikers who visit the offices are hoping for a **last-minute cancellation**. Even in peak season, your chances of being able to hike within a day or two are pretty good, especially if you're flexible as to which trail you'd like to explore. Your name will be added to a waiting list, and each morning at 8am that day's cancellations are reassigned – though you must be present to get one.

Where to camp

The most popular campgrounds within the canyon are the three along the rim-to-rim Corridor Trails – *Indian Garden* on the Bright Angel Trail, *Bright Angel Campground* near the river and *Cottonwood Campground* on the North Kaibab Trail. Camping in other areas varies between similar permanent campgrounds, designated campsites – where the spots at which you can camp are specified by the Park Service, though they hold no facilities – and wilderness camping. Wherever you camp, minimize your impact on the canyon. Camp where someone else has camped before and make no additional physical changes.

No **fires** are permitted within the canyon, except in emergencies, though camping stoves are allowed. Human waste should be buried from four to six inches deep, at least 200ft from the nearest water supply, while you must take all rubbish, including toilet paper, out of the canyon with you. Never use soap in or near a water source.

Flash floods, which can appear from nowhere, are most likely in July and August. Fatalities are rare, but they have occurred over the last decade on both the Bright Angel and North Kaibab trails. Survivors often report having had just a few minutes' warning, in the form of a loud rumble heading downstream along the nearest watercourse. The most important precaution you can take is always to camp well above the bed of even the driest-seeming wash. If you hear any ominous noise, head immediately for high ground and don't attempt to cross flooded areas until the water has receded.

What to take

Exactly what **equipment** you'll need depends on which trail you're taking, for how long and in what season. Bear in mind that it's usually around 30°F warmer beside the river than it is up at the rim; be prepared for extremes of both hot and cold.

For a **day hike**, essentials include dependable **hiking boots** that you've already broken in, worn for blister protection either with purpose-made hiking **socks** or two pairs of ordinary socks, thick on the outside and thinner within; a **long-sleeved shirt** and trousers for sun protection, together with a broad-brimmed **hat**, **sunblock** and **sunglasses**; containers for carrying up to a gallon of **water**, plus, if necessary, a water purification system; substantial **food**; a **pocket knife**; a **torch**; and a **signal mirror** and/or **whistle** for emergencies. On trails without pit toilets, you'll also need **toilet paper** and **Ziploc bags** in which to store that and other waste.

All hikers should carry a **first-aid kit**, at its most basic including bandages and moleskin for blisters, painkillers and anti-inflammatories such as Advil, and knee and ankle bandages. A great deal of hikers' lore surrounds feet in particular; many people

Grand Canyon Field Institute

The perfect way for novice hikers to get a first taste of the canyon, or for more experienced ones to improve their skills, is to join one of the many expeditions led each year by the **Grand Canyon Field Institute** (☎928/638-2485, ⓦgrandcanyon.org /fieldinstitute). Co-sponsored by the Grand Canyon Association and the National Park Service, this friendly, enthusiastic organization offers an extensive programme of well-priced, expert-led **guided tours and hikes** in and around the canyon. All participants receive detailed advice on how to prepare and what to bring.

Different tours, some of which are restricted to women only, specialize in geology, history, natural history, photography, wilderness techniques and other topics. Most involve camping and backpacking, while others include lodge stays or even llama trekking; all are graded according to the difficulty of any hiking involved, and your acceptance is subject to completion of a detailed health questionnaire. Typical prices include $495 for a three-night hike down to Indian Garden; $675 for a five-night rim-to-rim backpack, including shuttle service; and $725 for a nine-night off-trail adventure in the wilderness of the northeastern canyon.

swear by duct tape as additional precaution against blisters, and everyone agrees that you should trim your **toenails** as much as possible before a downhill hike. A hiking **stick** or pair of trekking poles can be invaluable on knee-jarring downhill stretches.

While you're unlikely to lose your way on the main trails, a good **map** will greatly improve your sense of where you are. National Geographic–Trails Illustrated's wide-ranging *Grand Canyon National Park* (1:73,530) is recommended.

The major decision for **backpackers** is whether to bring a **tent**. While it's certainly necessary in winter, protection against cold is not a factor in summer. However, rain is always a possibility, in July and August especially, and you may also prefer to be sealed away from the desert wildlife, so a **rain fly** or waterproof **bivvy sack** may suit you. A **sleeping bag** is always recommended – though in summer it could simply be a light cotton sleeping sack – as are a foam pad or air mattress to put it on and a groundsheet beneath it all. As for a cooking **stove**, hot food may be more bother than it's worth in summer, but it's a lifesaver in winter. **Sandals** are a welcome indulgence for camp use.

Equipment rental

Outfitters the world over should sell any specialized equipment you need, and you'll find several good stores in nearby **Flagstaff** (see p.152). The **General Store** beside the *North Rim Campground* (see p.72) stocks a fairly limited range, while the **Canyon Village General Store** on the South Rim (see p.49) has a very good selection. The latter also **rents** equipment, including day packs and backpacks, stoves, sleeping bags and tents; typical rates for a tent would be $15 for the first day and $10 each subsequent day. Rental reservations are only accepted between one and five days in advance (☎928/638-2262).

The Corridor Trails

So called because they form the only continuous routes between the South and North rims, the three **Corridor Trails** – the **Bright Angel**, **South Kaibab** and **North Kaibab** trails – are deservedly the most popular hiking routes within the park. All provide a wonderful inner-canyon baptism for **backpackers**, featuring well-equipped campgrounds en route and the lure of **Phantom Ranch** down by the river, while also offering good, short **day hikes** for novice canyoneers who lack either the time or the energy to complete the entire routes. Again, as previously explained, it's crucial not to try to hike down to the river and back up again in a single day.

Because most hikers want to start from and finish at the South Rim, the most common itinerary is to hike **down the South Kaibab**, spend a night or two by the river, then return **up the Bright Angel**. That's certainly better than doing it the

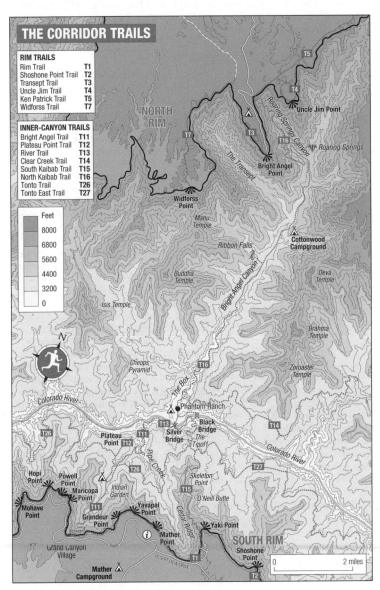

THE CORRIDOR TRAILS

RIM TRAILS

Rim Trail	T1
Shoshone Point Trail	T2
Transept Trail	T3
Uncle Jim Trail	T4
Ken Patrick Trail	T5
Widforss Trail	T7

INNER-CANYON TRAILS

Bright Angel Trail	T11
Plateau Point Trail	T12
River Trail	T13
Clear Creek Trail	T14
South Kaibab Trail	T15
North Kaibab Trail	T16
Tonto Trail	T26
Tonto East Trail	T27

Feet

	8000
	6800
	5600
	4400
	3200
	0

NORTH RIM

Uncle Jim Point

Roaring Springs Canyon

Roaring Springs

The Transept

Bright Angel Point

Widforss Point

Manu Temple

Ribbon Falls

Cottonwood Campground

Buddha Temple

Deva Temple

Isis Temple

Bright Angel Canyon

Brahma Temple

N

Cheops Pyramid

The Box

Zoroaster Temple

Colorado River

Phantom Ranch

Black Bridge

Silver Bridge

The Tipoff

T14

Plateau Point

Colorado River

Pipe Creek

T26

Skeleton Point

T27

Hopi Point

Powell Point

Maricopa Point

Indian Garden

O'Neill Butte

Mohave Point

Grandeur Point

Yavapai Point

Cedar Ridge

Yaki Point

Grand Canyon Village

Mather Point

SOUTH RIM

Shoshone Point

DESERT VIEW DRIVE

T1

Mather Campground

T2

0   2 miles

other way round, as the climb up the South Kaibab is a real killer. The reason more people don't do the **rim-to-rim** hike, from the South Rim to the North or vice versa, is largely because it's longer – the North Kaibab alone takes at least two days – and also because you end up more than two hundred driving miles from where you began. However, the **Transcanyon Shuttle** ($80 one-way; see p.115) does offer daily minibus service between the rims.

Finally, the Corridor Trails are also the only ones on which **mules** are allowed; for details of mule trips, see p.56 (South Rim) and p.69 (North Rim). Hikers are expected always to give way to mule trains, by standing still and quiet beside the trail.

T11 The Bright Angel Trail

Trailhead Grand Canyon Village (6860ft)
Water Mile-and-a-Half Resthouse (May–Sept)
Three-Mile Resthouse (May–Sept)
Indian Garden at 4.6 miles
Stream water (treat before use)

Day hike to Indian Garden (3800ft)
Difficulty Difficult
Distance 9.2 miles round trip
Estimated time 5–7hr

Day hike to Plateau Point (3665ft)
Difficulty Very strenuous
Distance 11.2 miles round trip
Estimated time 8–10hr

Phantom Ranch (2486ft)
Difficulty Strenuous
Distance 9.6 miles one-way
Estimated time 5–6hr descent, 7–9hr ascent

By far the busiest inner-canyon hiking route, the **Bright Angel Trail** starts in Grand Canyon Village, beside the wooden shack that once served as the Kolb photographic studio (see p.55). Although the side canyon immediately below the village makes access to the Tonto Platform relatively straightforward, it's still a long hard climb, with **water** available in the topmost 4.6 miles between May and September only. Most **day hikers** content themselves with walking to either of the two resthouses in the first three miles, but with an early start you should be able to manage the round trip of nine miles to **Indian Garden**, or even the eleven miles to **Plateau Point**. Just don't consider hiking to the Colorado and back in a single day, and only try to reach the river if you've reserved lodgings there for the night.

The "Bright Angel" name, first ascribed by John Wesley Powell to the tributary stream that flows down from the North Rim, is so ubiquitous in the Grand Canyon that it's easy to get confused. The Bright Angel Trail doesn't start from Bright Angel Point, which lies on the North Rim, and it doesn't quite reach, let alone follow, Bright Angel Creek. Technically, it ends where it meets the Colorado, 7.8 miles from the rim, and the 1.8-mile hike from there to **Phantom Ranch**, beside the creek, is on the separate **River Trail** (see p.96). The Bright Angel Trail does, however, launch itself into the canyon a couple of hundred yards west of *Bright Angel Lodge*, and most crucially of all, it owes its existence to the geologic fault line that makes rim-to-river access possible at this point, the **Bright Angel Fault**.

As one of the "easiest" natural routes into the canyon, the trail down to Indian Garden was known to Ancestral Puebloans a thousand years ago and was still in use by the **Havasupai** when prospectors Pete Berry and Niles and Ralph Cameron improved it in 1890. Ralph took it over in 1903, exploiting spurious mining claims to charge riders a toll of $1 each. It was finally passed over to the park in 1928.

The initial descent

There's no gentle introduction to the Bright Angel Trail, which hurtles straight into a long, exposed set of switchbacks down the dry rocky hillside. Be careful if you're coming this way in **winter**; conditions can be very icy. Each of the two short **tunnels** within the first mile marks a transition between geologic layers, the first from Kaibab Limestone to the Toroweap Formation, the second on to Coconino Sandstone.

Soon after dropping down that steep, dark cliff, you reach **Mile-and-a-Half Resthouse**, a basic waystation that offers water (May–Sept), restrooms and emergency phones. By now, wildlife is much more abundant, including pesky squirrels and ravens. A similar onward haul, past first the Hermit Shale and then the Supai Formation – look out for rock surfaces along the way that hold a few Ancestral Puebloan **pictographs**, all but obscured by graffiti – brings you to the equally self-explanatory **Three-Mile Resthouse**, which has water (again in summer only) and phones but not restrooms.

As is readily apparent from its sweeping canyon views, Three-Mile Resthouse marks the final boundary between forest and desert. Below it lies the precipitous **Redwall Limestone**, the major obstacle to inner canyon access throughout the park, breached here thanks to the Bright Angel Fault. Even so, it takes the forty tight switchbacks of **Jacob's Ladder** – the most murderous stretch of the return journey – to carry you down to the gently sloping bed of Garden Creek.

Indian Garden

Though you'll almost certainly have spotted it from the rim, the verdant green strip of **Garden Creek** still makes a welcome surprise at the foot of those baking-hot switchbacks. Just past a patch of prickly pears and other yellow- and red-blossomed cacti, you hear the astonishing sound of trickling water. The streambed is lined with dazzling green cottonwood trees.

Native peoples really did grow crops at **Indian Garden**, 4.6 miles from the rim. As well as the creek, there's also a perennial **spring**, where seepage from the more porous rock layers above collects atop the impervious Bright Angel Shale. Originally planted in prehistoric times, the "garden" was continuously used by the Havasupai from around 1300 AD until the modern era; early tourists admired the ancient stone granaries. In 1905, Theodore Roosevelt is said to have curtly instructed the Havasupai leader to "get your people out"; they were eventually evicted in 1928, by which time they were no longer farmers but dependent on the tourist trade.

These days this unexpected little oasis holds a year-round water supply, a ranger station, restrooms, separate **camping** and day-use areas, and a staging post for mules. Forever busy with hikers, backpackers and mule riders, it's not exactly pristine wilderness, but it's such a well-shaded and attractive staging post for weary trail users that no one's complaining.

T12 The Plateau Point Trail

The Bright Angel Trail continues its descent to the river from Indian Garden, as described below. However, if you turn left across Garden Creek at Indian Garden and head west three-quarters of a mile on the **Tonto Trail**, you'll reach an obvious spur trail to the right. This spur threads its way out 0.8 mile to **Plateau Point**, a superb overlook above the Granite Gorge, from which it's not possible to descend any farther.

Forged to allow day-tripping mule riders a glimpse of the river – though such trips are not currently offered (see p.56) – the **Plateau Point Trail** also makes an ideal route for hikers. However, although it involves almost no additional elevation change, the round trip still adds three very exposed miles to any day hike. For that reason, it's not recommended between June and August. At other times, allow at least eight hours to get to Plateau Point and back from the rim.

Barren even by inner-canyon standards, the Tonto Platform landscape is spectacular, with agave and yucca plants shooting up from the sandy soil and the mighty
red buttes and mesas of the canyon now framed against the blue sky. Shortly after
you get your first awesome glimpse of the black tumbling walls of the gorge, the
trail comes to a dead end. From a precarious perch atop the rocky outcrops, you
can admire a long stretch of the dark-green Colorado, though both the bridges and
Phantom Ranch lie out of sight around the next promontory to the east. With
binoculars, you can just make out the buildings back at the top of the South Rim,
six miles away.

Devils Corkscrew and The Colorado River

As it flows down from Indian Garden, Garden Creek has cut a narrow cleft into
the Tapeats Sandstone below. With the Bright Angel Trail alongside, it swiftly
enters a secluded little gorge known as the **Tapeats Narrows**. This is among the
most delightful segments of any inner-canyon trail – if you could somehow
arrive here without having hiked down, you'd never imagine you were deep in
the Grand Canyon. The temptation to linger beside the babbling stream is
irresistible, but don't drink from it – you've just seen where it's been, beside the
mule pen.

At the lower end of the narrows, Garden Creek veers into a tangle of rocks as it
rushes to meet **Pipe Creek**. Humans, however, have to take the slow way down,
along one last searing set of switchbacks, the **Devils Corkscrew**, which were
hacked into the rock as a shortcut to the river during the 1930s (before that, river-
bound Bright Angel hikers took the Tonto Trail 4.1 miles east from Indian
Garden to join the South Kaibab Trail at the Tipoff). Beyond the **Columbine
Spring** waterfall at the bottom, the gradient becomes much less severe, and you
crisscross Pipe Creek repeatedly as it meanders down its own pleasant side canyon
to reach the Colorado at **Pipe Creek Beach**, 3.2 miles from Indian Garden. The
small **River Resthouse**, with a phone but no water or restrooms, is located just
before the river.

It's a breathtaking moment when you first find yourself in the **Granite Gorge**,
with thousand-foot walls of gnarled gray **Vishnu Schist** soaring to either side of
the river. Only here at its very bottom, the rims obscured from sight and only the
occasional butte or temple rearing its head above the inner walls, can the Grand
Canyon ever feel at all gloomy or oppressive, though a more common response
among hikers is exhilaration at finally being down in the ancient bowels of the
planet. It takes a good ten-minute walk along the **River Trail** (**T13**), undulating
over rocky debris slopes, before you round a corner to see a bridge in the distance,
and another mile or so through sandy dunes before you reach it.

The slender, see-through **Bright Angel Suspension Bridge**, also known as the
Silver Bridge, was built in the 1960s to carry the **pipeline** from Roaring Springs,
high on the North Kaibab Trail (see p.103), by which the South Rim receives all
its water. Mules quite sensibly balk at the way both pipeline and river are clearly
visible between the slats, and how the whole bridge bounces at every step. Mule
trains therefore continue east less than a mile along the River Trail to the South
Kaibab Trail. Hikers invariably cross here, however, eager to reach the **Phantom
Ranch** area on the far side.

The Phantom Ranch area

The only place where inner-canyon hikers and mule-riders can not only cross
the Colorado River, but also camp, and even sleep in a real bed, at the bottom
of the canyon, lies at the confluence of the Colorado with **Bright Angel**

Creek. **Phantom Ranch**, at the rendezvous of the Bright Angel, South Kaibab and North Kaibab trails, is a venerable Park-Service lodge that provides individual and dorm accommodation in log cabins, and also has a restaurant. In addition, up to 92 campers per night can enjoy the stream-side **Bright Angel Campground**.

Although **Bright Angel Creek**, which flows down Bright Angel Canyon from the North Rim, is usually just a few feet wide by the time it meets the Colorado,

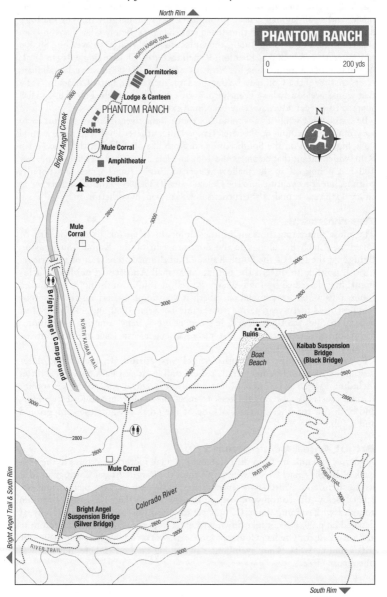

the sandy deposits around its mouth stretch for a few hundred yards in either direction. The journals of John Wesley Powell, who spotted it on August 15, 1869, record "We discover a stream entering from the north, a clear beautiful creek coming down through a gorgeous red canyon". He named it Bright Angel to contrast with the muddy Dirty Devil River, upstream in Utah.

Hikers who arrive on the North Kaibab Trail will be prepared for the rich riparian habitat of the riverbanks; if you've come down the South Kaibab, though, this feels like an amazing oasis. Majestic willows and cottonwoods offer welcome shade, and small animals scurry through the dense undergrowth. The **ecology** down here, however, is both threatened and changing. Before Glen Canyon Dam was completed in the mid-1960s, the Colorado would carry an average 380,000 tons of earth and rock past Phantom Ranch each day. On one single day in 1921, 27 million tons went hurtling by. Now it's more like 40,000 tons per day, all from rivers that meet the Colorado below the dam, such as the Little Colorado. Trees that would previously have been swept away establish themselves instead, and fish adapted to suit muddy waters are becoming extinct.

Be warned that while it's always a relief to reach the river, it's often too **hot** to do very much of anything down here. Temperatures at river level tend to be around 20°F higher than on the South Rim, and more like 30°F higher than the North Rim, which means that between mid-May and late September it's likely to be over 100°F. Cooling off in the shallow waters of Bright Angel Creek is a popular pastime, but don't venture into the Colorado itself. Thanks to the dam, that stays at an icy 45°F year-round; if the currents don't kill you, hypothermia may.

The riverbank

The most interesting portion of the Colorado riverbank in the vicinity of Phantom Ranch lies alongside the northern end of the **Kaibab Suspension Bridge**, at the foot of the South Kaibab Trail. Immediately west of the bridge, it's still possible to discern the outline of a small **Ancestral Puebloan settlement**, first described by John Wesley Powell in 1869. Consisting of five linked rooms plus a *kiva* (ceremonial chamber), it was home to perhaps three or four families for a forty-year period some time between 1060 and 1150 AD. Just beyond that lies the **Boat Beach**, in frequent use by canyon rafting expeditions, for whom this represents the first place passengers can leave the river in the 87-mile run from Lees Ferry.

If you arrive across the **Bright Angel Suspension Bridge** instead, after descending the Bright Angel Trail, a short trail leads past Park Service facilities including ranger accommodation, a small mule corral and public restrooms. It then crosses Bright Angel Creek to meet the trail from the Kaibab bridge, and both run together up the east side of the creek towards the campground and ranch.

Bright Angel Campground

A quarter of a mile up from the confluence, a small footbridge crosses to the west bank of Bright Angel Creek, where you enter the **Bright Angel Campground** at its northern end. Thirty-two separate sites, each with its own picnic table, are ranged below the cottonwoods beside the creek, and there's a central restroom complex with running water. Camping at this beautiful spot is by **permit** only, as detailed on p.90. Do not hike down without a reservation. The site started out in 1933 as a base for Civilian Conservation Corps workers, who were improving the park's trail network. They even built a swimming pool down here, but that was filled in, in 1972.

Phantom Ranch

Another quarter of a mile north of the campground, and thus set half a mile back from the Colorado, **Phantom Ranch** itself is the only accommodation option within the canyon. Clustered around a central lodge, its various cabins, corrals and outbuildings stand amid huge cottonwoods and fruit orchards that were planted early in the twentieth century to shade a group of tents known as Rust's Camp. Renamed Roosevelt's Camp after a visit by Theodore Roosevelt in 1913, this was in turn replaced by Phantom Ranch in 1922. Designed by Mary Jane Colter (see box, p.54) as something of a dude ranch for the Fred Harvey Company, the lodge incorporates uncut river stone and natural timbers to blend in with the surroundings. More buildings were added over the succeeding years until the complex reached its present size.

Priority booking for Phantom's eleven fully equipped individual **cabins** (⑤) goes to riders on Fred Harvey **mule trips** – full details, including prices, appear on p.56. When available, however, which is more likely in winter, they're also let to hikers, and rafters who need to spend a night here before or after a river trip. You can also get a bed in one of the four ten-bunk, single-sex **dormitories** (❷) – two for men and two for women – with bedding, showers, towels and soap provided.

Reservations, as for the South-Rim lodges, are handled by Xanterra (advance reservations ☎303/297-2757 or 1-888/297-2757, same-day reservations ☎928/638-2631, ⓦwww.grandcanyonlodges.com). Once again, you must not hike down without a reservation; even if you do have one, it's essential to **reconfirm** between one and three days in advance of your stay, either in person at the transportation desk at *Bright Angel Lodge* or by calling ☎928/638-3283.

As a rule, Phantom Ranch books up well in advance, but if you're spending a few days at the canyon, it's worth enquiring about **cancellations** for dorm beds and, conceivably, cabins. These are handed out first-come, first-served at *Bright Angel Lodge* early each morning. The night before, check what time the desk will open – it can be as early as 6am.

Phantom Ranch's main lodge building acts as a **dining room**, **bar** and **store**. Meals are served communally at long tables, and at set times; all must be reserved in advance, ideally at the same time as you book your accommodation, and they're also available to campers. All supplies get here the same way you do, so food is expensive. The price for **dinner** depends on your main course, and includes vegetables, salad, dessert and coffee. The 5pm sitting offers either a 12oz steak for $42 or a vegetarian alternative, with lentil loaf, for $26, while a beef stew is served at 6.30pm, again for just over $26. **Breakfast**, served in two separate sittings well before dawn, includes eggs, pancakes and bacon for about $19.50, and you can also pick up a **sack lunch** to carry with you on the trail for just over $12. Note that the lodge closes between breakfast sittings, so if you've ordered a sack lunch, make sure you can pick it up when you want.

Outside meal times, the counter in the lodge sells simple snacks, like trail mix and cookies; drinks including beer and wine; first-aid supplies such as bandages and sun cream; and accessories like camera batteries, torches and sunhats (daily: April–Oct 8am–4pm & 8–10pm, Nov–March 8.30am–4pm & 8–10pm). They'll also have details of the daily programme of **ranger talks** about different aspects of the canyon, mostly held in the grounds nearby. There's also an outdoor payphone, for credit-card and calling-card calls only.

Finally, via the *Bright Angel* transportation desk, you can arrange to have a large bag carried in or out of the canyon for you, by some unfortunate mule. So-called **duffel service** costs around $65 each way, though as you'll still have to carry your own food and water you may not be able to reduce your load all that significantly.

T14 The Clear Creek Trail

Trailhead Off North Kaibab Trail, 0.5 mile north of Phantom Ranch (2640ft)
Water Stream water after 8.5 miles (treat before use)
Difficulty Strenuous
Distance 8.7 miles one-way
Estimated time 5hr each way (at least two days)
Elevation gain 1600ft

Inner-canyon trails are few and far between on the north side of the canyon, and fewer still offer the chance to explore parallel to the river rather than simply heading to or from the rim. The **Clear Creek Trail**, which heads east from the North Kaibab Trail just under half a mile north of **Phantom Ranch**, is therefore the most popular side-hike for backpackers basing themselves in the ranch area.

Not that it's an easy option: it starts with a very stiff thousand-foot climb from the Granite Gorge up to the Tonto Platform, and continues for a total of almost nine miles one-way as it meanders eastwards beneath the Brahma and Zoroaster temples. The views are superb, both down into the gorge and also across the vastness of the inner canyon.

When the trail was built by the Civilian Conservation Corps in 1933, the idea was to provide access to the canyon's highest free-falling waterfall, **Cheyava Falls**, which cascades off the Walhalla Plateau and achieves peak flow in late spring. However, the falls lie another four miles of fierce scrambling up the bed of Clear Creek from the official end of the trail, so it requires a 26-mile round trip from Phantom Ranch – and thus a multi-day wilderness camping expedition – even to get a glimpse of them.

T15 The South Kaibab Trail

Trailhead Yaki Point (7200ft)
Water None

Day hike to Cedar Mesa (6060ft)
Difficulty Strenuous
Distance 3 miles round trip
Estimated time 2–4hr

Day hike to Skeleton Point (5160ft)
Difficulty Very strenuous
Distance 6 miles round trip
Estimated time 4–6hr

Phantom Ranch (2486ft)
Difficulty Strenuous
Distance 7.1 miles one-way
Estimated time 4–6hr descent (ascent not recommended)

The **South Kaibab Trail** – the most direct route from the South Rim to **Phantom Ranch** – is the only major park trail never to have been used by the canyon's ancient inhabitants. Rangers hacked it out of the bare rock in 1924, when it looked as though they'd never wrest control of the Bright Angel Trail away from Ralph Cameron (see p.94). Whereas all Ancestral Puebloan trails follow natural drainage channels down into the canyon, the South Kaibab stays atop the narrow, exposed **Cedar Ridge**. Sure, the views are fabulous, but with a pitiless lack of shade and not a drop of water en route, it's a gruelling trek. The Park Service recommends that no one should try to hike up it in summer, and all year it's used principally by backpackers who descend this way and return via the Bright Angel Trail, and day hikers venturing a short way down to enjoy those views. On all but the very shortest day hikes, carry a gallon of water per person.

You can only drive to the trailhead at **Yaki Point**, four miles east of Grand Canyon Village, between December and February. Year round, however, you can get there on the free park shuttle buses – either the **Kaibab Trail Route** (also known as the **Green Line**), or, ideally, the early-morning **Hikers' Express**, both of which are detailed on p.43 – or by taxi (p.44).

Although avoiding the midday sun is advisable in summer, it's a shame to start down the trail much before dawn; the views as the sun rises are superb.

Descent to Cedar Mesa and Skeleton Point

Starting from the Yaki Point mule corral – not the main overlook – the trail drops down the western flank of the promontory, negotiating the off-white Kaibab Limestone layer via a long but not too steep switchback. This first stretch is easy going underfoot, on a recently upgraded path that's lined with neat boulders. Three-quarters of a mile along, it reaches the tip of the promontory, where for the first time massive views open to the east as well as the west. The Park Service has taken to calling this **Ooh Aah Point**; it's a dramatic enough spot, but the new name was bestowed partly to give day hikers the sense of having reached an important destination.

Turn back now, and you've had a satisfying taste of what it's like to see the canyon from the inside. For anyone who intends to press on, the scale of the task that lies ahead is readily apparent. Reaching the level plateau of **Cedar Mesa**, down below, involves a sharp, three-quarter-of-a-mile zigzag descent of the red Coconino Sandstone layer. Allowing an hour to get there from the trailhead, and two hours to climb back up again, that makes a good half-day hike. Once again, the views from this scraggy, exposed russet mesa-top – which holds pit toilets but no water or phone – are tremendous. As well as seeing thirty miles up the canyon in either direction, and straight up Bright Angel Canyon towards the North Rim, you can gaze down to the Tonto Trail, snaking across the Tonto Platform, and the Devils Corkscrew on the Bright Angel Trail to the west. To cap it all, it's also a popular hangout for **condors**.

Although the Park Service discourages day hikers from continuing beyond Cedar Mesa, the next segment of the trail, as it drops off the mesa's east side, is relatively mild. After a forty-minute traverse along the flank of the mesa, which skirts the 6071ft pinnacle of **O'Neill Butte**, it levels out on another small plateau dotted with towering agave. Just after you plummet off **Skeleton Point**, the tip of this little plateau, you'll get your first glimpse of the Colorado.

Below Skeleton Point

From Skeleton Point a succession of major switchbacks, interspersed with a brief saddle or two where you can catch your breath, now cuts down through a notch in the Redwall. After perhaps three hours of hiking from the trailhead, a distance of 4.4 miles, you emerge on the **Tonto Platform**, to meet the **Tonto Trail** a short distance ahead.

While hardy backpackers can connect with the Grandview Trail (see p.106) by hiking 18.5 miles **east** along the Tonto Trail, the obvious way to go is **west**. Were you to continue for four miles, you'd reach **Indian Garden** (see p.95), where you could join the Bright Angel Trail and follow it back up to the village. At this point, however, you're much more likely to be heading for the river. It's now less than two miles away, but the most hair-raising section of the South Kaibab Trail still lies ahead.

The launch pad for Granite Gorge hikers is a spot known as **the Tipoff**, a cleft in the rock that's located just beyond a set of pit toilets, and is equipped with an emergency phone. Turn right off the Tonto Trail here, descend a couple of grey switchbacks, and you're suddenly confronted by a long, alarmingly vertiginous traverse, where the trail seems barely scraped into the red dust of the Hakatai Shale as it curves above an abysmal drop. Here and there, a few mighty blocks of blackened Tapeats Sandstone teeter above your head. Walking this stretch is not quite as bad as it looks, but then little here could be. Attaining the haven of the broad promontory at the far end, you're rewarded with a prospect of the full majesty of the **Granite Gorge**, with Phantom Ranch spread out invitingly below.

Further steep switchbacks fly by during the final descent, which culminates first with a rendezvous with the **River Trail** (which connects with the Bright Angel Trail, as described on p.96) and then with the forty-yard tunnel that brings you to the broad, green Colorado itself. Hanging from eight 1.5-inch-thick cables, the slender 400ft **Kaibab Suspension Bridge** here, also known as the **Black Bridge**, was erected in 1928 to replace a makeshift cable car. Each cable weighs more than a ton and was carried down the Kaibab Trail on the shoulders of 42 Havasupai. The bridge of choice for the canyon's skittish mules, who prefer its rubberized, non-see-through floor, it stands 78ft above the water and makes a great vantage point for spotting exhilarated river runners as they round the last curve before **Phantom Ranch** (described on p.96 onwards).

T16 The North Kaibab Trail

Trailhead North Kaibab Trailhead (8241ft)
Water Supai Tunnel (May–Oct) at 1.7 miles
Cottonwood Campground (May–Oct) at 6.8 miles
Stream water (treat before use)

Day hike to Supai Tunnel (6800ft)
Difficulty Strenuous
Distance 4 miles round trip
Estimated time 3–5hr

Day hike to Roaring Springs (5220ft)
Difficulty Very strenuous
Distance 9.4 miles round trip
Estimated time 7–9hr

Day 1: to Cottonwood Campground (4080ft)
Difficulty Strenuous
Distance 6.8 miles one-way
Estimated time 4–5hr descent, 6–8hr ascent

Day 2: Cottonwood Campground to Phantom Ranch (2486ft)
Difficulty Moderate
Distance 7.2 miles one-way
Estimated time 4–5hr each way

Some version of the **North Kaibab Trail**, which follows **Bright Angel Creek** from the North Rim to the Colorado, has been in use for more than a thousand years. At one time, the Park Service trail started several miles east of Bright Angel Point and traced the creek's entire course to the river; the present route, which begins with a descent through **Roaring Springs Canyon**, was established in the late 1920s, to be more accessible from the epicentre of North Rim tourism, and also to shorten its overall length to 14.5 miles from rim to river. Old and new routes combine at the actual **Roaring Springs**, almost five miles down, which is the very furthest you should aim for on a day hike. In fact, as the first few miles are the steepest of all, it's more realistic to settle for the four-mile round trip as far as the Supai Tunnel. Be aware that the trail does not necessarily open when the North Rim itself opens for the season, in mid-May; it can take rangers a few weeks to clear away winter rockslides and fallen trees.

The trail starts from a wooded car park at a curve in AZ-67 less than two miles north of *Grand Canyon Lodge* (see p.70). In summer, when the car park tends to fill early, many hikers simply leave their vehicles by the roadside, but even that alternative is soon exhausted, in which case you'll have to park at the lodge or campground and walk from there. A limited, early-morning **hiker shuttle** to the trailhead leaves *Grand Canyon Lodge* at 5.45am and 7.10am daily, and costs $7 per person. Notices at the trailhead, filled with sombre advice about heat and water, recommend all hikers set off by 6am.

Initial descent

At first, the trail remains within the pine forest, with thick sandy dust underfoot as it zigzags steadily downwards through the Kaibab Limestone layer. Views at this stage are mostly of Roaring Springs Canyon itself, which was created by its own separate geological fault.

Many people go no further than the **Coconino Overlook**, a flat slab of rock just off the trail 0.7 miles down. Marking the bottom of the Toroweap Formation and the top of the Coconino Sandstone layer, this high eminence overlooks the junction of Roaring Springs and Bright Angel canyons. Just over a mile beyond that, a total of around an hour's walking from the top, you'll reach a clearing beneath magnificent Coconino cliffs that are stained dark by natural mineral secretions to create the effect known as "desert varnish". Equipped with a summer-only water tap and pit toilets, this is the turnaround point for mule trains on their half-day trips (see p.69).

The Supai Tunnel and Roaring Springs
Immediately around the corner from the mule turnaround point lies the brief **Supai Tunnel**, bored through the sandstone in the 1930s. Though less than twenty yards long, it seems to carry you into another world. Below it, long and very exposed switchbacks take roughly half an hour to plummet down the red Supai Sandstone layer, until they come to the **Redwall Bridge**. After a flash flood destroyed much of the trail here in 1966, the bridge was built to provide a safer crossing over Roaring Springs Creek.

Once across the bridge, you come to a gentle but consistently spectacular traverse of the Redwall Limestone, following a man-made ledge carved halfway up a mighty cliff with a sheer drop-off to your left. The scenery in this area, with its bizarre limestone outcrops, is more reminiscent of some strange, sacred Chinese mountain than of the Grand Canyon, and is best enjoyed from a huge fern-bedecked alcove further along.

It takes about an hour to reach **Roaring Springs**, which is much the tallest of several waterfalls that cascade down the opposite wall of Roaring Springs Canyon. A worthwhile quarter of a mile detour off to the left of the trail leads down to the lovely little streamside oasis that's fed by all this water, where you'll find several picnic tables and a mule corral. No drinking water is available, and the pools are only deep enough to cool your toes rather than swim, but Roaring Springs makes the ideal point to head home on a day hike, or halt on a longer expedition.

It's the water from Roaring Springs that supplies the lodges and amenities on both rims of the canyon, being pumped straight up to *Grand Canyon Lodge* on the North Rim, as well as piped down the trail and up to the South Rim. If anything goes wrong with the pumphouse, it has to be repaired immediately, so the park-service employee responsible lives a minute or two's walk away, down here in the canyon. From 1973 until 2006, that employee was painter **Bruce Aiken**, whose resplendently glowing canyon canvases sell for as much as $60,000 (Ⓦbruceaiken.com).

Not far on, Roaring Springs Creek is subsumed into the much more substantial stream of Bright Angel Creek. The trail remains on its western side through the slender Tapeats Narrows, then crosses a bridge over to the east bank just after its confluence with the lesser Manzanita Creek.

Cottonwood Campground and beyond
Cottonwood Campground, 1.4 miles past the bridge mentioned above and 2.5 miles beyond the springs, is a major overnight halt for trans-canyon hikers. Laid out in the 1930s by the Civilian Conservation Corps, it's an attractive spot, located at one of the canyon floor's broader moments, right beneath Bright Angel Point. It holds a summer-only water faucet and restrooms, but only the ranger station benefits from the shade of the eponymous Fremont cottonwoods; the actual campsites stand amid rather sandy scrub.

The highlight of the final seven-mile segment to Phantom Ranch is lacy **Ribbon Falls**, 1.5 miles below the campground and 0.3 miles up a spur trail west into a side canyon. Of the two alternative trails that lead across the creek to the falls, only the first, at a very obvious junction where the main trail is about to climb a short hill, is recommended. That one has a footbridge, whereas the other involves a dangerous fording of the water. Ribbon Falls is a beautiful spot, a double cascade tumbling around a hundred feet over shiny, moss-stained cliffs wreathed in rich vegetation. Small wonder that one clan of the Zuni people, who now live two hundred miles southeast in New Mexico, proudly traces its origins here.

The North Kaibab Trail finally enters the Grand Canyon's Inner Gorge through **the Box**, squeezing for almost four muddy miles between twin thousand-foot walls of ancient black Vishnu Schist. Four footbridges cross the stream before the Box eventually opens out again a mile or so short of **Phantom Ranch**, with the last stretch of trail consisting of a level, sandy stroll alongside the delightful babbling creek. Your first intimation of the ranch ahead comes with the sudden reappearance of dramatic cottonwood trees; the area is described in detail on p.96 onwards.

In **winter**, after the North Rim closes (see p.67), it's still possible to walk *up* the North Kaibab from Phantom Ranch. What's unpredictable is quite how far you'll get; you'll probably be stopped by heavy snow and ice somewhere above Roaring Springs. Ill-equipped hikers who have climbed too high on this trail have been known to die from hypothermia.

Other South Rim trails

While the two corridor routes, the Bright Angel and the South Kaibab, are always the busiest South Rim trails, there are plenty of appealing alternatives even for first-time hikers. All the trails described below – which are listed from east to west – are officially "unmaintained", which means they can be hard to follow and may even be blocked altogether by rockfalls. They're unarguably more demanding to walk on, and it's unfortunate that the times when the main trails are most crowded, and you're most likely to want to try the lesser-known ones, are also of course the hottest seasons of the year. Don't be too deterred, however; these trails do see regular traffic, and in their upper reaches especially, where they're frequented by day-hikers, you're unlikely to run into difficulties. The two most obvious day hikes are as far as **Santa Maria Spring** via the **Hermit Trail**, and down to **Horseshoe Mesa** on the **Grandview Trail**.

T17 The Tanner Trail

Trailhead Lipan Point (7360ft)
Water None

Day hike to Seventy-Five-Mile Saddle (5600ft)
Difficulty Strenuous
Distance 3.8 miles round trip
Estimated time 4–5hr

Day hike to the Redwall (5600ft)
Difficulty Very strenuous
Distance 7 miles round trip
Estimated time 6–8hr

Colorado River (2700ft)
Difficulty Very strenuous
Distance 7.6 miles one-way
Estimated time 5–6hr descent, 7–9hr ascent

The easternmost of the South Rim's inner-canyon trails, the **Tanner Trail**, follows a former Hopi route that was improved by prospector Seth Tanner (see p.117) during the 1880s to provide access to his copper-mining claims. Fortune seekers in search of John D. Lee's supposed hidden gold mines also passed this way, and it's said that rustlers and bandits combined it with the Nankoweap Trail on the far side to make the self-explanatory Horsethief Trail. Today, as an unmaintained park trail, it's in pretty poor condition, and makes a steep haul. With no water and precious little shade en route, it's used almost exclusively by hardened canyon backpackers.

From the trailhead at **Lipan Point** – see p.62 – the path swiftly drops down the eastern flank of the promontory. Numerous rockfalls make it easy to lose your way here, and even at its clearest the path is very uneven, but there are no dangerous drop-offs in the first stretch (it's actually easier going up than coming down, or at least it would be were it not for the extreme fatigue). Once the terrain begins to level out, after around an hour of stiff switchbacks, it's absolutely essential that you stay on the west – left – side of Tanner Creek, rather than follow, let alone cross, the streambed. A rough traverse will soon bring you to the **Seventy-Five Mile Saddle**, named after Seventy-Five Mile Creek which starts to the west and joins the Colorado just after river mile 75.

While the trail proper doesn't lead along the red sandstone neck that stretches out towards 6536ft **Escalante Butte**, the crumbling, eroded spur that does is a must for day hikers and the ideal turnaround point on a half-day trek. Stroll out a few hundred yards to enjoy superb views west, between the towering ruddy walls that frame Seventy-Five-Mile Creek, to the Granite Gorge of the Colorado. To the east, you should be able to see the Watchtower at Desert View up on the rim, and even hear the gleeful cries of tour groups.

The Tanner Trail continues by dropping once again eastwards, but the surface is in notably better condition, and there's little elevation change for the next 1.6 miles, as it skirts around the bases of first Escalante Butte and then **Cárdenas Butte** (6281ft) – Don García López de Cárdenas being the Spanish would-be conquistador credited with first seeing the Grand Canyon from somewhere nearby (see p.200). Grassy natural depressions near both buttes make ideal campsites for backpackers on the long climb out of the canyon.

Hardy day-hikers choose to press on as far the top of the **Redwall**, just beyond Cárdenas Butte. While that seven-mile round trip makes a gruelling trek in the heat of summer, the views from here, down to where the river makes its crucial westward bend at **Tanner Rapid**, are magnificent.

The most difficult stretch comes immediately afterwards, as the trail plummets down a steep crack in the crumbling Redwall Limestone. The river itself is four miles down, and the gradient barely relents. Traversing the Dox Sandstone layer, the trail dwindles to a foot wide and sits at an angle to the slope, with steep drop-offs.

At the bottom, sandy, dune-fringed **Tanner Beach** is a popular campsite for both hikers and rafters. It also marks the start of a twenty-mile round trip hike to the north along the **Beamer Trail (T18)**, which runs parallel to the Colorado and leads to the mouth of the Little Colorado River.

T19 The New Hance Trail

The most demanding of all the South Rim trails, the **New Hance Trail** bears the name of one of the Grand Canyon's great characters, **Captain John Hance**. The very picture of the eccentric white-bearded prospector, Hance spent his old age as a treasured Fred Harvey employee, spinning tall tales of his adventures for any tourists who would listen. In 1883, he created the Old Hance Trail to help him reach his asbestos mine across the river; building a cabin at the trailhead, he became the canyon's first white resident. He went on to guide pioneer sightseers down his trail, though by the turn of the century it had eroded and collapsed so completely that not a trace now remains.

Trailhead Near Moran Point (6982ft)
Water Seasonal streams after 5.1 miles (treat before use)

Day hike to Coronado Butte Saddle (5900ft)
Difficulty Strenuous
Distance 2.4 miles round trip
Estimated time 3–4hr

Day hike to the Redwall (4850ft)
Difficulty Very strenuous
Distance 5.8 miles round trip
Estimated time 6–8hr

Colorado River (2600ft)
Difficulty Very strenuous
Distance 6.6 miles one-way
Estimated time 5–6hr descent, 7–9hr ascent

By all accounts the old trail was exceptionally steep and dangerous; Hance's replacement, originally known as the Red Canyon Trail but now named after its creator, remains extremely difficult. Sections of its switchbacks have crumbled away, and you often have to scramble over minor rockfalls. It's not a hike to undertake lightly, and if you're using it as part of a longer itinerary, by combining it for example with an expedition along the Tonto Trail, it's one much better used to go down rather than up.

Parking is prohibited at the unmarked New Hance trailhead, which lies a quarter of a mile off the highway along a disused road. Leave your vehicle either at Moran Point, and walk the 1.6 miles southwest from there, or at the Buggeln Picnic Area another mile southwest. As with the Tanner Trail, the route consists of two distinct sets of fierce switchbacks, one down to the saddle below **Coronado Butte**, and the other two miles further on where it drops off the **Redwall**. This time, though, the stretch in between the two is hardly less demanding, so even a day hike to the brink of the Redwall is far from easy. The final couple of miles to the river, beside the verdant Red Canyon Wash – which doesn't flow year-round – are the most attractive part of the hike, but even those involve some difficult scrambling. At the far end, the roiling waters of **Hance Rapid** await.

T20 The Grandview Trail

Trailhead Grandview Point (7406ft)
Water None
Day hike to Horseshoe Mesa (4932ft)
Difficulty Strenuous
Distance 6.4 miles round trip
Estimated time 5–7hr

The **Grandview Trail** provides a rare opportunity to explore one of the many wooded mesas that dot the inner canyon, the double-pointed **Horseshoe Mesa**. Although it's possible, by connecting with other trails, to use the Grandview to find your way down to the Tonto Platform and thus eventually to the Colorado, this is not a rim-to-river route. Involving a shorter trek, and less of an elevation change, than the other major South Rim trails, it's therefore one of the most popular **day hikes** in the park. Which doesn't mean it's easy; the trail itself is in worse condition than you'll be used to if you've only tackled the Corridor Trails, and the climb back out is tough by any standards. Allow about six hours for the whole round trip.

Peter Berry first improved this trail in 1892, to aid operations at his Last Chance copper mine out on the Horseshoe Mesa. He made enough money to finance construction of the *Grandview Hotel* at the top, which lasted a little longer than the copper but was eventually bankrupted by the arrival of the railroad to the west. While the trail is no longer officially maintained, evidence of Berry's work remains very visible. Many of its switchbacks were constructed by inserting metal rods deep into the canyon wall, then covering them with juniper logs, stones and dirt. The whole thing has stayed surprisingly sturdy for over a century, though several of its upper portions had to be reconstructed in 2005, following landslides. Hiking can at times be a little hair-raising, but it's certainly easier than both the New Hance and the Tanner trails.

As described on p.61, the best views come at and just below the trailhead, beside the car park at Grandview Point. Below that, narrow cobbled switchbacks cling to the canyon's wall of Kaibab Limestone, with steep drop-offs to the side. It takes something under an hour to reach the refuge of the **Coconino Saddle**, a spur between Grapevine Canyon to the west and Hance Canyon to the east where the trees offer some very welcome shade. In due course the switchbacks grow shallower, and you're faced instead with some long, exposed traverses along the red Supai Sandstone layer, where the path dwindles to just a couple of feet wide and gravel skitters over the edge with every step.

Another saddle, three miles from the rim, leads onto Horseshoe Mesa, with a short drop still to go before you reach the pit toilets (with no water) that mark the start of what used to be the active mining area. The ruddy soil is scattered with mineral-rich flecks and outcrops of copper ore, and the ruins of miners' cabins are everywhere you look. Makeshift trails meander around the whole mesa-top, passing abandoned workings and mysterious caves; investigating any of these is officially forbidden, and would be an extremely perilous undertaking.

If you're planning to backpack further into the canyon, the best route down from the mesa – signed to Cottonwood Creek – heads off to the left (west) close to the restrooms. Below on the Tonto Platform, a seven-mile **loop** around the foot of Horseshoe Mesa rejoins the Grandview Trail a few hundred yards higher up. Alternatively, you could join the **Tonto Trail**, and head either seven miles east on what's officially the **Tonto East Trail** (see p.110) to meet the New Hance Trail beside the Colorado, or twenty miles west to join the South Kaibab Trail.

T21 The Hermit Trail

Equally appealing to both day hikers and long-distance backpackers, the **Hermit Trail** is another unmaintained trail that dates from the days when the obstreperous Ralph Cameron controlled access to most of the prime rim-edge sites (see p.203). Having started life as the El Tovar Trail, used from 1912 onwards by the Fred Harvey Company for its mule excursions, it was soon renamed in honour of the reclusive French-Canadian prospector Louis Boucher, a familiar figure in its early days.

Though abandoned in 1931, much of the trail's engineering remains in good shape, and even if the views are seldom as spectacular it makes a good alternative to

| Trailhead Hermits Rest (6640ft)
| **Water** Santa Maria Spring at 2.3 miles (seasonal; treat before use) Year-round stream at 7.7 miles (treat before use)
| **Day hike to Santa Maria Spring** (5000ft) **Difficulty** Moderate **Distance** 4.6 miles round trip **Estimated time** 3–4hr
| **Colorado River** (2400ft) **Difficulty** Strenuous **Distance** 9.7 miles one-way **Estimated time** 6–7hr descent, 7–9hr ascent

the often-overcrowded Bright Angel and South Kaibab trails. The major appeal tends to be the wildlife, in the form of birds, butterflies, and, in spring and autumn, abundant wild flowers. The best **day hikes** go to either Santa Maria Spring on the main trail (4.6 miles round trip), or Dripping Spring on the side trails described below (6.5 miles round trip). Water from both is drinkable if treated.

The trail begins from Hermits Rest, at the far western end of Hermit Road (see p.59). While summer day hikers have to use the park shuttle buses to get here (see p.43), hikers with backcountry permits specifically issued for the Hermit Trail – *not* day hikers, who don't need permits – are allowed to drive to a car park beyond the shuttle stop year-round. In winter, when the shuttles aren't running, all trail users can drive to the car park.

Immediately rough and rocky underfoot, it starts by switchbacking down the eastern flank of Hermit Basin, feeling a long way removed from the central Grand Canyon as it slowly descends a high rock wall far above Hermit Creek. Upheavals in the cobbled pathway, and rockfalls from above, make for slow progress at first, but in due course the trail levels out along a sandy floor. It's joined from the south by the **Waldron Trail** (T22) 1.5 miles along – mapped out in 1896 as the original route down into Hermit Basin but now seldom used – and then passes the spur trail to **Dripping Spring** a quarter of a mile further on.

Make sure you stick to the main trail beyond the Dripping Spring turn-off; the streambed leads over a waterfall. Just over half a mile along, having slowly traversed down a crumbling red ledge, you reach **Santa Maria Spring**. The spring itself seldom amounts to much more than a steady drip from a standpipe into an artificial and unattractive trough, but it's enough to feed a delightful oasis of flowering plants, and there's also some very welcome shade in a gorgeous resthouse, with an open front that's all but smothered in creeping vines. Inside, you'll even find a comfortable rocking bench.

Day hikers should turn back at Santa Maria Spring. The trail onwards is gentle at first, but after around a mile it reaches further steep switchbacks and then a tricky downward scramble through fallen rocks, where it's easy for inexperienced hikers to lose their way. It eventually hurtles down the Redwall below Pima Point by means of the cramped **Cathedral Stairs** switchbacks, to meet the Tonto Trail a total of seven miles from the trailhead.

Between 1913 and 1931, mule-riders would spend the night deep in the inner canyon at the permanent **Hermit Camp**, a mile west of the Tonto Trail junction, which was provisioned by cable car from Pima Point. Only the outline of its sturdy stone walls remains in place, however, so modern backpackers congregate instead at the **Hermit Creek Campground**, a few hundred yards on. Though its much-loved natural swimming pool was destroyed by a flash flood in 1996, it's still a spectacular spot, with dramatic views of the cliffs that soar above it to the rim.

The most direct route down to the Colorado on the Hermit Trail has you turning right into Hermit Creek just before Hermit Camp, but you can also get there by following the creek down from the campground. Either way, you reach the river in a little over a mile, at the rocky beach just short of **Hermit Rapid**, whose wave-like surge can reach over twenty feet high.

T23 The Dripping Spring Trail

Trailhead Hermits Rest (6640ft)
Water Dripping Spring at 3.25 miles (treat before use)

Day hike to Dripping Spring (5800ft)
Difficulty Moderate, with high drop-offs
Distance 6.5 miles round trip
Estimated time 3–5hr

The delightful and none-too-strenuous expedition to **Dripping Spring** ranks among the best mid-length day hikes in the Grand Canyon. The spring itself, which was home to the "hermit" Louis Boucher between 1891 and 1912, sits only a few hundred yards beneath the rim, but the nearest road-accessible trailhead is at **Hermits Rest**, and it's necessary to approach the spring from below, so it's still a round trip of 6.5 miles.

Begin by taking the Hermit Trail, as described above, then turn left at the clearly-marked junction almost two miles down. Follow the narrow path as it ventures out in a high sweeping curve that's barely scraped into a steep cliff of red Hermit Shale – anyone with a fear of heights would do better to turn back and head for Santa Maria Spring instead (see above). Assuming you do keep going, a mile along, beyond two successive wooded amphitheatres, you turn left again, joining the **Boucher Trail** on its upward course back towards the rim. Not far up, the spring cascades from the ceiling of a large overhanging alcove in the Coconino Sandstone wall, amid eruptions of ferns and tiny blossoms. Boucher used this perennial water supply to irrigate gardens and orchards along the creek.

T24 The Boucher Trail

Strictly speaking, the **Boucher Trail**, which runs a mile or so west of, and roughly parallel to, the Hermit Trail, begins at a remote trailhead above Dripping Spring. Pronounced *boo-shay*, it began life as Louis Boucher's "Silver Bell Trail", the most direct route down to his stream side base. These days, however, access is so much easier from Hermits Rest that it's used almost invariably as part of longer, multi-trail itineraries, which most commonly involve

> **Trailhead** Hermits Rest (6640ft)
> **Water** Dripping Spring at 6.5 miles (treat before use)
> Boucher Creek at 8.5 miles (treat before use)
>
> **Colorado River** (2325ft)
> **Difficulty** Very strenuous
> **Distance** 10.8 miles one-way
> **Estimated time** 7–9hr descent, 9–11hr ascent

going down to the river via the Boucher Trail and then climbing back out again on the Hermit.

In its earlier stages especially, the Boucher Trail is not a hike for canyon novices. As soon as you turn right onto the trail, three miles down the Dripping Spring itinerary described above, you're obliged to totter along the very brink of an extremely steep drop. In icy winter conditions, this long traverse of the west wall of **Hermit Basin** is truly terrifying. Conditions improve when you round the headland beneath **Yuma Point** at the far end, but you still have to negotiate long, difficult scrambling descents before you meet the **Tonto Trail**, which westwards of this point officially becomes the **Tonto West Trail** (see p.110). There's an extra disadvantage in that this far west you're beneath the permitted flight path for sightseeing helicopters, and the noise during daytime can be incessant.

Half a mile on from there, turn right and pick your own way along the boulder-strewn Boucher Creek streambed to reach the river close to the **Boucher Rapid**. Alternatively, a 4.5-mile eastward hike on the Tonto Trail will bring you to the **Hermit Creek Campground** on the Hermit Trail (see opposite).

T25 The South Bass Trail

Over a century ago, the **Bass Trail** was the most important trans-canyon hiking route. Now located way to the west of the current centre of tourist activity, and all but reverted to wilderness, it no longer even crosses the canyon at all. Its early promoter, former cowboy **William Bass**, set up the long-defunct **Bass Camp** tent village near **Havasupai Point** in 1885,

> **Trailhead** Bass Camp (6646ft)
> **Water** None
>
> **Colorado River** (2200ft)
> **Difficulty** Strenuous
> **Distance** 8 miles one-way
> **Estimated time** 5–6hr descent, 6–8hr ascent

and soon instigated a regular stagecoach service from Williams. He would lead intrepid visitors down the ancient Indian trail he had improved to reach his copper and asbestos mines, and ferry them over the river either by boat, when the water was low, or via cable car.

Bass went out of business after the railroad reached the South Rim, but his trail remains in reasonable condition for experienced inner-canyon hikers who have the route-finding abilities to negotiate its occasional obliterated segment. Many do still complete the rim-to-rim trip by hitching a ride with the river runners they chance upon down by the Colorado. However, that route is generally regarded as two separate hikes – the **South Bass Trail**, described here, and the **North Bass Trail**, as outlined on p.112.

The main impediment to hiking the South Bass Trail is not the absence of water anywhere above the river, but the sheer remoteness of the trailhead. When you ask about current trail conditions at the park visitor centre, get a ranger to describe the access route in detail. It's a thirty-mile drive west of Grand Canyon Village or Tusayan, of which the first 26 miles are on Forest Service road 328, which heads west from Tusayan just south of the abandoned *Moqui Lodge*, and the final four, north from Pasture Wash, are so rough that a **high-clearance 4WD** vehicle is essential. You have to enter the Havasupai reservation near the end; if the tribe have bothered to post a guard at the entrance, you'll have to pay a $35 fee.

Havasupai Point, two miles east of the trailhead, is reachable via an equally problematic dirt road that branches off to the right shortly before Bass Camp. It marks a natural boundary between the eastern Grand Canyon, characterized by massive indented amphitheatres, isolated buttes and generally tangled topography, and the western canyon, which consists of a much simpler, broad valley known as the **Esplanade**, with the deep **Granite Gorge** still at its core. That's why the ridge immediately east of the trailhead is known as the **Grand Scenic Divide**.

The trail takes almost three miles to zigzag down through the woods and reach the edge of the Esplanade, alongside the towering butte of **Mount Huethawali**. This spot offers the first and best views of the vast sweep of the canyon, making it clear how abruptly the mesas and buttes disappear as the river heads west. Down below you, the trail plunges deep into **Bass Canyon**, whence it emerges after three miles to meet the Tonto Trail. Follow the bed of the often dry wash for two miles downwards, and it ends at a lovely little riverside **beach**, often used by passing rafters for overnight stays.

⟦T26⟧ The Tonto Trail

The **Tonto Trail** is an exception to the other South Rim trails described here, in that it has no contact with the canyon rim. Neither, for the vast proportion of its length, does it approach the river. Instead it runs parallel to both rim and river, meandering along the Tonto Platform at a typical elevation of around 4000 feet. That means it stays mostly on the parched, cactus-strewn Bright Angel Shale layer, which spreads out below the Redwall and Muav Limestone strata and above the Tapeats Sandstone layer and the Granite Gorge. It doesn't mean, however, that it's an easy hike. With streams and earthquake faults forever cutting down towards the Colorado, the Tonto Trail is repeatedly forced either to cut down into lesser gorges and then climb out again, or to circle endlessly back around the head of each successive amphitheatre. Water is scarce and facilities non existent.

As it stretches for a phenomenal 92 miles, almost no one walks the full length of the Tonto Trail. Canyon hikers tend simply to cross it at some point en route to or from the river, or at best join it for a small connecting stretch between two major trails. There's no trailhead as such, but technically it begins, as the **Tonto East Trail** (⟦T27⟧), at the foot of the **New Hance Trail**, heading west to meet the **Grandview Trail** in seven miles and the **South Kaibab Trail** another twenty miles after that. Its central portion, the part officially called the Tonto Trail, runs for four miles from the Tipoff on the South Kaibab to Indian Garden on the Bright Angel Trail; thirteen more miles to join the Hermit Trail; and six miles beyond that to connect with the Boucher Trail. The **Tonto West Trail** (⟦T28⟧) then takes up the baton, running for a full thirty miles to connect with the South Bass Trail, and another twelve miles to Garnet Canyon, where it meets the Royal Arch Route for the lengthy climb out.

Other North Rim trails

While the **North Kaibab Trail** is by far the most popular inner-canyon trail to start from the North Rim, two others lie within reach of seasoned hikers eager to experience greater solitude – and a tougher physical challenge. Both the **Nankoweap Trail** and the **North Bass Trail** demand considerable confidence and self-sufficiency, and are much more suitable for backpackers planning multi-day itineraries than they are for day hikers. Be sure to ask about current conditions when you pick up your permit.

T29 The Nankoweap Trail

Located far to the north of all other Grand Canyon trails, the dramatic **Nankoweap Trail** is unique in not only providing access to the seldom visited upper reaches of the canyon, but also offering tremendous panoramas out across the Marble Platform and upstream towards Lees Ferry. With its hair's-breadth ledges and sickeningly high drop-offs, however, it's not recommended for anyone with even the slightest fear of heights. **Charles Doolittle Walcott**, who with John Wesley Powell improved the trail during their geological expedition of 1882, called it "utterly frightful", and its early stages remain every bit as terrifying. Only true canyon veterans should even consider attempting it.

> **Trailhead** Saddle Mountain (8848ft)
> **Water** Nankoweap Creek at 10.6 miles (treat before use)
> **Colorado River** (2800ft)
> **Difficulty** Very strenuous, with high drop-offs
> **Distance** 13.9 miles one-way
> **Estimated time** 9–12hr descent, 12–14hr ascent

The official **trailhead**, at **Saddle Mountain**, is less than three miles north of Point Imperial (see p.75), so it's possible to start your hike from there, following the **Point Imperial Trail**. Saddle Mountain itself can only be reached by car if you drive fifteen miles along the gravelled Forest Service road 610, which heads east from AZ-67 a mile south of *Kaibab Lodge* (see p.132); the route is normally passable in ordinary vehicles.

From Saddle Mountain, it takes a mile for the trail to begin in earnest; first you have to negotiate a steep little hill, which involves a brisk climb. Then comes the hard part, a heart-stopping sidle along a narrow exposed ledge of Esplanade Sandstone. A brief respite comes at **Marion Ridge**, a camping spot overlooked by some striking misshapen rock pillars. At times, seasonal water is available here; in any case, it's recommended that you cache water for your return hike nearby.

Yet more tremulous ledge work will take you from Marion Ridge as far as **Tilted Mesa**, 6.8 miles down at the outer limit of the Redwall. Beyond there, a very steep set of switchbacks – which are at least in good condition – leads down onto the terrace where at length you meet the verdant **Nankoweap Creek**, a total of 10.6 miles from the trailhead.

Three more miles down the trackless but mostly gentle streambed, at spreading, sandy Nankoweap Delta, you arrive at the Colorado itself, to be confronted by the towering eastern wall of Marble Canyon on the far side. Minor trails lead downstream beside the river for around a mile, but in due course you have to turn around and climb back the way you came. Note that there are no designated campsites along the trail; instead you're free to select your own site in the wilderness.

T30 The North Bass Trail

> **Trailhead** Swamp Point (7520ft)
> **Water** Muav Saddle Spring at
> 1.2 miles (treat before use)
> Seasonal streams (treat before use)
>
> **Colorado River** (2200ft)
> **Difficulty** Very strenuous
> **Distance** 13.5 miles one-way
> **Estimated time** 8–10hr descent,
> 2-day ascent

The North Rim counterpart to William Bass's South Bass Trail (see p.109), the **North Bass Trail**, starts from the overlook at **Swamp Point**, which as described on p.81 is a twenty-mile dirt-road drive west of AZ-67 that's only suitable for 4WD vehicles. As with the South Bass, this trail is recommended for veteran inner-canyon hikers only – in many places, the trail is liable to have vanished completely, so you'll need route-finding skills, considerable energy for scrambling down talus slopes and through thick brush, and a head for heights.

From Swamp Point, a mile of comparatively well-maintained switchbacks drop down to the **Muav Saddle**, where a long-abandoned Park Service cabin dating from 1925 is still used by overnighting backpackers. A minor dead-end trail leads up from the cabin onto **Powell Plateau**, but the main route now descends **Muav Canyon** in earnest, along the rocky bed of **White Creek**.

When you've covered the total of almost five miles to the top of the **Redwall**, you've cleared the most difficult section of the trail – several short *uphill* stretches won't have improved your mood – and you've also finally reached some superb inner-canyon views. Swift switchbacks then carry you down the Redwall, where you rejoin White Creek via a stretch of trail that was restored and realigned in 2005.

In theory the trail strays away from the creek onto the nearby plateau, but it's much easier simply to follow the streambed all the way down to **Shinumo Creek**, another five miles on. William Bass planted melons, corn and squash down here, along with peach orchards, at a spot he found by tracing ancient Indian irrigation ditches; in his day, intact cliff-dwellings and granaries were still visible nearby.

Access to the Colorado is via a final steep descent, which ends at a sheltered riverside grove much frequented by rafters (and ringtail cats hungry for your provisions). Both here and all along the trail, there are no officially designated campsites, so follow usual wilderness-camping protocols.

Hiking the Grand Canyon

If there's one sure remedy for the oft-voiced complaint that it's hard to appreciate or even comprehend the Grand Canyon from the rim, it's to hike down into it. A descent along any of the park's five hundred miles of magnificent trails is rewarded with much more than just another view of the same thing. Instead, one passes through a sequence of utterly different landscapes, each with its own distinct topography, climate and wildlife. But while the canyon is certainly a sublime, enticing wilderness, it can also be a hostile, unforgiving environment, gruelling even for expert hikers.

The unique demands of canyon hiking

Whatever experience you may have gained elsewhere, the Grand Canyon is different. Most hikers are far more familiar with walking *up* hills and mountains, when it's the initial climb that's most demanding, and if your energy levels start to flag, you can simply turn around and walk back to base. Canyon hiking is deceptively seductive. The **descent** seems easy, and your progress quick. There's always another great view a little farther on, and the lure of the river beckons you forward. Eventually, however, you have to pay; start your **ascent** when you're already tired, and the midday heat of the inner canyon has set in, and you're in for a murderously long haul. With the South Rim rising 7000ft above sea level, and the North Rim 8000ft, the altitude alone is fatiguing.

Most people spend twice as much time climbing back up as it took to hike down. That means turning back after a third of your allotted time; if you plan a six-hour hike, allow two hours to hike down and four hours to hike up. Rangers say the average speed is two miles per hour on the way down and just one on the way up.

North Kaibab Trail ▲

Hikers at Indian Garden, Bright Angel Trail ▼

PLATEAU POINT 1.5 M.

RIGHT ANGEL CG 4.5 M.

PHANTOM RANCH 5 M.

Prickly pear cactuses on North Kaibab Trail ▼

When to hike

The best hiking seasons are spring and autumn, when temperatures are cooler, the trails less crowded and water is more available. Summer, on the other hand, offers far from ideal conditions, though of course that's when most people visit. At that time of year especially, avoid hiking in the middle of the day. Set off very early in the morning – well before 7am if you're heading down, and before 5am if you're climbing out.

The shape of the trails

The main trails from the **South Rim** involve a seven- to ten-mile descent to the Colorado. An initial burst of steep switchbacks culminates in overlooks atop the Coconino Sandstone layer, 1.5 miles down. The flat Tonto Platform lies a further 1.5 miles along; trails continue a couple of miles to its edge, for views of the Granite Gorge, before the final plunge to the river. All follow watercourses, and thus offer intermittent views, except for the South Kaibab, which crests a high ridge, with views most of the way down.

Trails from the **North Rim**, which is further from the river, are longer, averaging fourteen miles. At least one overnight stop is necessary en route to the Colorado.

Inner-canyon wildlife

Below the rim, the Grand Canyon is far from a lifeless desert. Inner-canyon hikes offer a wonderful opportunity to experience its unique **flora and fauna**. As you descend, the vegetation changes from spruce and fir to dense ponderosa woodlands and piñon-juniper "pygmy forest", followed by cacti, yucca and mesquite. Though the lush banks of the Colorado are rich with wildlife, the river itself is such an impassable barrier that separate species have evolved on either side. Thus reddish Abert's squirrels pester picnicking hikers on the Bright Angel Trail, while greyer Kaibab squirrels scavenge the North Kaibab Trail across the river. Similarly, different rattlesnakes inhabit the two rims – none has ever seriously harmed human visitors.

Great trails for wildlife enthusiasts include the **Hermit Trail**, rich in birds and butterflies, and the **South Kaibab Trail**, which is popular with soaring California condors, especially in the early morning.

▲ Hikers descending the South Kaibab Trail

▼ Bighorn sheep

▼ Bright Angel Point, North Rim

Hikers on the Bright Angel Trail ▲

Sunrise on the South Kaibab Trail ▼

The canyon's best day hikes

The most important advice for would-be hikers is **don't try to hike to the Colorado River and back in one day**. Several hikers each year die in the attempt. However, plenty of rewarding **day hikes** venture into the inner canyon. The following six round trips are highly recommended; see the map on p.86.

▶▶ **South Kaibab Trail to Cedar Mesa** (3-mile round trip): The canyon's most instantly rewarding hike, this stark, exposed trail sets off from Yaki Point, not far east of Grand Canyon Village on the South Rim. The views are especially sublime at dawn, but in summer the heat further down can be oppressive. See p.101

▶▶ **North Kaibab Trail to Supai Tunnel** (4-mile round trip): The North Rim's best-loved trail is demanding from the word go; only the very fittest should venture further than this dramatic viewpoint atop the Redwall. See p.102

▶▶ **Hermit Trail to Santa Maria Spring** (4.6-mile round trip): Leaving the South Rim from the end of Hermit Road, this peaceful trail descends through verdant scenery to a lovely little oasis. See p.107

▶▶ **Bright Angel Trail to Three-Mile Resthouse** (6-mile round trip): The canyon's oldest and busiest trail drops down steep switchbacks from the South Rim; fabulous panoramas open up at every twist. See p.94

▶▶ **Grandview Trail to Horseshoe Mesa** (6.4-mile round trip): Despite not descending all the way to the Colorado River, the superbly engineered Grandview Trail offers some of the South Rim's finest hiking. See p.106

▶▶ **North Kaibab Trail to Roaring Springs** (9.4-mile round trip): It takes a major physical effort to hike to and from this stunning North Rim waterfall in a single day, but the scenery en route is utterly breathtaking. See p.102

The road between the rims

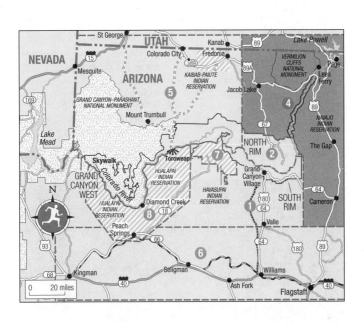

CHAPTER 4   # Highlights

❋ **Cameron Trading Post**
This historic Navajo trading
post offers lodgings of a
surprisingly high standard.
See p.118

❋ **Antelope Canyon** Arizona's
most famous slot canyon gets
very crowded with tour groups,
but remains extraordinarily
beautiful. See p.120

❋ **Horseshoe Bend** A rare
glimpse of the Colorado
as it makes an amazing
180-degree turn, just before
entering the Grand Canyon.
See p.121

❋ **Glen Canyon Dam** Visit the
massive and controversial
dam that stopped the
Colorado River, drowned Glen
Canyon and transformed the
Grand Canyon. See p.121

❋ **Marble Canyon Lodge** This
attractive roadside stop
enables weary drivers to
spend the night in the heart of
the desert. See p.126

❋ **Lees Ferry** Haunting Wild
West ruins overlook the exact
spot where the Grand Canyon
begins. See p.126

❋ **Lonely Dell Ranch** Lovely
little oasis, established by
ferryman and convicted killer
John Doyle Lee. See p.127

❋ **Vermilion Cliffs** This towering
escarpment glows an unearthly
red as the sun rises over the
Grand Canyon. See p.128

❋ **DeMotte Park** Meadow-like
forest clearing, just short of
the North Rim, which holds
appealing lodging options.
See p.132

▲ Horseshoe Bend

The road between the rims

lthough the South and North rims of the Grand Canyon stand just eleven miles apart, the impossibility of constructing a road across the canyon means that the shortest driving route between the two is 215 miles long, and takes at least four hours to drive. Starting from Grand Canyon Village, you have to follow first Desert View Drive and then AZ-64 east until you meet US-89 at **Cameron**. From there you head north to cross **Marble Canyon** on Navajo Bridge, then double back west to **Jacob Lake** to join the 44-mile AZ-67 south to the North Rim.

Although there are very few towns along the way, the scenery is seldom less than spectacular. Highlights include the twin escarpments that blaze to either side of the Colorado as it emerges from Glen Canyon only to plunge into the Grand Canyon – **Echo Cliffs** on the east bank, and the **Vermilion Cliffs** to the west – and the fascinating historical site of **Lees Ferry**, the official start of the Grand Canyon. Several lodges and motels, dotted in splendid isolation, make for atmospheric overnight stays en route. In addition, a short detour northeast of the Echo Cliffs can take you up to **Page**, a humdrum town that's nonetheless close to a couple of compelling natural wonders in the shape of **Antelope Canyon** and **Horseshoe Bend**, and near too to **Glen Canyon Dam**, responsible for stopping the Colorado River in its tracks and creating the unearthly **Lake Powell**.

The first explorers to attempt a Colorado crossing in this region were two Spanish friars, padres **Domínguez and Escalante**, who did so back in 1776. However, the

The Transcanyon Shuttle

Between mid-May and mid-October, **Transcanyon Shuttle** (☎928/638-2820, ⓦtrans-canyonshuttle.com) runs a daily minibus service along the route described in this chapter.

Departing the North Rim from *Grand Canyon Lodge* at 7am, it calls at *Marble Canyon Lodge* at 9am and reaches the South Rim at 11.30am. The return trip departs the South Rim at 1.30pm, stops at *Marble Canyon Lodge* at 4.15m and arrives back at the North Rim at 6.30pm. A one-way ride costs $90, and a return ticket $150; no credit cards are accepted.

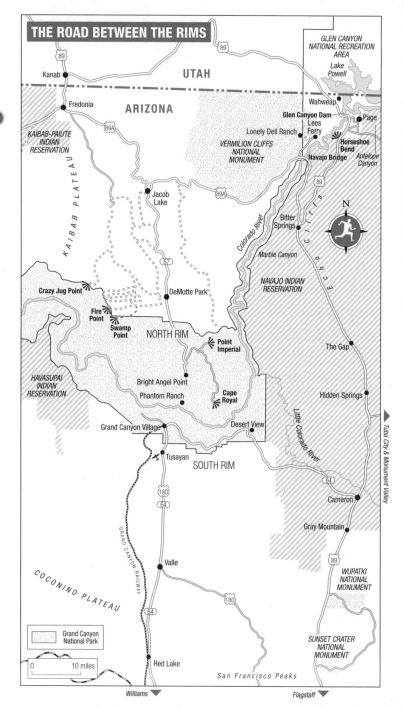

route only began to see regular traffic a century later, with the establishment of the **Mormon Trail**. Linking Mormon settlements in Utah with new (and for the most part unsuccessful) "colonies" in Arizona, the trail was kept busy in part by Mormon newlyweds, who, having married in civil ceremonies in Arizona, would head at the next opportunity to have their vows sealed at the nearest Temple, in St George, Utah. Hence its alternative name – the **Honeymoon Trail**.

Little Colorado River Gorge

In its 34-mile run between Desert View on the South Rim (described on p.63) and its junction with US-89 just south of Cameron, AZ-64 descends more than three thousand feet. Once past the first dozen miles, which lie within the pine forests of the Coconino Plateau, vast views open up across the Painted Desert to the northeast. Closer at hand, a crack in the flatlands betrays the presence of the **Little Colorado River**, snaking northwards at the bottom of its own deep canyon to meet its bigger brother.

Ten miles out of Cameron, between mile markers 285 and 286 – by which time both road and river are running parallel east to west – the **Little Colorado River Gorge Navajo Tribal Park** gives visitors their best chance to catch a glimpse of the river. Though there's no admission charge, per se, you can only reach the end of the promontory that offers the finest views by running the gauntlet of several dozen **Navajo craft stalls**, mostly selling good-quality jewellery and trinkets.

The drop down into the chasm here measures around 1200ft, though the cliffs are so sheer that it's hard to lean out far enough to see the river itself. In any case, for several months of the year – especially in spring and early summer – the Little Colorado is liable to dry up altogether. At other times, however, it's capable of powerful flash floods. The fact that the river remains undammed, despite repeated early Mormon attempts, has acquired an added significance since the completion of the **Glen Canyon Dam** in 1963. Now that the Colorado itself carries almost no sediment into the Grand Canyon, certain river species, such as the humpback chub, can only breed in the muddy waters of the Little Colorado.

The Little Colorado continues to play a crucial role in **Hopi** cosmology. Modern Hopi still follow in the steps of their ancestors, travelling from their mesas sixty miles to the east along the ancient **Salt Trail**, which leads beside the Little Colorado into the Grand Canyon. Not far up the Little Colorado from its confluence with the Colorado proper lies the legendary *sipapu*, the hole through which the Hopi believe that human beings first entered this, the Third World. You won't find this natural dome-shaped hot spring marked on any map; only the Hopi are allowed access.

Back on the highway, further crafts stalls, some at lesser overlooks, are dotted along the roadside for the rest of the way down to Cameron.

Cameron and around

Tiny **CAMERON**, which amounts to little more than a handful of buildings, lies a mile or so north of the intersection of AZ-64 and US-89. The Mormon Trail originally crossed the Little Colorado River at a rocky ford six miles upstream. That became known as **Tanner's Crossing**, in honour of Seth Tanner, a Mormon prospector from Tuba City who built a house nearby in the 1870s. He later expanded his operations into the Grand Canyon area, where he also gave his name to the Tanner Trail.

After the danger from quicksand and flooding at Tanner's Crossing led to the construction of the first **suspension bridge** across the gorge in 1911, Cameron – named after another legendary canyon prospector, Ralph Cameron – sprang into being on the south side of the span. The original one-lane bridge is still there; now it only carries an oil pipeline, having been superseded by a broader modern highway bridge.

Cameron Trading Post

Clustered beside the two bridges, the ever-expanding **Cameron Trading Post** remains at heart what it started out as in 1916 – a trading centre for the Navajo Nation. Reservation residents still flock in to stock up on wool, flour and other supplies, catch up with friends, fill up their gas tanks and pick up their mail, and some of the trading post's business is still conducted by barter.

That Old West tradition is now complemented by a brisk **tourist** trade, however. A large **motel** complex (☎928/679-2231 or 1-800/338-7385, ⓦcamerontrading post.com; March–April ❹; May–Oct ❺; Nov to Feb ❸), which perhaps surprisingly offers some of the highest standard accommodation in the region, sits amid beautifully landscaped gardens that slope towards the river. All the rooms are smartly presented, and those on the upper floors have large balconies that look out across the Little Colorado to the open desert. There's also **RV** parking for $15.

In the complex's main building, an atmospheric tin-roofed **dining room** (daily: summer 6am–10pm, otherwise 7am–9.30pm), centring on a massive fireplace, serves all meals. As its principal customers are tour groups in a hurry to be somewhere else, the food's OK but nothing special – the $10 Navajo taco is probably your best bet, for a filling lunch, while dinner dishes range up to $20 steaks – and here on the reservation **no alcohol** is served. The adjoining **souvenir store** sells a huge array of Southwest arts and crafts, both authentic and mass-produced. For a real treat, it's worth crossing to the nearby **Gallery**, which stocks such Native American pieces as genuine Hopi *kachinas* and museum-quality Navajo rugs. The prices are incredible, but so is the stock; even a small rug from the 1890s can go for up to $20,000, while an Apache shirt from the 1850s costs $75,000.

Gray Mountain

When there's no room at Cameron, the nearest alternative lodging is nine miles south on US-89 (and forty miles north of Flagstaff), in the even smaller community of **GRAY MOUNTAIN** (population 68). Just outside the reservation, it's a lonely desert outpost, attractive in its own desolate way, consisting almost entirely of the *Anasazi Inn* (☎928/679-2214 or 1-800/678-2214, ⓦanasaziinn.com; ❸). This boasts three separate **motel** blocks – all the rooms are of a reasonable standard, with prices varying according to how close you are to the pool – plus the *Gray Mountain Restaurant* across the highway, which serves Mexican specialities and Navajo tacos as well as steaks.

Echo Cliffs

Driving north from Cameron on US-89 is a delight, with unfolding views of the unearthly, multicoloured Painted Desert marred only by rows of mighty electricity pylons marching across the plateau from the Navajo Generating Station at Page. Though it's far from fertile country, much of this is open ranchland, so watch out for cattle if you're driving at night.

Fifteen miles north of Cameron, US-160 climbs away northeast via **Tuba City** towards Monument Valley and Colorado. Continuing north, US-89 passes through **Hidden Springs** in another five miles, the home of a small group of **San Juan Southern Paiute**, who were recognized as a separate tribe in 1990.

By now, the rich orange **Echo Cliffs** – the visible face of the Echo Cliffs Monocline – have started to climb to the east of the road. Over the next fifty miles, they reach well over 2000ft above the Colorado. Their name was given by members of John Wesley Powell's second expedition in 1871, who fired a shot at the river from the top of the ridge, and heard the echo come back 24 seconds later.

The one natural break in the cliffs, ten miles on from Hidden Springs, is logically enough called **The Gap**, though sadly its small trading post (daily 7am–9pm) cannot claim to have spawned the multi national clothing chain. A dirt road climbs up through the notch, leading to a defunct copper mine and, eventually, Page, but it's not recommended for ordinary vehicles.

Page

US-89 eventually veers to the right at **Antelope Pass**, twenty empty miles beyond The Gap, and heads another 25 miles along the top of an all but barren mesa to reach the town of **PAGE**, Arizona. Before Glen Canyon Dam was constructed four miles west, from 1956 onwards, this area belonged to the Navajo Nation. Thanks to a small spring, however, the mesa made the best site to house the dam's workforce. The Navajo agreed to swap it for a similar-sized chunk of desert between Bluff and Hatch in Utah, the route now followed by US-89 was blasted through the Echo Cliffs, and Page was born on Thanksgiving Day 1958.

While Page is home to almost ten thousand people, which makes it the largest community in a 720-mile stretch of the Colorado River, it's a dull and unattractive little place that simply happens to make a convenient base for visitors to Lake Powell. It originally seemed destined to wither away once the dam was completed. Ironically, it gained a new lease of life when Congress decided that instead of building more dams, the Southwest could meet its power needs by burning coal instead. The **Navajo Generating Station**, which creates electricity using coal from Black Mesa and pumps water from Lake Powell to Phoenix, went up four miles southeast of town, and has kept Page in work ever since.

Arrival and information

Helpful staff at Page's **visitor centre**, 608 Elm St (April–June Mon–Sat 8am–6pm; July–Oct same days 7am–7pm; Nov–March Mon–Fri 8am–5pm; ☎928/645-2741 or 1-888/261-7243, ⓦpagelakepowelltourism.com), can advise on local amenities and attractions. Several other offices in town purport to be information centres but are in fact tour operators offering trips to Antelope Canyon, as detailed on p.120.

Page is not served by any scheduled buses or flights, though charter airlines do occasionally fly into the local **airport**, a mile east of town on Hwy-98.

Accommodation

While no one would choose to spend much time in Page itself, Lake Powell is enough of an attraction to keep its **motels** busy for most of the year, and able to charge surprisingly high rates.

Best Western Arizonainn 716 Rim View Drive ℡928/645-2466 or 1-800/826-2718, ⓦbestwesternarizona.com. Smart motel on the outskirts of Page, commanding a massive desert panorama from the poolside. ❹

Courtyard by Marriott 600 Clubhouse Drive ℡928/645-5000 or 1-877/905-4495, ⓦcourtyard .com/pgacy. Page's most incongruous splash of luxury – a 153-room resort, complete with golf course – is below the mesa in view of the dam. ❻

Holiday Inn Express 751 S Navajo Drive ℡928/645-9000 or 1-800/465-4329, ⓦhiexpress .com. Good-quality chain motel, with a pool and free continental breakfast. ❺

LuLu's Sleep Ezze Motel 208 N Lake Powell Blvd ℡928/608-0273 or 1-800/553-6211, ⓦlulussleepezzemotel.com. Tiny, very welcoming little motel in central Page, with simple but nice rooms. ❸

Downtown Page

The view as you descend towards Page is utterly surreal. The five power plant chimneys stand silhouetted amid sandstone outcrops and similarly stark pylons, while the misty hump of Navajo Mountain rises in the distance. As you approach, the waters of Lake Powell emerge from the haze, with drowned buttes poking their heads here and there above the surface.

Page itself, on the other hand, resembles a dull suburban mall writ large; if it has a redeeming feature, you'll have a hard time finding it. Permanent structures have replaced most of its original trailer homes, but the only sight of any interest is the **John Wesley Powell Memorial Museum**, 6 N Lake Powell Blvd (Mon–Fri 9am–5pm; $5; ⓦpowellmuseum.org). As well as charting the exploits of the first man to raft down the Colorado (see p.201), the museum celebrates subsequent river runners and recounts Page's own brief history. It also holds a locally excavated plesiosaur fossil and an amazing collection of fluorescent rocks.

Antelope Canyon

A couple of miles southeast of Page on AZ-98, mile marker 299 marks the trailhead for magnificent **Antelope Canyon**, Arizona's most famous **slot canyon**. The canyon actually comprises two separate sections, on either side of the highway, and both are on Navajo land.

Immediately north of the highway, **Lower Antelope Canyon** achieved worldwide notoriety in 1997, when the tragic deaths of eleven hikers in a flash flood proved just how dangerous such places can be. Nevertheless, they're also irresistibly, astonishingly beautiful. Having realized quite what an invaluable tourism asset Antelope Canyon is, the Navajo now control all access (March–Oct daily 8am–5pm; Nov daily 9am–3pm; ℡928/698-3347, ⓦnavajonationparks .org/htm/antelopecanyon.htm).

In summer, tourists can visit both sections of the canyon simply by turning up at the car park. However, not only is there a $6 entry fee, but you also have to pay an outrageous $13 for a "guide" service that consists either of pointing you to the entrance of Lower Antelope or driving you in a shuttle van down to **Upper Antelope Canyon**, a matter of perhaps two miles.

You're deposited just outside a slender, unprepossessing crack in a red sandstone wall. Stepping inside is like entering both a cathedral, in that you find yourself in a majestic chamber adorned with delicate glowing colours, and a pinball machine, in that you can just imagine that any second some mighty and unavoidable boulder will come thundering down the narrow passageway. Walking the full length of the canyon and back takes barely twenty minutes, even with frequent pauses to admire the interlacing fins of multihued rock that swirl overhead, in places to a height of 120ft. A flash flood is capable of filling the slot to the brim with water and spilling over the top; once such a flood recedes, on the other hand, it leaves the canyon floor scrubbed bare of its usual 8ft layer of fine soft sand.

Be warned that while Antelope Canyon is every bit as beautiful as photos suggest, it offers little of the wilderness feel of other desert highlights. It's both short and narrow enough to feel *very* crowded at busy times, and as the main priority for all visitors is to take photographs, it can feel like a working film set rather than a place to contemplate beauty.

Given the high cost of an unaccompanied visit, you may prefer to join a guided **tour** from Page, where several competing companies have offices. One-hour trips typically cost about $30, longer photography tours up to $50. Highly recommended for his personalized small-group excursions is the affable, self-styled Chief Tsosie of Antelope Slot Canyon Tours, 55 S Lake Powell Blvd (closed Sun; ☏ 928/645-5594, ⊛ antelopeslotcanyon.com), who also leads day-trips to lesser-known canyons and overlooks, while Overland Canyon Tours, 48 S Lake Powell Blvd (☏ 928/608-4072, ⊛ overlandcanyontours.com), offers extended trips into the backcountry.

Horseshoe Bend

An easy self-guided hike not far south of Page leads to an amazing view of **Horseshoe Bend**, where the Colorado River makes an extravagant 180-degree turn in the depths of Marble Canyon, roughly halfway through its short course between Glen Canyon Dam and the official start of the Grand Canyon at Lees Ferry.

To reach the overlook, drive south on US-89 and turn west on the dirt road just past mile marker 545, exactly 2.6 miles south of the Wal-Mart in Page. That road soon stops at a car park at the foot of a small sandy hill. Climb the railed path to the top of that hill, and from there you'll see it wind its way down another 0.4 miles to the lip of the gorge. The river itself only becomes visible once you're at the very edge, which is unrailed, windy and pretty hair-raising. Its huge curving sweep, far below, barely fits into the widest-angled lens. Be sure to carry water, and allow around an hour for the exposed round trip hike.

Eating

With the arguable exception of a couple of plain hotel dining rooms, Page offers a poor choice of restaurants; a *KFC* across from the visitor centre is as good a bet as anything else.

Beans Gourmet Coffee House Dam Plaza, 644 N Navajo Drive ☏ 928/645-6858. Espressos and light snacks, plus picnic lunches takeaway. Daily 7am–6pm.
Bonkers 810 N Navajo Drive ☏ 928/645-2706. Something for everyone, with a full menu of Italian specialities, plus burgers and sandwiches. Daily 11am–2pm & 5pm onwards.

Dam Bar & Grille Dam Plaza, 644 N Navajo Drive ☏ 928/645-2161. Themed diner and bar, appealingly designed to echo the days when Page was populated solely by dam-building hard-hats. Steak and pasta main courses for around $18. Daily 3–11pm.

Glen Canyon Dam

Glen Canyon Dam plugs **Marble Canyon** not at its narrowest point, but at its northern end, just downstream from Wahweap Creek. As US-89 crosses Glen Canyon Bridge four miles outside of Page, the vast curve of the dam is to the north, while Marble Canyon drops 700ft below you.

The western half of the United States would sustain a population greater
than that of our whole country today if the waters that now run to waste were
saved and used for irrigation.

President Theodore Roosevelt, State of the Union address, 1901

The twentieth-century growth of the American West was largely the story of the
"taming" of the **Colorado River**. If the Colorado were to run dry, Los Angeles, Las
Vegas and Phoenix would die, and the exodus from the Southwest would dwarf
anything from the Dustbowl era.

In terms of volume, the Colorado does not rank among the top 25 rivers in the US.
However, the sheer aggression with which it hurtles from 13,000ft up in the Rockies
makes it the fastest and fiercest of them all. That's why it's responsible for so many
magnificent canyons; and that's also why civil engineers can't bear to leave it alone.
They yearn to harness its energy with hydroelectric dams and divert its flow to irrigate
the desert instead of rushing uselessly to the sea.

Early in the twentieth century, the sparsely populated Southwestern states began
to fear that southern California's ever-increasing thirst might drain them dry. The 1922
Colorado River Compact divided the river between an **Upper Basin**, consisting of
Utah, Wyoming, Colorado and New Mexico, and a **Lower Basin** comprising of
Arizona, Nevada and California. Each basin was to receive 7.5 million acre-feet (an
acre-foot being the amount of water it takes to cover an acre of land one foot deep)
of the estimated annual flow of 16.8 million, with the dregs left over for Mexico. This
was the first of fifteen such agreements in fifty years, largely because the estimates
were wrong; the correct figure is more like 13.9 million acre-feet.

The task of distributing the water fell to a new federal agency, the **Bureau of Reclamation**. Its engineers saw their mission as being to "reclaim" the West to the way it
ought to be; the main tool at their disposal was the **dam**. They began in 1935, by
damming Black Canyon, on California's doorstep, with the **Hoover Dam**. That
project inspired a dam-building spree, in the US and all over the world. The Bureau's
subsequent plans for the Colorado Plateau were clear from the subtitle of one report:
A Natural Menace Becomes A Natural Resource. Proposals included damming the
Green River in northwest Colorado, the San Juan in New Mexico, and the Colorado
itself in both Bridge Canyon in Arizona and Utah's Glen Canyon.

Almost a century earlier, in 1869, John Wesley Powell had been entranced by the
idyllic canyon that stretched southwest from the confluence of the Green and
Colorado rivers: "A curious ensemble of wonderful features – carved walls, royal
arches, glens, alcove gulches, mounds, and monuments…We decide to call it **Glen
Canyon**". Those few river runners who had seen it since knew it as a cool, tranquil
haven, bursting with luxuriant vegetation and desert wildlife – a far cry from the
cataract-filled canyons both up- and downstream. Theirs were lone voices in the
wilderness, however; too little known to have earned federal protection, Glen
Canyon's remoteness was to work against it.

The environmental movement was in its infancy in the 1950s, and its strategy
concentrated on defending national parks. The Green River dam-site being within
Dinosaur National Monument, **David Brower**, executive director of the Sierra Club
conservation organization, told Congress that damming Glen Canyon was a far better
idea – in fact, he originally endorsed construction of a dam in the Grand Canyon *on
condition* that a dam was built in Glen Canyon as well.

Conservationists prided themselves on a job well done when it was decided to dam
the Green River outside Dinosaur, at Flaming Gorge to the northwest, and to go ahead
with damming Glen Canyon. The one concession to "the abominable nature lovers",
as one Utah senator termed them, was that water would not be allowed to encroach
upon the magnificent sandstone arch at Rainbow Bridge National Monument.

President Eisenhower triggered the first blast at the dam-site in September 1956. Meanwhile, with Glen Canyon doomed but not yet drowned, archeologists, artists and photographers set out to chronicle its disappearing treasures. These included the glowing, fern-dripping alcove known as the **Cathedral in the Desert**, and the **Crossing of the Fathers,** where Spanish friars Domínguez and Escalante forded the river in 1776.

On January 21, 1963, the same day that the Colorado River was brought to a halt, President Kennedy's Secretary of the Interior, Stewart Udall – great-grandson of John D. Lee, of Lees Ferry (see p.128) – announced plans to build two further dams within the Grand Canyon. By now, the Sierra Club had realized its mistake; and it promptly made another. This time it argued for building coal-burning power stations instead of hydroelectric dams. The Navajo, thinking nuclear power might soon render its mineral resources worthless, decided to cash in by permitting the strip-mining of Black Mesa, and the construction of the Navajo Generating Station outside Page.

It took seventeen more years for Lake Powell to fill to the brim, on June 22, 1980. At its maximum depth, the lake is 561ft deep at the dam and holds enough water to cover all of Arizona five inches deep. The water backs up 186 miles on the Colorado River and 72 miles on the San Juan River, as well as inundating 96 side canyons formed by rivers such as the Escalante and the Dirty Devil. Its total shoreline of 1960 miles is longer than the entire US Pacific coast. Despite the searing sun, it loses only 2.5 percent of its volume each year to evaporation.

Although many people consider the lake a loathsome abomination, many more see it as a thing of beauty, and Lake Powell has become Utah's number one tourist attraction, drawing around four million visitors per year. It is, undeniably, an extraordinary spectacle, its turquoise waters rippling against a stark red-rock rim and cradling islands that once were buttes and mesas. No one could ever mistake this for a natural landscape, however, and you don't have to be an out-and-out environmentalist to be disturbed by the transformation of America's last great wilderness into a playground.

David Brower, who left the Sierra Club to found Friends of the Earth in 1969, came to see his support for Glen Canyon Dam as "the greatest sin I have ever committed". Shortly before his death, in 2000, the 87-year-old "Archdruid" hosted a Day of Action Against Dams at the dam site, during which he called once again for Lake Powell to be drained so the canyon could regenerate. One original argument for the dam had been that the Colorado's phenomenal load of silt would otherwise fill Lake Mead, behind Hoover Dam, within a few years. Brower argued that the floodgates at Glen Canyon should remain open until that really does happen, perhaps two hundred years from now. Other activists would go much further. The central fantasy of Edward Abbey's *The Monkey Wrench Gang* involved dynamiting the dam, and Abbey was among the demonstrators who in 1981 signalled the birth of the **Earth First** movement by suspending a 300ft strip of plastic down the face of the dam to simulate an almighty crack. To some extent, the argument has been won; no major dam has been built since the 1960s, and the general consensus is that Glen Canyon Dam will be the last.

The debate over the future of Lake Powell was given an extra spin when **droughts** in the early twenty-first century threatened to restore Glen Canyon by default, and demonstrated how rapidly flora and fauna could re-establish themselves. Some argued that the lake would never refill, others that this latest dry spell was typical of long-term weather patterns, and showed precisely why the dam was necessary. In any case, though drought may be a natural phenomenon, the level of the lake is dictated by political decisions, and specifically the amount of water released to the Lower Basin states. Proposals to renegotiate the Colorado River Compact are forever being advanced, as for example by Arizona senator John McCain during his unsuccessful presidential campaign in 2008, and the future seems as uncertain as ever.

You can't stop on the bridge, so if you want a better look, call in at the ultramodern **Carl Hayden Visitor Center** (daily: March–Oct 8am–6pm; Nov–Feb 8.30am–4.30pm; ☎928/608-6404, ⓦnps.gov/glca) on the west bank, which doubles as the main source of information on the **Glen Canyon National Recreational Area**. Regular free **tours** of the actual dam take 45 minutes to drop via two elevators first to the walkway along the top, and then a further 500ft to the generating station at the bottom. Beneath the roar of the 1.3-million kilowatt turbines, a digital counter steadily ticks off the billions of dollars earned thus far by the sale of power.

Just before the bridge, a spur road on the east bank tunnels down through the cliffs to the river; rafters use it as an access point for the gloriously lazy fifteen-mile **float trip** down to Lees Ferry. There's no whitewater along the way, and strictly speaking you never enter the Grand Canyon, but it's still a very pleasant drift between imposing high-canyon cliffs. Half-day trips are run by Colorado River Discovery, 130 Sixth Ave, Page (daily: May–Sept 7.30am & 1pm; March, April Oct–Nov 11am; $84 adults, $74 ages 4–11; ☎928/645-9175 or 1-888/522-6644, ⓦraftthecanyon.com; see also p.196); the company also offers full-day oar-powered rowing trips between March and May, and September and November (departing 8.30am from Page, Mon, Wed & Sun; adults $161, children $151).

Wahweap

Unlike Page, **WAHWEAP**, a couple of miles west of Glen Canyon Dam, has never become a town. Lake Powell's principal **marina** has, however, grown steadily since it was established in 1963, coordinating most of the boat rental and tour business and also offering several hundred motel rooms.

To the fury of the federal authorities, the first man to appreciate Wahweap's potential did so long before the dam was ever built. Art Greene, the owner of the *Marble Canyon Lodge* (see p.126), ran boat trips upriver to Rainbow Bridge from the 1940s onwards; when he got wind of plans to dam Glen Canyon, he shrewdly leased the land at the mouth of Wahweap Creek at a knockdown rate. Knowing it made the perfect site for a marina, Greene refused to budge, and wound up making a killing as official concessionaire.

Boat tours from Wahweap

The prime attraction of staying at Wahweap, if you have time, is to take a boat tour fifty miles north to stunning **Rainbow Bridge National Monument**, where the world's largest natural bridge spans beautiful Forbidden Canyon. Tours operate year-round (daily: April–Oct 7.30am & 12.30pm; Nov–March 9am if numbers sufficient; adults $100, under-13s $72; ☎928/645-2433 or 1-888/896-3829, ⓦlakepowell.com). These schedules are open to considerable variation, as the length of the trip depends on the level of the lake; what's currently a six-hour trip has often been an eight-hour one in recent years when certain deep-water channels become no longer navigable. For much of the year, the tours are booked well in advance, so reserve your boat trip before you finalize your accommodation.

Shorter cruises from Wahweap include ninety-minute excursions to Antelope Canyon ($31.50, under-12s $18).

Practicalities

Only half the rooms in the plush *Lake Powell Resort* (☎928/645-2433 or 1-888/896-3829, ⓦlakepowell.com; ⓖ) overlook Lake Powell. Its *Rainbow Room* restaurant, however, provides huge lakeside windows and serves smart resort food daily for all meals, with prices kept relatively low to cater to the many tour groups that pass through. The same management also operates an adjacent first-come, first-served **campground** ($23), as well as an **RV park** (April–Oct $38; Nov–March $23).

Marble Canyon

If you drive north along US-89 from Cameron and fork left at Antelope Pass, rather than heading up towards Page, you join **US-89A**, which presses on for another fifteen miles at the foot of the Echo Cliffs before finally dropping down to reach Navajo Bridge. Although the spot where US-89A finally crosses the Colorado is often loosely referred to as **Lees Ferry**, the highway bridge actually stands six miles downstream from the ferry crossing it superseded.

By this point, the Grand Canyon has officially begun, and is already almost 500ft deep. John Wesley Powell named this segment of the gorge **Marble Canyon**, on account of its highly polished walls, indented with caverns and carvings that appeared almost architectural. Marble Canyon stretches a total of 61.5 miles from Lees Ferry to the Colorado's confluence with the Little Colorado, but it's another fifty miles from the bridge before the chasm reaches a mile deep. Here, near its starting point, it's such a narrow interruption in the vast flat plains – which have become known in turn as the **Marble Platform** – that you can barely tell it's there until you're right on top of it.

Navajo Bridge

Even though Prohibition meant that the newly built **Navajo Bridge** could only be baptized in ginger ale and not champagne, its opening in 1929, as the world's highest steel arch bridge, marked a turning point in Arizona history. Until then, no bridge spanned the Colorado for its entire length between Searchlight, Nevada, and northern Utah, while the ferry crossing near this spot was so dangerous that it had been abandoned altogether. When a crucial piece of equipment needed to finish Navajo Bridge was stranded on the wrong side of the river, the only way to get it across was to take it eight hundred miles by road, via Las Vegas.

Nowadays, the nearest bridge to Navajo Bridge is a mere fifty yards away. The original span was joined by a modern replica – all but identical, but at 44ft more than twice as wide – in 1995. The old bridge is reserved for pedestrians, so you can walk out to the middle and gaze 470ft down to the Colorado, green with algae, at the bottom of Marble Canyon. Just to add to the spectacle, this spot is popular with **condors** too.

Land ownership here is extraordinarily convoluted, by the way. The top of the west bank belongs to the Glen Canyon National Recreation Area, though Bureau of Land Management holdings start not far beyond; the top of the east bank belongs to the Navajo Reservation; and both bridge and river are in Grand Canyon National Park.

On the west bank, the **Navajo Bridge Interpretive Center** (daily: April–Sept 8am–6pm; closed Oct–March; restrooms always open; ☎928/355-2319, ⓦnps .gov/glca) is not so much a visitor centre as a good bookstore, stocking literature about the Glen Canyon region. The large viewing area outside is festooned with all sorts of plaques, including the one honouring John Doyle Lee that's mentioned on p.128.

Marble Canyon Lodge

Not far west of Navajo Bridge, just past the turn-off for Lees Ferry, the **Marble Canyon Lodge** (☎928/355-2225 or 1-800/726-1789, ⓦmarblecanyoncompany .com; ❸) provides more than fifty conventional motel-style rooms, with TVs but no phones, in low-slung buildings at the foot of the cliffs. The central lodge holds a gift store with the feel of a trading post, which sells Navajo rugs and other Native American crafts, and an adequate but unexciting **restaurant** that's open for all meals daily. Main dishes cost $8–14, with a Navajo taco salad for $9 and inexpensive house wine. While the lodge as a whole can be a little slapdash, it's a romantic enough overnight halt, what with its spectacular desert setting and roadrunners scurrying through the sands.

Marble Canyon Lodge has always catered to adventurers here for rafting and fishing trips on the Colorado. It gears up at 6am each day to meet the needs of river rats, and coin-op showers and laundry facilities are available at the gas station alongside the lodge. An array of plaques and monuments across the highway honours river pioneers, from the 1776 Domínguez and Escalante expedition (see p.130) onwards.

Lees Ferry

Reached via a gently sloping six-mile spur road that branches right (north) from US-89A just west of Navajo Bridge, **LEES FERRY** is little more than a dot on the map; it's not a town, and has a population of zero. Nonetheless, it boasts the geographical distinction of being the official starting point of the Grand Canyon, and even greater hydrological significance as marking the boundary between the upper and lower basins of the Colorado River. That's actually a political rather than a geographical concept; broadly speaking, under the Colorado River Compact of 1922, half the water in the river "belongs" to the states upstream from Lees Ferry, and the other half to those downstream. The complications and contradictions concealed within that simple formula are far too convoluted to go into here, though you'll notice that none of the river is thereby left in peace to flow into the ocean.

The practical importance of Lees Ferry stems from the fact that it's the only place within hundreds of miles that offers easy land access to both banks of the Colorado. That's because it stands at the confluence of the **Paria River**, flowing southeastwards from southern Utah, with the Colorado.

Mormon elder Jacob Hamblin was guided to this remote spot by a Paiute named Naraguts in 1858, while John Doyle Lee's eponymous **ferry** service – see box on p.126 – was instigated in 1871. After Lee's death, his wife Emma remained in the vicinity, but sold the ferry back to the Mormon Church for $3000 worth of cattle. Always a hazardous operation, with the boats in constant danger of being swept downstream, the ferry was finally abandoned after an accident in June 1928, in which three lives, plus a Model T Ford, were lost.

Four miles down from Marble Canyon, the road passes the fairly basic **Lees Ferry Campground**, which belongs to the Glen Canyon National Recreation Area ($10/night; ☎928/355-2334). It's an exposed spot, perched on a mesa above the river, but each pitch has its own shelter with table; water and toilets are available, but not showers.

After crossing the Paria River 0.7 miles farther on, the road continues another 0.6 miles to reach to a large car park and launch ramp beside the Colorado. It's the concrete gauging station visible on the far bank that counts as the exact start – **Mile 0** – of the Grand Canyon. This is where **whitewater rafting** expeditions set off into the canyon; passengers can leave the river at Phantom Ranch, five or six days downriver, but the first point where the boats can be taken out again is at Diamond Creek, around twelve days away by muscle power.

Some boats do, however, leave the water at Lees Ferry. As detailed on p.124, commercial operators based in Page run half-day **smooth-water** trips that float here from just below Glen Canyon Dam. That 15.8-mile stretch, fed by the cold, clear water released from the dam – and not yet muddied by the influx from the Paria – has became famous for its **trout fishing**. All the local lodges, including Lees Ferry Anglers, based at *Cliff Dweller's Lodge* (☎928/355-2261 or 1-800/962-9755, ⓦleesferry.com), organize guided fishing expeditions at varying prices. There's an official daily catch limit of two trout per person.

Lees Ferry trails

Rudimentary trails from the far end of the car park lead within a couple of hundred yards to an assortment of buildings left over from the ferry era. Most were constructed, not surprisingly, using slabs of red sandstone. They include a small post office, and the sturdy **Lees Ferry Fort**, erected in 1874 as a stronghold against Navajo attacks that never materialized.

The most prominent remains, however, date from an abortive experiment by **Charles H. Spencer**, who set out in 1910 to mine **gold** from the Chinle shale exposed on the slopes above Lees Ferry. Spencer's elaborate scheme, under which he'd sluice the shale down the hillside using pressurized hoses, required him to haul coal to the site, which he attempted both by **mule train** over the Echo Cliffs, and by **steamboat** along the river. While the boiler of his abandoned boat lies rusting in the Colorado, his precipitous **Spencer Trail** is still there, switchbacking up the cliffs – though not regularly maintained, it's open to hikers and offers a gruelling 1700ft climb. What ultimately stymied Spencer's endeavour was that something kept clogging his amalgamators, making them unable to extract gold. Only fifty years later did he find out that the problem was caused by **rhenium**, a metal unknown to science back in 1912. Amazingly enough, he returned to Lees Ferry, now aged over 90, and embarked on another unsuccessful mining venture, this time in pursuit of rhenium itself.

Keep walking beyond Spencer's employee bunkhouse and more derelict machinery, and after about a mile you'll come to the actual launch point of Lee's famous ferry. It's a hard, thirsty hike, however, with little reward at the far end.

Lonely Dell Ranch

John Lee lived not at the ferry site, which receives an average of six inches of rain per year, but in the much more congenial surroundings of the **Lonely Dell Ranch**, nestled in a fertile curve of the Paria River half a mile up from the confluence. Having crossed the river on your way back from the modern boat ramp, head immediately right on the unpaved road and you'll swiftly reach the

Park Service's replanted approximation of Lee's orchards, rich with apple, pear, plum and peach trees.

His original **log cabin** stands not far beyond, constructed largely of driftwood and chinked with thick, red river mud. The smaller **blacksmith shop** alongside it was also Lee's, and is shaded by a large mulberry tree planted to help raise silkworms. Various other structures were added by Lee's successors, who were also responsible for the green farm machinery left to rust in the fields, and some of whom now themselves lie in the tranquil little **cemetery** at the end of the road. Uninhabited since the 1940s, the ranch these days has the feel of a desert oasis, and is a popular halt for migratory birds.

For serious backpackers, Lonely Dell Ranch marks the end of an epic four- to six-day hike that traces the full length of the Paria Canyon, starting at the White House trailhead off AZ-89 between Kanab and Page. The canyon forms part of the Paria Canyon-Vermilion Cliffs Wilderness, which is itself subsumed within Vermilion Cliffs National Monument (see below).

Vermilion Cliffs

For the first thirty miles west of Marble Canyon, US-89A curves at the foot of the **Vermilion Cliffs**. In 2000, in one of his final acts as president, Bill Clinton designated a vast 280,000-acre expanse that includes the cliffs, the Paria Plateau above and Paria Canyon, as **Vermilion Cliffs National Monument**. Administered

John Doyle Lee (1812–77)

Travellers who read the plaque at Navajo Bridge that hails **John Doyle Lee** as "a man of good faith, sound judgment and indomitable courage" might never realize that the man who put the Lee in Lees Ferry was also a prime mover in one of the most notorious episodes in Western history. While the precise truth remains in dispute, the generally accepted story runs something like this:

In 1847, Mormons fleeing persecution in Illinois ventured west beyond the United States and founded Salt Lake City. Almost immediately, however, the US extended its boundaries to the Pacific, and California-bound pioneers began to stream through Mormon territory. By 1857, tensions were such that a "Mormon War" was seen as inevitable.

That August, finding that no one would sell them supplies, a wagon train of settlers from Arkansas and Missouri resorted to raiding Mormon farms. One even claimed to be carrying the very gun with which Mormon founder Joseph Smith had been killed in Missouri. Camping at **Mountain Meadows** in southern Utah, the settlers were ambushed, and then besieged, by warriors dressed as Native Americans. Whether the attackers were genuine Utes, or white Mormons in disguise – as Mark Twain reported in *Roughing It* – is still open to question. Clearly, however, local Mormons saw the wagon train as a threat to be eliminated. Their commander, John Lee, rode up to the beleaguered Gentiles on September 11, claiming to have negotiated a truce with the "Indians", and stated that if they laid down their guns they would be allowed to proceed west in peace.

Desperately short of ammunition, the migrants agreed. Each was assigned a Mormon escort, and together they set off west. Within a mile, Lee called the order **"Halt! Do your duty!,"** whereupon the Mormon militiamen, possibly with assistance from Native Americans, killed the entire group, amounting to 120 unarmed men, women and children.

by the BLM in St George, Utah (☎ 435/688-3200, ⓦ blm.gov/az), it's not expected to change significantly, let alone open up for tourism.

Although the road itself is all but featureless, and the desert almost entirely devoid of vegetation, the drive along the Vermilion Cliffs is superbly dramatic, with the soaring sandstone walls glowing a magnificent red at sunrise and sunset. However, only a couple of small **motels** offer any incentive to get out of your car. You'd never know the Grand Canyon was out there to the east, slicing through the Marble Platform, unless you detour two miles down a dirt road that leaves the highway a couple of hundred yards south of *Lees Ferry Lodge* to reach the clifftop **Badger Canyon–Marble Canyon Overlook**.

Lees Ferry Lodge

Enjoying great views from a very pretty location three miles west of *Marble Canyon Lodge*, the small **Lees Ferry Lodge** complex dates from 1929 (☎ 928/355-2231 or 1-800/451-2231, ⓦ leesferrylodge.com; ❹). Besides offering appealingly rustic guest cabins of varying sizes, the lodge centres on the friendly little *Vermilion Cliffs Bar & Grille* (summer daily 6.30am–10pm; shorter hours in winter) which serves good food washed down with an extraordinary range of bottled beers.

Cliff Dweller's Lodge

Originally built in 1890 as a mocked-up "ancient ruin", but now run as a standard-issue Western motel, the **Cliff Dweller's Lodge** (☎ 928/355-2261 or 1-800/962-9755,

When reports of the massacre reached the rest of the country, it was widely believed to have been carried out on the orders of Mormon President **Brigham Young**. No serious legal investigation ever took place, however, and most of the perpetrators lay low in remote desert outposts. In due course, Young bowed to national pressure; Lee was excommunicated in 1870, arrested in 1874 and **executed** by firing squad in Mountain Meadows on March 23, 1877.

Lee's own version of events was quite different. He claimed to have acted as a loyal servant of the Church; not to have actually killed anyone; to have given Brigham Young the names of all involved; and to have been made a scapegoat.

It was during his years on the run, albeit in answer to a request from Brigham Young, that Lee set up the first **ferry** service across the Colorado. He arrived here in 1871, with just two of his eighteen wives still standing by him. Lee initially utilized three boats abandoned by John Wesley Powell before building his own boat, *Colorado*, big enough to carry four wagons. The boat was swept across the river in both directions by the current, and then towed back upstream to its starting point; the fare was $3 per wagon, 75¢ per animal.

Many legends surround Lee's years in the Grand Canyon. Tales that he planted the peach orchards of the Havasupai are untrue – though he did visit them in his wanderings – while persistent stories of **lost gold mines** have never been proved. He's said to have been in the habit of disappearing for days at a time and returning with cans filled with gold nuggets. His wife Emma believed he'd struck lucky, but none of the prospectors who followed her suggestions ever found a thing.

Haunting photos of Lee on the day he died show a gaunt old man sitting on his coffin, waiting for the firing squad – hidden beneath a blanket to prevent reprisals – to do its work. He suffered one final indignity: the US Congress, determined not to honour a convicted murderer, formally stripped Lee's Ferry of its apostrophe.

Domínguez and Escalante

On July 29, 1776 – three weeks after Congress endorsed the Declaration of Independence – a party of twenty explorers set off from Santa Fe, the capital of the Spanish province of New Mexico. Led by two Franciscan friars, **Atanasio Domínguez** and **Silvestre Vélez de Escalante**, they hoped to establish a route to the Spanish mission at Monterey, California. Knowing that the Grand Canyon blocked their path, but not knowing how far it stretched, they headed north, planning to turn west once they felt confident the canyon had petered out. They eventually crossed the Colorado River somewhere east of modern Grand Junction, Colorado, then continued north and west as far as what's now Provo, Utah, which they named San Antonio de Padua. By October, they were in southern Utah, at what they calculated was the same latitude as Monterey. However, the distant western horizon was lined by snow-capped mountains, and winter blizzards were setting in.

By casting lots, the expedition made the difficult decision to head home, and attempt to blaze a more direct trail back to Santa Fe. Their Indian guides steered them across the Kaibab Plateau, and down through House Rock Valley to the Vermilion Cliffs. A roadside plaque, eighteen miles southwest of Navajo Bridge near mile marker 557, commemorates the **San Bartolome Campsite** where they halted on October 25.

The following day, they approached the Colorado at Marble Canyon, a spot described as "a corner all hemmed in by very lofty bluffs and big hogbacks of red earth which...present a pleasingly jumbled scene". Crossing the mouth of the Paria River, they then made their camp amid the more difficult terrain of what's now Lees Ferry, roughly a hundred yards downstream from the present-day boat-launch site. Two members of the party managed to swim across the Colorado – at the cost of losing all their clothes – but returned having been too exhausted to climb the cliffs on the far side. Next they built a raft, but three times failed to pole it all the way across. After eleven days, convinced of the impossibility of coaxing their horses (some of which they were in any case by now having to eat) through quicksand and onto makeshift rafts, they gave up.

They headed north instead, managing to climb out of Paria Canyon a few miles along, and eventually forded the Colorado on horseback on November 7 at what became known as the **Crossing of the Fathers** in Glen Canyon. That uniquely shallow ford was dynamited by Mormon settlers in the 1870s to thwart its use by Navajo cattle raiders, and now lies drowned beneath the waters of Lake Powell.

The Franciscans eventually returned to Santa Fe on January 2, 1777, having promised to return to Utah to set up a mission among the Laguna. Thanks to general cutbacks by the government in Spain, however, they never did so, meaning that the vast new lands explored by the expedition remained virgin territory until the arrival of the Mormons seventy years later.

Ⓦleesferry.com; ➍) occupies another dramatic spot amid the jumbled rocks half a dozen miles beyond *Lees Ferry Lodge*. Like its neighbours, it's geared primarily towards river runners, so its restaurant – which has an attractive shady patio – makes a very early start (Mon–Thurs 5–10am & 4–10pm, Fri–Sun 5am–10pm; shorter hours in winter). It's also the base for Lees Ferry Anglers (see p.127), which runs river fishing expeditions.

House Rock Valley

US-89A rounds the southernmost promontory of the Vermilion Cliffs just under twenty miles out from Navajo Bridge. Not far beyond, as the highway begins its arrow-straight run across the desert towards the Kaibab Mountains, a dirt road sets off south between mile markers 559 and 560. It leads to the House Rock Buffalo

Ranch, headquarters for a hundred-strong herd of buffalo that roams free across House Rock Valley. In recent years the buffalo have also wandered up onto the Kaibab Plateau and along the North Rim, so your chances of spotting them are pretty minimal; you'd have to be very keen indeed to think it worth driving the slow fifty-mile round trip to road's end and back.

Another five miles up the highway, a northbound gravel road just past mile marker 565, which closely parallels the streambed of House Rock Wash, leads within three miles to the **Condor Release Site**. This is mission control for the Peregrine Fund's attempt to repopulate Arizona with wild condors, as detailed on p.40. A roadside pavilion commands views of the precise spot, high on the Vermilion Cliffs, where the first six birds were released from a glorified coop on December 12, 1996. As the abundant guano stains prove, they and their siblings regularly return "home". With powerful binoculars, you may well see them perched on the clifftops, or flying far overhead, but you're actually more likely to get close-up views at Grand Canyon Village on the South Rim.

Shortly after the release-site turn-off, AZ-89A finally hits the **Kaibab Mountains**, and begins the final eleven-mile climb to Jacob Lake. A panoramic viewpoint after the first few switchbacks, before the road plunges for good into the thick forests of the Kaibab Plateau, commands a superb prospect of the cliffs, the Marble Platform and the slender crack of Marble Canyon.

Jacob Lake

Set deep in the forest forty miles up from Navajo Bridge, the crossroads community of **JACOB LAKE** looks more like a Canadian logging camp than anything you'd expect to find in Arizona. Named after Jacob Hamblin, a Mormon missionary to the Paiute and Navajo, it guards the sole access route to the North Rim of the Grand Canyon: **AZ-67**, whose 44-mile run southbound to *Grand Canyon Lodge* is closed to all traffic between the first serious snowfall of each winter and the following spring's thaw. Jacob Lake thus goes into a state of quasi-hibernation in the winter, emerging in summer to make its living from the constant stream of tourists.

The *Jacob Lake Inn*, a sprawling but very welcoming complex of timber-frame buildings at the road junction, stays open all year round (☎928/643-7232, ⓦjacoblake.com). As well as its simple **motel** rooms (❺) and log cabins (❹), it incorporates some pricier family units capable of sleeping up to six (❻), plus a gas station. The main lodge building, invitingly festooned with hanging rugs, holds a general store, an old-fashioned diner counter and a **restaurant**, where lunch sandwiches and burgers cost under $10, while most dinner dishes, including the house speciality *jagerschnitzel*, a breaded pork cutlet pounded with juniper berries, are priced at $17–20.

Alongside the inn, the Forest Service's **Kaibab Plateau Visitor Center** contains displays and information on the surrounding area (daily 8am–5pm; ☎928/643-7298, ⓦfs.usda.gov).

The Forest Service also oversees the lovely *Jacob Lake Campground*, on US-89A just west of the intersection, which has facilities for **tent campers** only ($17; mid-May to Oct; ☎928/643-7395). **RVs** can stay instead at the equally attractive *Kaibab Camper Village*, well off AZ-67 a mile southwest of the inn, near the eponymous lake itself, which is actually a collapsed limestone sinkhole (tents $17, RVs $34, cabins ❹; mid-May to mid-Oct; ☎928/643-7804, ⓦkaibabcampervillage.com).

DeMotte Park

Mormon settlers made little use of the forests that lie south of Jacob Lake, other than grazing their cattle in the large meadow-like clearings that punctuate the road to the canyon. No one knows quite how these came into being; the theory that some natural mechanism deters trees from encroaching is undermined by the observable fact that the trees are in fact doing just that, year upon year.

One especially idyllic such meadow, **DEMOTTE PARK**, 27 miles down AZ-67 from Jacob Lake, is now the site of the *Kaibab Lodge* (mid-May to Oct only; ☎928/638-2389 in summer, 928/526-0924 in winter or 1-800/525-0924, ⓦkaibablodge.com). This offers three different kinds of cabin – characterful older ones with bare wooden floors (❹), a few slightly more expensive ones with motel-style trimmings (❺) and three larger family units with their own sitting rooms (❼) – plus a simple restaurant that's open for all meals daily, from breakfast blueberry pancakes to $25 dinner steaks. Immediately south, there's another Forestry Service campground, the first-come, first-served, tent-only *DeMotte Park Campground* ($17; late May to Oct; ☎928/643-7298). The **gas station** nearby is the last before the canyon; the park's North Entrance Station is five miles down the road, while visitor facilities, including a gas station, lie nine miles beyond that.

With a good map – ideally the Forest Service's *North Kaibab Ranger District* and not AAA's otherwise reliable *Guide to Indian Country* – it's possible to navigate the dirt roads that branch off of AZ-67 near DeMotte Park to several dramatic viewpoints. These include overlooks of the Marble Platform to the east, as well as the canyon views from Parissawampitts, Crazy Jug and Monument points (see p.81 onwards) to the west. For advice on conditions along these backcountry roads, call in at the Forest Service visitor centre in Jacob Lake.

5

The Arizona Strip

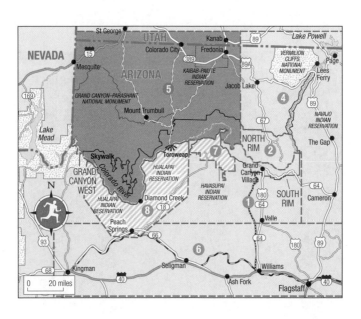

CHAPTER 5 # Highlights

✳ **Kanab** Just across the state line in Utah, this former movie town provides plentiful food and lodging options in an otherwise underpopulated region. See p.137

✳ **Pipe Spring National Monument** Desert outpost that owes its tangled and fascinating history to its precious perennial water supply. See p.140

✳ **Toroweap Overlook** The remotest canyon overlook within the national park offers unique and extraordinary views of the inner gorge. See p.143

✳ **Lava Falls Overlook** Spectacular viewpoint, commanding the spot where a vast volcanic lava flow once blocked the entire Grand Canyon. See p.145

▲ View from Toroweap Overlook

The Arizona Strip

Thanks to its sheer remoteness, the **Arizona Strip** – the anomalous area of northern Arizona that's sandwiched between the North Rim and the Utah state line – remains one of the least visited regions in the Southwest. Nonetheless, it makes a very rewarding destination for travellers eager to get the full Grand Canyon experience. Writer Wallace Stegner described it as "scenically the most spectacular and humanly the least usable of all our regions… as terrible and beautiful wasteland as the world can show", and much of it remains absolute wilderness. Almost no one ever sees the colossal canyon formed by **Kanab Creek**, which splits this region in two, while the million-acre **Grand Canyon–Parashant National Monument**, created in 2000, makes no provision for tourism whatsoever.

Virtually no roads cross the Strip, and those that do hold just a few tiny, secretive and often semi-derelict hamlets. Although you have to pass this way in order to complete a full tour around the Grand Canyon, the majority of visitors tend rather to be racing between the Grand Canyon and the national parks of southern Utah. Few are aware that they're missing perhaps the most spectacular section of Grand Canyon National Park: the **Tuweep** district, home to two stunning overlooks at **Toroweap Point** that provide a rare opportunity to see the canyon's innermost core.

The Arizona Strip has never held more than five thousand inhabitants. Roughly that many **Kaibab Paiute** were living here – mostly as nomads, but also farming what little arable land exists – when **Mormon** explorers arrived in the 1850s, and set up ranches wherever they found water. By 1909, decimated by diseases and the inevitable conflicts, the Paiute population had dwindled to just 89. However, the ranchers in turn largely gave up by the mid-twentieth century, and only a couple of their settlements, **Fredonia** and **Colorado City**, ever grew to any significant size.

By any logic, you'd expect the Strip to belong to Utah rather than Arizona. In 1864, Mormon leader Brigham Young called on Congress to grant the Mormons all territory that lay within two degrees of latitude of either side of the Colorado; the boundary was drawn instead along the 37th parallel, and that remains the Utah–Arizona border. At least four attempts to incorporate the Strip into Utah failed, largely because many of those Mormons who chose to remain in this remote region were renegades who didn't accept their church's reversal of its doctrine on multiple marriage. Effective isolation from the state authorities of both Utah and Arizona continues to suit these die-hard **polygamists** just fine.

Other than plenty of time, and a reliable vehicle, the principal requirement needed to explore the Arizona Strip is a good **map** – ideally, the BLM Arizona Strip Field Office's *Visitor Map*.

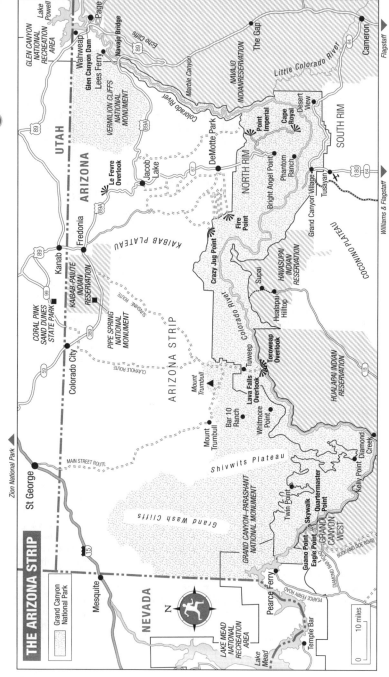

THE ARIZONA STRIP

Grand Canyon National Park

NEVADA

N

Zion National Park

St George

Mesquite

MAIN STREET ROUTE

LAKE MEAD NATIONAL RECREATION AREA

Pearce Ferry

Temple Bar

Lake Mead

PEARCE FERRY ROAD

DIAMOND BAR ROAD

Guano Point

Eagle Point

Skywalk

GRAND CANYON WEST

Quartermaster Point

Twin Point

BUCK AND DOE ROAD

GRAND CANYON-PARASHANT NATIONAL MONUMENT

Grand Wash Cliffs

Shivwits Plateau

Kelly Point

Diamond Creek

HUALAPAI INDIAN RESERVATION

Mount Trumbull

Bar 10 Ranch

Whitmore Point

Lava Falls Overlook

Mount Trumbull

Tuweep

Toroweap Overlook

18

Colorado River

Supai

Hualapai Hilltop

HAVASUPAI INDIAN RESERVATION

Crazy Jug Point

KAIBAB PLATEAU

Fire Point

COCONINO PLATEAU

Grand Canyon Village

Tusayan

180

64

Williams & Flagstaff

Bright Angel Point

Phantom Ranch

NORTH RIM

SOUTH RIM

DeMotte Park

Point Imperial

Cape Royal

Desert View

Jacob Lake

89

Le Fevre Overlook

NAVAJO INDIAN RESERVATION

Little Colorado River

Flagstaff

64

Cameron

The Gap

Echo Cliffs

Marble Canyon

89A

VERMILION CLIFFS NATIONAL MONUMENT

Colorado River

Lees Ferry

Glen Canyon Dam

Navajo Bridge

Wahweap

Page

Lake Powell

GLEN CANYON NATIONAL RECREATION AREA

UTAH

ARIZONA

89

Fredonia

Kanab

89

Colorado City

389

59

PIPE SPRING NATIONAL MONUMENT

KAIBAB-PAIUTE INDIAN RESERVATION

CORAL PINK SAND DUNES STATE PARK

99

SUNSHINE ROUTE

CLAYHOLE ROUTE

ARIZONA STRIP

15

Tuba City & Monument Valley

89A

66

0   10 miles

136

Le Fevre Overlook

The Kaibab Plateau extends for a good fifty miles north of the Grand Canyon's North Rim. Only once you've driven the full length of AZ-67, and then continued northwest on US-89A from the intersection at **Jacob Lake** (see p.131), does the ground finally begin to slope downwards.

Ten miles along, between mile markers 590 and 591, the roadside **Le Fevre Overlook** presents a jaw-dropping panorama across the Arizona Strip and into southern Utah. Tier upon tier of cliffs rise one behind the other into the distance, making it abundantly clear why the entire region is known to geologists as the **Grand Staircase**. First comes the red sandstone of the Vermilion Cliffs, the formation pierced by **Zion Canyon**; next are the White Cliffs, which form the **Kolob Canyons** district of Zion National Park; and beyond them, forty miles away, stand the softer Pink Cliffs, sculpted into the hoodoos of **Bryce Canyon**. Apart from the occasional jewellery seller, the lookout holds no facilities of any kind.

Fredonia

US-89A eventually levels out at the foot of the Grand Staircase on **Muggins Flat**, reaching the very hot – in terms of temperature, not nightlife – little community of **FREDONIA** just over thirty miles from, and 3000ft lower than, Jacob Lake. While a population of around 1300 makes this the largest town on the Arizona Strip, the presence of the bigger and more interesting **Kanab** a mere seven miles north, across the Utah border, means that few visitors spend the night here. Fredonia was originally founded alongside Kanab Creek by Mormon farmers in 1885, under the more down-to-earth name of Hardscrabble, and remains a dusty and unadorned desert outpost. Sadly there's no Marx Brothers connection; the Republic of Fredonia lampooned in *Duck Soup* probably took its name from a Fredonia in New York State.

The very helpful **welcome centre**, on the east side of US-89A close to the state line at the north end of town (Tues–Sat 9am–5pm; ☎928/643-7241), is the best place to get advice on the Strip's backcountry routes, and to buy the necessary maps. There's also a Forest Service office at 430 S Main St (Mon–Fri 9am–5pm; ☎928/643-7395).

Practicalities

Fredonia holds a handful of tiny but adequate **motels**. Driving south to north on US-89A, you pass the *Blue Sage*, 330 S Main St (☎928/643-7125; closed winter; ❷), which also accommodates RVs, and the ivy-covered *Grand Canyon*, just where AZ-389 heads west to Colorado City, at 175 S Main St (☎928/643-7646; ❷), which boasts a very dilapidated, red British telephone box in the garden.

Nedra's Café, 165 N Main St (☎928/643-7591), is a surprisingly good **Mexican restaurant**, where, if you're a newcomer to this neck of the woods, you might want to sample your first Navajo taco; for the uninitiated, it's a pizza-like cheese-topped slab of frybread.

Kanab

Until new roads were pushed through the region in the 1950s, **KANAB**, Utah, just two miles north of the Arizona state line, was renowned as perhaps the most inaccessible town in the US. Now it's a significant tourist halt, thanks to its location halfway between the Grand Canyon, 80 miles southeast, and Bryce Canyon, 83 miles northeast.

Kanab started life in 1864 as **Fort Kanab**, a frontier outpost so prone to Indian attacks that it was abandoned after just two years. Jacob Hamblin founded the town itself in 1870 as a God-fearing ranching community with a sideline in harbouring Mormons who fell foul of the federal government, among them several perpetrators of the Mountain Meadows Massacre (see p.128). Pulp novelist Zane Grey later cultivated that lawless image, setting many of his Westerns nearby, while Kanab's rugged surroundings earned it the nickname of "Utah's Little Hollywood", and made it a focus for Western movie-makers from Tom Mix, who filmed *Deadwood Coach* here in 1924, to Clint Eastwood with *The Outlaw Josey Wales* in 1976.

Ranching in southern Utah has long been in decline, but the citizens of Kanab would still much prefer to wrest their living from the earth. Their biggest payday came in the late 1950s, when this was the original base for the construction of **Glen Canyon Dam**. During the eighteen months it took to upgrade the 72-mile dirt road to the dam site, and build the new town of Page, Arizona, locals scurried to grab their share of the 200 million federal dollars that were pumped into the project. In November 1958, the workers decamped for Page, and the boom was over.

For many years thereafter, Kanab pinned its hopes on the prospect of large-scale coal-mining on the **Kaiparowits Plateau** to the northeast. The politicians and environmentalists who thwarted such plans in the 1970s were burned in effigy on the streets of Kanab – "victims" included Robert Redford, which might explain why not so many movies get made around here any more – while the town closed down in protest for an hour in 1996 when President Clinton's proclamation of Grand Staircase–Escalante National Monument precluded that possibility forever.

Kanab has thus been left to survive by catering for tourists, which it does with reasonably good grace. US-89 is lined with an above-par assortment of motels and restaurants, with the greatest concentration where the highway briefly doglegs to run east–west along **Center Street**. A few blocks south, US-89 proper branches off east toward Page, while US-89A continues south into Arizona.

Apart from a few large Western-themed souvenir stores, such as Denny's Wigwam, opposite *Parry Lodge* at 78 E Center St (☎435/644-2452), there's almost nothing to do in Kanab, though hikers may enjoy the views from the **Squaw Trail**, which climbs the escarpment just north of town.

Information and tours

Operating under the slogan "The Greatest Earth on Show", Kanab's **visitor centre** stands just south of Center Street at 78 S 100 East (March–Oct Mon–Fri 9am–7pm, Sat 10am–6pm, Sun 9am–4pm; Nov–Feb Mon–Fri 9am–5pm; ☎435/644-5033 or 1-800/733-5263, ⓦkaneutah.com). Interesting displays relate the town's filmmaking past. The local **BLM** office, 318 North 100 East (mid-March to mid-Nov daily 8am–4.30pm; mid-Nov to mid-March Mon–Fri 8am–4.30pm; ☎435/644-4600, ⓦblm.gov/ut), carries full information on nearby public lands, including Grand Canyon–Parashant National Monument, and up-to-date details on driving conditions.

Local **tour operators** offering wilderness trips include Dreamland Safari Tours, whose all-day Toroweap tour costs $350 for two people in Kanab (☎435/644-5506, ⓦdreamlandtours.net).

Accommodation

Kanab holds several good-value budget **motels**, so don't feel compelled to pay extra for a fancier name. All are within easy walking distance of downtown.

Aiken's Lodge 74 W Center St ☎435/644-2625 or 1-877/644-2105, ⓦaikenslodge.com. This low-slung and far from pretty option is nonetheless the ideal budget motel: crisp and clean, right in the heart of town and with its own pool. ❸
Kanab Comfort Inn 815 E AZ-99 ☎435/644-8888 or 1-800/574-4061, ⓦhikanabutah.com. Large new motel, set atop a bluff on the eastern edge of town. Somewhat isolated, but with the best rooms in Kanab, plus a free breakfast bar. ❹
Parry Lodge 89 E Center St ☎435/644-2601 or 1-888/289-1722, ⓦparrylodge.com. Opened in

1931, Kanab's oldest motel has an undeniable air of romance. Photos of celebrity guests festoon the lobby and restaurant, while nameplates identify the rooms in which they slept; you can even bathe in John Wayne's extra-large bathtub. *Parry's* isn't *that* great, though, and some of the newer rooms are dingy and noisy. Rates include a full cooked breakfast. ❹
Shilo Inn 296 W 100 North ☎435/644-2562 or 1-800/222-2244, ⓦwww.shiloinns.com. Large, presentable motel at the north end of town. Some rooms have kitchens, and there's a breakfast buffet, pool and spa. ❺

Eating

Twenty or so largely formulaic **restaurants** cling to the edge of the highway as it passes through Kanab. One or two make the effort to be distinctive, while the others rest safe in the knowledge that however bad they may be, there's precious little choice for a hundred miles in any direction.

Houston's Trails' End 32 E Center St ☎435/644-2488, ⓦwww.houstons.net. Western-themed family diner, serving chicken-fried steaks, ribs, fish and fried breakfasts at low prices. Open daily for all meals, but closed mid-Nov to mid-March.
Linda Lea's 4 E Center St ☎435/644-8191. Good central bakery, with sidewalk patio seating to enjoy its fine breads, pastries and coffee. Mon–Sat 6am–2pm.
Nedra's Too 310 S 100 East ☎435/644-2030. Informal local hangout at the junction of US-89 and US-89A on the south side of town, with a sister restaurant in Fredonia (see p.137). The unifying factor of the Mexican/American menu is the fryer; even the ice cream comes deep-fried. Mexican dishes cost around $11, steak and seafood more likc $20. Open daily for all meals.

Parry Lodge 89 E Center St ☎435/644-2601. Attractive dining room where the menu occasionally hints at the healthy, in the form of dishes like poached salmon; unlike most places in Kanab, it has a licence to sell alcohol. Typical main dishes cost $15 or less. Open for all meals in summer, breakfast and dinner only in spring and autumn, and closed Nov–March.
Rocking V Café 97 W Center St ☎435/644-8001. This valiant and largely successful bid to improve Kanab's culinary reputation is housed in a former bank, one of the town's oldest buildings. Open for dinner only, it serves daily "taste of the Planet" specials like Thursday's *chana masala* vegetarian stew, for around $10.

Coral Pink Sand Dunes State Park

No area in the Grand Canyon region conforms so exactly to the popular notion of a desert – graceful dunes of fine sand, their parallel crests sweeping towards the horizon – as **CORAL PINK SAND DUNES STATE PARK** (daily 24hr; $5 per vehicle; ☎435/648-2800). This pseudo-Saharan landscape is roughly ten miles west of Kanab, but can only be reached by a circuitous route; drive eight miles north of Kanab on US-89, then turn left, southwest, onto a paved road that takes a dozen miles to reach the park itself.

The only dune field in the Colorado Plateau lies at the foot of a seven-mile bluff of the Vermilion Cliffs, which here unusually face the northwest. Its sand grains are eroded from Navajo sandstone, itself originally deposited in the form of dunes.

Hikers who launch themselves from the boardwalk near the entrance station usually find that a few minutes of wading knee-deep in sand sates their *Lawrence of Arabia* fantasies. However, in marked contrast to Utah's federal parks, **off-road vehicles** are positively encouraged. The park was created in response to campaigns by local off-road enthusiasts, and plays host to countless formal and informal dune buggy races, most notably each July 4.

The well-shaded **campground** ($16; reservations on ☎1-800/322-3770) remains open all year, though it only has water in summer. Spending a night here offers the enticing prospect of seeing not only kangaroo rats but, more to the point, the snakes that prey on them. The tiny rats are named for their squatting postures, and the snakes are not a danger to humans.

Pipe Spring National Monument

Immediately south of Coral Pink Sand Dunes, across the state line in Arizona and only accessible via a turning off AZ-389, thirteen miles west of Fredonia, **Pipe Spring National Monument** (daily: June–Aug 7am–5pm; Sept–May 8am–5pm; $5, under-16s free; ☎928/643-7105, ⊛nps.gov/pisp) marks the site of one of the few water sources on the Arizona Strip. Not surprisingly, ownership of this precious spring has been much contested: it has spent time in both Utah and Arizona, and belonged to three different counties. In 1863, a Mormon rancher, Dr James Whitmore, appropriated it from the Paiutes, who knew it as *Mu-tum-wa-va*, or Dripping Rock. After Whitmore was killed three years later by Paiute and Navajo raiders, Brigham Young ordered the Mormons to withdraw. However, they returned in 1870 and enclosed the spring in a fort, named **Winsor Castle** after its first superintendent, which was personally dedicated by Young in a ceremony attended by John Wesley Powell.

In 1907, the federal government established the **Kaibab Paiute Indian Reservation**, which measured eighteen miles by twelve miles and included the spring. No provision was made concerning its water, however, and Mormon cattle ranchers continued to bring their herds here. The situation was further confused in 1923, when spring and fort were designated as **Winsor Castle National Monument**, thanks to the first director of the National Park Service, Stephen Mather, who had discovered its charms after his car broke down nearby. The idea was ostensibly to preserve the fort as a "memorial to Western pioneer life", though the declaration owed as much to its standing halfway between the Grand Canyon and Zion National Park as to any intrinsic interest.

Bitter legal disputes between cattlemen, Paiutes and the Park Service dragged on for another fifty years, before use of water from Pipe Spring was largely assigned to the Paiutes. By then, overgrazing had reduced the surrounding rich grassland to virtual desert. Debates over local history still endure; the Paiute argue that the fort was built not so much to protect valiant Mormon settlers from Native Americans, as defiant polygamists from the government, and that the Mormon practice of recruiting Paiute into "indentured servitude" was little different from the earlier Navajo and Ute tradition of kidnapping them into slavery.

Considerable care has been taken to ensure that the monument reflects both Paiute and Mormon history. Its visitor centre doubles as an interesting museum where staff can also advise on the state of local roads. The fort itself, a short walk away, remains in good condition, and is open for half-hourly guided tours that illuminate early ranching life. An Ancestral Puebloan ruin that's said to lie beneath its outbuildings has yet to be excavated. With its small herd of longhorn cattle, scattered old wagons and farming implements, and long-range views across the desert, the monument is a pleasant enough little spot, but not one where you're likely to spend very much time.

A quarter of a mile north of the monument, the Paiute run a small **campground** (☎928/643-7245), where a site costs $5 per tent or $10 for RVs. At the peak of the 1990s Indian gaming boom, they also had a casino, but that is now defunct.

Colorado City

Continuing northwest from Pipe Spring, AZ-389 serves as the most direct route between the North Rim and I-15, which in turn connects Las Vegas and Salt Lake City. A mile or so before it reaches Utah, a spur road to the right runs up to the renegade and notoriously polygamist Mormon community of **COLORADO CITY**. Set beneath the towering bluffs of the Vermilion Cliffs, and devoid of either accommodation or dining options, this is a surreal-looking place, laid out with a small grid of extremely broad, largely unpaved streets that see very few cars but plenty of gingham pinafores. Massive homes built to house multiple marriages and even more multiple families stand on every corner, and with much of the male population currently in jail, on the run or hounded out of town (see box, pp.142–143) you're only likely to see female faces. As young women are forbidden to cut their hair before marriage, most are surmounted by extraordinary swept-back quiffs. Everyone will assume you're a magazine journalist hoping to write a sensational article about polygamy, and there's no encouragement to linger.

Toroweap

The Arizona Strip holds one tremendous prize for visitors prepared to venture off the paved highways: **Toroweap Point**, the only place where you can drive to the very lip of the canyon's Granite Gorge and peer down sheer 3000ft cliffs to the Colorado River. As the crow flies, the overlook lies slightly under sixty miles west of Bright Angel Point, the main focus for North Rim tourism. By road, however, it's almost 150 miles, as you have to circumvent the full length of Kanab Canyon by heading all the way north to Fredonia.

Is it worth it? An unequivocal yes – Toroweap is not just another overlook. However, don't underestimate the amount of time and effort it takes to get there. Even a fleeting visit requires at least six hours of laborious driving on gravel roads.

There are two main routes: the eastern **Sunshine Route**, which starts on AZ-389 seven miles west of **Fredonia** and runs for 61 miles southwest, and the more scenic but longer western **Main Street Route**, which takes a total of 90 miles from the heart of **St George**, Utah, but is closed by snow for much of the winter. The account below follows the obvious east–west itinerary for a road trip, by getting there from Fredonia and heading back via St George. A third possibility, the sixty-mile **Clayhole Route** from Colorado City, is not recommended here because it's less convenient for onward travel and it's liable to become impassable not only during wet weather, but also, thanks to drifting sand, after prolonged dry spells too.

When open, which in the case of the Sunshine Route is usually all year, these roads are generally passable in ordinary vehicles. If 4WD is necessary at all, it will be for the last few miles only, so if you don't have 4WD you can still reckon on

Polygamy on the Arizona Strip

Although it was not officially founded until 1913, as **Short Creek**, Colorado City had long been an important centre of Mormon settlement. After the Mormon church disavowed **polygamy** in 1890, the Arizona Strip was a major refuge for recalcitrant polygamists. During the 1930s, Short Creek became the home of the Fundamentalist Church of Jesus Christ of Latter-Day Saints, who preached that by maintaining polygamy they were keeping true Mormonism alive. The community's location, straddling the state line, made it easier to avoid outside investigation; residents could simply cross between Arizona and Utah to escape police enquiries. Nonetheless, repeated state and federal enquiries culminated in the **Short Creek Raid** of 1953, when Arizona governor Howard Pyle ordered a massive police swoop that saw 23 polygamist men hauled off for trial in Kingman.

Pyle's anti-polygamy campaign backfired, amid much negative publicity about separated families and children left without their fathers. Each of the accused menfolk of Short Creek received a year's probation, while Pyle lost his bid for re-election. To erase the name from public memory, Short Creek residents voted in 1958 to divide the town in two, becoming **Colorado City** in Arizona, and **Hildale** in Utah.

The issue of polygamy in Colorado City has returned to the national headlines in recent years, sparking furious political controversy in both Arizona and Utah. In the first few years of the twenty-first century, exposé after exposé revealed that despite continuing to benefit hugely from state and federal funding, Colorado City was the virtual fiefdom of a small group of Mormon polygamists. The Fundamentalist Church of Latter Day Saints was run by the self-styled "Prophet" **Rulon Jeffs**. Not only did he assign the town's young women, often in their early teens, as brides to his middle-aged and already multiply-married cronies – and conduct the wedding ceremonies

being able to hike along the remainder of the road as far as the overlooks. Be sure to enquire locally about current driving conditions before you set off; the best sources of information are the visitor centres at Pipe Springs, Fredonia, Jacob Lake and the Grand Canyon North Rim. In addition, carry all the food, water and gas you might need, plus a spare tyre and emergency repair kit for your vehicle.

Sunshine Route

The **Sunshine Route** to Toroweap begins with a southward turn off AZ-389 seven miles west of Fredonia, onto **BLM road 109**. This is a broad, well-surfaced gravel road, albeit subject to "washboarding" (becoming corrugated by bone-jarring little undulations), that passes through a succession of wide open valleys first recorded by the Domínguez and Escalante party of 1776 (see p.130). Much of the country here is rangeland, grazed within an inch of its life. You don't see so much as a tree during the first hour, and precious few thereafter.

Thirty miles in, the road leaves the plain and enters a range of smooth volcanic cinder cones. Ten miles farther, it meets **BLM road 5** – the Clayhole Route mentioned above – coming down from Colorado City. The final thirteen miles south to the national park lie just within the eastern boundary of **Grand Canyon–Parashant National Monument**. Halfway along, BLM road 5 veers west towards Mount Trumbull, as described on p.145, so the last few miles to Toroweap are on **BLM road 115**.

Tuweep

A sign just over six miles short of Toroweap Point welcomes visitors to the **Tuweep Area** of Grand Canyon National Park. While the conspicuous roadside himself – but he also presided over a system in which as many of four hundred of its young men, their own children, were run out of town as they came of age so they could not become rival bridegrooms. Many ended up as homeless addicts in neighbouring towns, while the prevalence of cousin marriages has ensured that the child population of Colorado City displays high levels of severe mental retardation.

After Rulon's death in 2002, his son **Warren Jeffs** succeeded him as Prophet, and within a week married all but two of his nineteen wives (not his own mother). A federal warrant for Warren's arrest was issued in 2005, on charges of sexual conduct with a minor and conspiracy to commit sexual conduct with a minor. During his subsequent fifteen months on the run, he's known to have performed further marriages in Colorado City, while figuring on the FBI's "Ten Most Wanted" list.

Along with many of the town's menfolk, Jeffs spent time in a linked polygamist community in Eldorado, Texas, which became notorious following federal raids in 2008. Jeffs himself was, however, arrested in Nevada in 2006, and found guilty in St George in 2007 of two charges of first degree rape for authorizing the marriage of a fourteen-year-old girl to her nineteen-year-old cousin. As this book went to press, Jeffs was still in prison, though his Utah conviction was overturned in 2010 on the basis of erroneous instructions to the jury and he was awaiting extradition to Texas to face charges similar to those that had already landed seven men from the Eldorado compound in jail.

Meanwhile Colorado City is in complete chaos. Evidence of widespread financial fraud resulted in the dismantling of the church's property holdings, but with its inhabitants and law enforcement officials alike refusing to implement or respect court decisions, the town's Department of Public Safety was closed down in 2010.

ranger station immediately beyond is not open to any fixed hours, and cannot be contacted by phone, a ranger is in residence year round, though not always available on site. General information about the area is available on the main park website, Ⓦnps.gov/grca.

The last six miles to the overlook from here are by far the roughest stretch of the drive. Expect to take a little under two hours to reach the ranger station from the highway, and then another half-hour to nurse your protesting vehicle to the canyon rim. A mile before the end, you come to the main section of the Park Service's exposed **primitive campground**, which holds a total of ten sites. All are free; nine are first-come, first-served, while one is a group site, which can be reserved by emailing Ⓔgrca_bic@nps.gov up to four months in advance. Fires are allowed, but you have to bring your own firewood, and there are composting toilets but no water. **No fee** is charged for day use or overnighting at the campground, but you do need to buy a permit in advance, as detailed on p.90, for **backcountry camping**.

Incidentally, although the Paiute terms "Tuweep" and "Toroweap" are used more or less interchangeably in these parts, strictly speaking, "Toroweap", which means "dry valley," is applied to a valley, the geological fault that created that valley, one of the strata in the canyon as a whole and an overlook, while "Tuweep," meaning "the earth," referred first to a Mormon settlement in the valley and now to this district of the park.

Toroweap Overlook

What doesn't quite sink in until you reach the end of the road at Toroweap is that this is an utterly unique segment of the Grand Canyon. Everywhere else, there are effectively two canyons in one, consisting of a towering rim, separated

Grand Canyon–Parashant National Monument

President Bill Clinton flew into Toroweap Valley by helicopter on January 11, 2000, to create the vast **Grand Canyon–Parashant National Monument**, covering over a million acres of northwestern Arizona. Such presidential proclamations skirt the normal legal requirements for public discussion and approval by state legislators; Theodore Roosevelt used the same strategy when he proclaimed the original Grand Canyon National Monument back in 1908. Both the governor of Arizona and the majority of its congressional delegation opposed the Clinton move.

The monument is bounded to the west by the Nevada border, and to the east and northeast by the drainage of the Virgin River (only a tiny portion of which crosses into Arizona). To the south, it either runs up against **Grand Canyon National Park** at or near the rim of the canyon, or meets, and shares jurisdiction with, the **Lake Mead National Recreation Area**. It's also scattered with parcels of Arizona state land; a few private landholdings; and several designated wilderness areas. The 808,000 of its acres that lie outside the Lake Mead NRA are administered by the **Bureau of Land Management**, and the rest by the **National Park Service**.

The point of creating Grand Canyon–Parashant was not to increase tourist visitation, but to preserve this little-known region's geological, archeological and natural resources. The new monument straddles the boundary between two major geological "provinces": the "Basin and Range" country to the west, and the Colorado Plateau to the east. Its central feature, the **Shivwits Plateau**, is the westernmost segment of the Colorado Plateau, which drops down the dramatic escarpment of the **Grand Wash Cliffs** on its western edge to meet the eastern **Mohave Desert**. While boasting a rich fossil record, it remains home to many rare animal and plant species; some sections have been set aside as sanctuaries for **desert tortoises**, and the programme of re-releasing **Californian condors** has been active here too (see p.40). Although few visitors are aware that the monument even exists, in terms of protecting the overall ecosystem of the Grand Canyon, ecologists insist it has effectively doubled the size of Grand Canyon National Park.

While the human presence has ranged from early hunters, via Ancestral Puebloans to Mormon ranchers, the region remains all but uninhabited and only minimally exploited. The monument is obliged to respect existing grazing and hunting rights, but no new mining or geothermal activity will be permitted.

Very few roads penetrate the monument, and none of them is paved. With a high-clearance 4WD vehicle, it's possible to visit remote western Grand Canyon viewpoints such as Whitmore Point, Twin Point and Kelly Point, but even without hiking, all involve demanding multi-day expeditions for which you'll need strong survival skills. Contact the visitor centres in Kanab or Fredonia before you set off, or visit Ⓦ blm.gov/az.

by mighty cliffs and, as a rule, a broad plateau, from the deep, narrow chasm that holds the Colorado River. Here, thanks to volcanic action along the **Toroweap Fault**, that high outer rim is absent on the north side of the river, and the road is able to follow the **Toroweap Valley** right to the brink of the inner Granite Gorge. From the end, it's therefore possible to gaze straight down upon the river.

You come to a halt at a wide, rocky hilltop that holds a couple of picnic tables. Anyone used to Grand Canyon viewpoints further east may find it hard to believe that this can really be the canyon; there are no buttes and pyramids, or labyrinthine spurs and mesas. Tiptoe to the southern edge of the car park, however, and the ground suddenly drops three thousand feet from your feet.

You're now at the **Toroweap Overlook**, which at 4600ft is the lowest viewpoint within the national park. Though you can see the river approaching from the east and flowing away to the west, it's so directly below that in places you may have to lie full length and peep over the edge to see it right here. The cliffs on the other side of the river, which belongs to the Hualapai reservation (see Chapter 8), soar thousands of feet higher.

Lava Falls Overlook

A five-minute hike over the boulder-strewn clifftop west of the Toroweap Overlook – there's no fixed trail – leads to the stupendous west-facing **Lava Falls Overlook**. The view of the river here, turning from green to blue as it recedes towards the horizon, and interspersed with mighty white rapids, is so spellbinding that you may not at first notice the most awesome feature of the landscape. Straight ahead, a few hundred feet below eye level, a colossal black **lava cascade** spills over the North Rim and pours down to within a few feet of the Colorado.

This lava bears witness to some of the most dramatic episodes in the canyon's history. On at least eight separate occasions, **volcanic eruptions** atop the Esplanade Plateau in this region have filled the Grand Canyon to a depth of as much as 2330ft, and thus **blocked the Colorado**. The largest flow, around 1.2 million years ago, created the long-vanished **Prospect Dam**, which backed the river up to form a lake that stretched all the way east to Lees Ferry. Geologists estimate that it would have taken 23 years to fill to the brim; then the Colorado burst over the top, and, eventually, wore the dam entirely away. Vestiges of such events can be seen at various heights on the canyon walls – the most recent was around 140,000 years ago – and make it possible to work out the speed at which the canyon grows deeper.

The same flow that dammed the Grand Canyon also filled a number of side canyons up to the brim, including **Prospect Canyon**, south of the river and **Toroweap Valley** here. That explains why it's flat enough for the road to run all the way to the rim, and also why you probably won't have noticed that Toroweap Valley even exists. What was once the valley mouth is now topped by a 567ft cinder cone known as **Vulcan's Throne**, which prevents any water that flows down the valley from reaching the river; instead, after heavy rains a small lake collects on its northern side.

Down below, a solitary black basaltic column known as **Vulcan's Anvil** sticks up 40ft from the middle of the river. For rafters, it's a telltale marker that the fearsome **Lava Falls Rapid**, created by debris washed down from Prospect Canyon, lurks just around the next bend. From here, however, you can both see the rapid and hear it roar. Until a flash flood radically redesigned Crystal Rapid in 1966 (see p.193), this was generally recognized as the most difficult whitewater challenge in the canyon.

Main Street Route

Though described here as an alternative route from Toroweap back to civilization, the **Main Street Route** is also the most direct way to approach Toroweap if you're coming from the west, as its terminus, **St George**, Utah, stands on the I-15 interstate between Las Vegas and Salt Lake City. A spectacular ninety-mile, three-hour desert drive on gravel roads, it's very straightforward in summer, but liable to be closed altogether in winter.

Starting from the Tuweep ranger station, you drive 7.5 miles north, and then turn left when you meet **BLM road 5**. This climbs west into the **Uinkaret Mountains**, the volcanic field responsible for all those eruptions. Uinkaret is a Paiute word meaning "place of pines"; you'll see why ten miles along, when you reach the high pine-forested saddle between **Mount Logan** to the south and the

8026ft **Mount Trumbull** to the north. In the late nineteenth century, timber from here was hauled north to construct the Mormon Temple at St George. In another five miles, you crest a final ridge to face a hair-raising descent into the huge **Hurricane Valley**.

Now located within but nevertheless not part of Grand Canyon–Parashant National Monument, Hurricane Valley used to be home to a Mormon ranching and mining community. Founded by Abraham Bundy in 1916 as **Mount Trumbull**, it was universally known as "Bundyville", as most of its peak of almost three hundred inhabitants seemed to be called Bundy. The settlement lasted for around fifty years, before being defeated partly by drought and partly by the fact that improved roads and vehicles meant ranchers could live in St George and commute to their land.

The flat desolate crossroads in the heart of the valley holds the last remaining vestige of Bundyville, the four-square **Mount Trumbull Schoolhouse**, which is generally open during daylight hours. Built in 1922, this was burned to the ground in 2000, but it has since been rebuilt from scratch, and holds old schoolbooks and an awful lot of photos of Bundys.

Make a right turn at the schoolhouse to stay on BLM road 5. Then head due north, on what eventually becomes **BLM road 1069**. After passing through the dramatic **Wolf Hole Valley** and down into some eerie gray badlands beside the **Mokaac Wash**, you'll reach the sanctuary of a paved tarmac road in suburban St George after another 49 miles.

6

Flagstaff and
Route 66

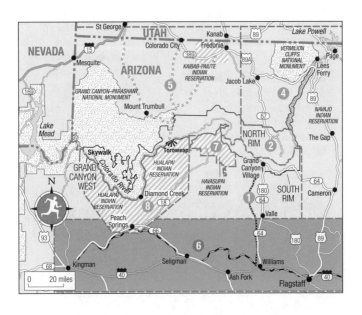

CHAPTER 6

Highlights

✳ **DuBeau and Grand Canyon International Hostels** These sister hostels in downtown Flagstaff offer budget travellers bargain lodging and cut-rate canyon tours. See p.153

✳ **Monte Vista** Characterful old Western hotel in Flagstaff with attractive rooms and a lively downstairs bar. See p.153

✳ **Downtown Flagstaff** Bisected by Route 66 and the Santa Fe Railroad, Flagstaff's bustling downtown abounds with Western atmosphere. See p.154

✳ **Museum of Northern Arizona** Just outside Flagstaff, this superb museum explains the history and geography of the Colorado Plateau in fascinating detail. See p.154

✳ **Wupatki National Monument** From these remarkably complete thousand-year-old pueblos in the remote desert, ancient astronomers plotted solar calendars. See p.159

✳ **Walnut Canyon National Monument** Extraordinary site east of Flagstaff, where the Sinagua people carved hundreds of homes into the canyon walls. See p.159

✳ **Pine Country Restaurant** The pies at this central Williams diner will leave your jaw dropping...and then munching furiously. See p.162

✳ **Seligman** Soak up genuine Route 66 ambience in this time-forgotten desert outpost. See p.163

▲ The Museum Club, on Route 66 in Flagstaff

6

Flagstaff and Route 66

T
hanks to the forbidding terrain of which the Grand Canyon is merely the most extreme example, Arizona's northernmost hundred miles remain impassable to east–west traffic. That makes the **I-40** interstate, which runs pretty much straight across the state roughly sixty miles south of the canyon, a crucial lifeline. Before the interstate was pushed through, the legendary **Route 66** followed much the same path; before either road, there was the Santa Fe Railroad; and before the railroad arrived, little more than a century ago, there were no significant Anglo settlements in the region at all.

The pick of the various communities along this corridor that compete to serve as "gateways" for Grand Canyon travellers is unquestionably the college town of **Flagstaff**. Set in the world's largest stand of sweet-smelling **ponderosa pine forest** – lumber from which provided the basis for the region's pioneer nineteenth-century economy – it ranks among the Southwest's most appealing small towns, while the deserts just to the east hold the intriguing ancient sites of **Wupatki** and **Walnut Canyon**.

While **Williams**, to the west, is closer to the canyon and acts as the starting point for excursion trains up to the South Rim, it's unlikely to hold your attention for any length of time. Both **Ash Fork** and **Seligman** are tiny desert outposts, while larger **Kingman** lacks much sense of identity. That said, all of these places became reliant on tourism during the heyday of **Route 66**, and driving through any one of them can always bring on a frisson of that era's romance.

Flagstaff

Northern Arizona's liveliest and most attractive town, **FLAGSTAFF**, occupies a superbly dramatic location beneath the San Francisco Peaks, halfway between New Mexico and California. Straddling the I-40 and I-17 interstates, it's a major waystation for tourists en route to the Grand Canyon, just eighty miles northwest, but it's also a worthwhile destination in its own right.

Downtown, where barely a building rises more than three storey, oozes Wild West charm. Its main thoroughfare, Santa Fe Avenue, used to be **Route 66**, while

FLAGSTAFF AND ROUTE 66

Tuba City & Monument Valley ▲

Winslow & Albuquerque ▲

Phoenix ▶

Las Vegas ▼

The Gap

NAVAJO INDIAN RESERVATION

Little Colorado River

Cameron

Gray Mountain

89

WUPATKI NATIONAL MONUMENT

SUNSET CRATER NATIONAL MONUMENT

WALNUT CANYON NATIONAL MONUMENT

San Francisco Peaks

Flagstaff

64

180

40

Desert View

Point Imperial

Cape Royal

NORTH RIM

SOUTH RIM

Phantom Ranch

Bright Angel Point

Grand Canyon Village

Tusayan

180
64

Valle

Red Lake

Williams

64

Fire Point

GRAND CANYON RAILWAY

Crazy Jug Point

Colorado River

HAVASUPAI INDIAN RESERVATION

Supai

Hualapai Hilltop

COCONINO PLATEAU

Ash Fork

89

Seligman

Toroweap Overlook

Tuweep

Lava Falls Overlook

Mount Trumbull

HUALAPAI INDIAN RESERVATION

18

HISTORIC ROUTE 66

66

Mount Trumbull

GRAND CANYON–PARASHANT NATIONAL MONUMENT

Diamond Creek

Peach Springs

Truxton

Valentine

40

Guano Point

Skywalk

Eagle Point

Quartermaster Point

GRAND CANYON WEST

BUCK AND DOE ROAD

HUALAPAI INDIAN RESERVATION

Antares Point

Hackberry

ANTARES ROAD

DIAMOND BAR ROAD

Pearce Ferry

LAKE MEAD NATIONAL RECREATION AREA

Temple Bar

Lake Mead

PEARCE FERRY ROAD

STOCKTON HILL ROAD

Chloride

Kingman

93

68

Oatman

Grand Canyon National Park

0   10 miles

N

before that it was the pioneer trail west. A stroll around its central few blocks is gloriously evocative of the past, though these days the diners and saloons are interspersed with outfitter stores and coffee bars, and the local cowboys and Indians share the sidewalks with liberal-minded students from Northern Arizona University. Just to add to the atmosphere, the tracks of the Santa Fe Railroad still divide downtown in two, so life in Flagstaff remains punctuated both day and night by the mournful wail of passing trains.

Flagstaff's first settlers arrived in 1876, lured from Boston by widely publicized accounts of mineral wealth and fertile land. Although they soon moved on, disappointed, towards Prescott, they stayed long enough to celebrate the centenary of American independence by flying the Stars and Stripes from a towering pine tree. This flagpole became a familiar landmark on the route west, and as the town grew it inevitably became known as Flagstaff. Right from the start, it was a cosmopolitan place, with a strong black and Hispanic population working in the (originally Mormon-owned) lumber mills and in the cattle industry, and Navajo and Hopi heading in from the nearby reservations to trade.

Modern Flagstaff, with a population of a little over fifty thousand, makes an ideal base for travellers. As well as the abundant hotels, restaurants, bars and shops within easy walking distance of downtown, outlets of the national food and lodging chains line the interstates slightly further afield, and budget travellers too are well catered for by hostels and student diners. There are also a couple of good museums nearby, together with some wonderful scenery and ancient sites in the close vicinity. Just one word of warning: the altitude here is almost 7000ft, which means the nights may well be colder than you're expecting. It can even snow in July.

Arrival, information and getting around

While the Santa Fe Railroad still hauls freight, Amtrak's daily **Southwest Chief**, between Chicago and Los Angeles, is now the only passenger **train** that stops at Flagstaff's venerable wooden stationhouse, in the heart of town. In summer, the eastbound service arrives from Los Angeles at 5.16am and the westbound arrives from Albuquerque at 8.51pm; winter times are one hour later.

Greyhound, a few blocks south of downtown at 399 S Malpais Lane (☎928/774-4573 or 1-800/231-2222, ⊛greyhound.com), runs five daily buses to Phoenix and also heads east towards Albuquerque and west to Las Vegas, LA, San Diego and San Francisco.

Flagstaff is also home to the tiny **Pulliam Airport**, six miles south of downtown at 6200 S Pulliam Drive, which is connected several times daily with Phoenix on US Airways (⊛usairways.com).

Getting to the Grand Canyon

As detailed on p.41, **Arizona Shuttle** (☎928/226-8060 or 1-877/226-8060, ⊛arizonashuttle.com) runs two or three **bus services** each day from **Flagstaff's** Amtrak station to *Maswik Lodge* in **Grand Canyon Village** (one-way $28, under-12s $20). Two buses follow a route via Williams; one leaves Flagstaff at 8am and reaches the *Maswik* at 9.45am, the other leaves Flagstaff at 3.45pm and gets to the *Maswik* at 5.45pm. Between March and October, a third bus leaves Flagstaff at 2pm and goes straight to the *Maswik*, arriving at 3.45pm. Arizona Shuttle also offers nine daily **buses** between Flagstaff and **Phoenix** ($39), and two to **Sedona** ($25).

Flagstaff companies offering **day-trip tours to the Grand Canyon**, at typical rates of just over $100 per day, include Around The Bend (☎928/213-5573 or

1-888/769-2269, Ⓦ walkgrandcanyon.com), Angel's Gate Tours (Ⓣ 928/814-2277 or 1-800/957-4457, Ⓦ seegrandcanyon.com) and Seven Wonders (Ⓣ 928/526-2501 or 1-888/298-7477, Ⓦ sevenwondersscenictours.com).

Two local hostels, the *DuBeau* and the *Grand Canyon*, also offer inexpensive Grand Canyon excursions, as described below.

Information

Flagstaff's helpful **visitor centre** occupies half of the Amtrak stationhouse at 1 E Route 66 (Mon–Sat 8am–5pm, Sun 9am–4pm; Ⓣ 928/774-9541 or 1-800/379-0065, Ⓦ www.flagstaffarizona.org). Even when it's not staffed, the building remains open for rail passengers, so visitors can still pick up brochures and **discount coupons** for local motels. You'll also find a courtesy phone in the Amtrak lobby for making hotel and hostel reservations (daily 8am–5pm).

Rentals and outfitters

Most of the major **car rental** chains have outlets in Flagstaff. Absolute Bikes, 202 E Route 66 (Ⓣ 928/779-5969, Ⓦ www.absolutebikes.net), rents **bikes** at $40 for the first day and $30 for subsequent days.

Several **outfitters** based in central Flagstaff offer equipment for outdoor activities and backpacking expeditions, including Aspen Sports, 15 N San Francisco St (Ⓣ 928/779-1935, Ⓦ flagstaffsportinggoods.com).

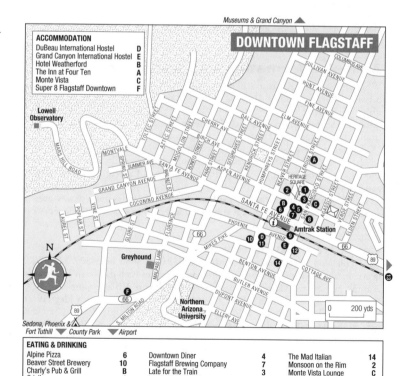

DOWNTOWN FLAGSTAFF

Museums & Grand Canyon ▲

ACCOMMODATION	
DuBeau International Hostel	D
Grand Canyon International Hostel	E
Hotel Weatherford	B
The Inn at Four Ten	A
Monte Vista	C
Super 8 Flagstaff Downtown	F

Lowell Observatory

Greyhound

Northern Arizona University

Amtrak Station

0   200 yds

Sedona, Phoenix & ▲
Fort Tuthill ▼ County Park ▼ Airport

EATING & DRINKING					
Alpine Pizza	6	Downtown Diner	4	The Mad Italian	14
Beaver Street Brewery	10	Flagstaff Brewing Company	7	Monsoon on the Rim	2
Charly's Pub & Grill	B	Late for the Train	3	Monte Vista Lounge	C
Criollo	8	Lumberyard Brewing		The Museum Club	13
Dara Thai	12	Company	9	Pasto	5
Diablo Burger	1	Macy's European Coffee House	11		

Accommodation

As Flagstaff is considerably more than just another interstate pit stop, its dozens of **motels** and **B&Bs** charge higher rates than its I-40 neighbours. They're still not bad value, however, while **budget** travellers can choose between two hostels. Most chain motels are clustered well to the east, but staying close to downtown is much more fun. It's worth knowing that if you do manage to find a room where the lonesome whistle of freight trains doesn't wake you up in the night, it's unlikely to be anywhere near Flagstaff.

If you arrive without a reservation, use the free **courtesy phones** in the visitor centre (see opposite) to compare options. Above all, plan ahead on summer weekends, when the town is likely to be booked solid.

The nicest local **campground** lies three miles south on US-89A, at *Fort Tuthill County Park* (May–Sept; ☏928/679-8000), though Flagstaff also holds a year-round commercial site, *Flagstaff KOA* at 5803 N AZ-89A (☏928/526-9926 or 1-800/562-3524, ⓦkoa.com). Best of all, contact the Coconino National Forest for details of its "Room With A View" **cabin rentals** in the nearby woods (☏928/527-3600, ⓦwww.fs.fed.us/r3/coconino).

DuBeau International Hostel 19 W Phoenix Ave ☏928/774-6731 or 1-800/398-7112, ⓦdubeauhostel.com. Welcoming independent hostel just south of the tracks, whose spotless, appealingly converted en-suite motel rooms serve as four-person dorms (❶) at $20 per bed, or private doubles (❷) at $45 Sun–Thurs or $48 Fri & Sat. Internet access is available, with free wi-fi, and breakfast is free too, but the common areas can get noisy at times. Free pick-up from Greyhound, car rental discounts and tours to the Grand Canyon ($75; Mon, Wed & Sat, plus Fri in summer only).

Grand Canyon International Hostel 19 S San Francisco St ☏928/779-9421 or 1-888/442-2696, ⓦgrandcanyonhostel.com. Independent hostel, under the same friendly management as the similar nearby *DuBeau*, but with a significantly quieter overall ambience. Dorm beds (❶) at $20 and six private rooms (❷) priced at $42–45. For tours, see the *DuBeau*, above.

Holiday Inn Express 2320 E Lucky Lane ☏928/714-1000, ⓦhiflagstaff.com. Large motel in a rather characterless area just off the interstate, with a handful of nearby diners. ❺

Hotel Weatherford 23 N Leroux St ☏928/779-1919, ⓦweatherfordhotel.com. Attractive old downtown hotel, with elegant wooden fittings, which has been progressively restored as a true labour of love. The finest rooms offer tasteful accommodation, with antique furnishings and clawfoot tubs plus phones and TVs; five more en-suite rooms are smaller and cheaper; and three large but basic ones share a bathroom. The upstairs lounge offers Wild West ambience, but can make for a noisy night. ❷–❻

The Inn at Four Ten 410 N Leroux St ☏928/774-0088 or 1-800/774-2008, ⓦinn410.com. Bright ranch home operating as a luxurious antique-furnished B&B; all nine rooms are en suite, most with fireplaces and three with whirlpool tubs. On summer evenings, the porch and patio make welcoming, convivial retreats. ❻

Little America 2515 E Butler Ave ☏928/779-7900 or 1-800/865-1401, ⓦflagstaff.littleamerica.com. Large motel-cum-resort near the interstate, where the 1950s-style ambience conceals a higher standard of accommodation than you might expect. Good pool. ❻

Monte Vista 100 N San Francisco St ☏928/779-6971 or 1-800/545-3068, ⓦhotelmontevista.com. Attractive landmark 1920s hotel in the heart of downtown. The assorted restored rooms, with and without attached bathrooms, are named after celebrity guests, from Bob Hope to Michael Stipe; Paul McCartney stayed here in 2008. Many of the guests are young international travellers, drawn by the local nightlife, including the hotel's own bar (see p.156). Weekend rates typically rise by $20. ❸–❻

Super 8 Flagstaff Downtown 602 W Route 66; ☏928/774-4581 or 1-800/800-8000, ⓦsuper8.com. Attractive chain motel centred on an enclosed swimming pool, adjacent to a Barnes & Noble bookstore less than a mile southwest of downtown, just past the US-89 turn-off towards Sedona. ❹

Super 8 I-40 Flagstaff Mall 3725 N Kasper Ave ☏928/526-0818 or 1-888/324-9131, ⓦsuper8.com. Decent budget motel four miles east of downtown, right where Route 66 joins US-89. ❹

The Town

Flagstaff's little-changed **downtown** stretches for a few red-brick blocks north of the railroad. Filled with cafés, bars and stores selling Route 66 souvenirs and Native American crafts, as well as outfitters specializing in tents, clothing and all sorts of contraptions for outdoor adventures, it's a fun place to wander around, even if it holds no significant tourist attractions. Although the visitor centre maps out walking tours, few specific buildings are especially historic; by the time you've browsed a few bookstores, downed a few coffees and peeped into the old *Weatherford* and *Monte Vista* hotels, you may well be ready to move on.

During the 1960s, when this whole area had become seriously run-down, it was about to be demolished to construct car parks for Route 66 visitors; the flaw in the plan was that it would have left no Route 66 to visit. Instead ongoing restoration efforts have brought the place back to life. The most recent development is a welcome open plaza known as **Heritage Square**, off Aspen Avenue between Leroux and San Francisco streets. While hardly inspiring architecturally, it makes a good venue for events of all kinds, from concerts by local bands to dance and music performances by Hopi Indians.

Ultimately, though, your most lasting impression of downtown Flagstaff is likely to be of the magnificent volcanic **San Francisco Peaks**, rising smoothly from the plains on the northern horizon, and topped by a jagged ridge.

Museum of Northern Arizona

The exceptional **Museum of Northern Arizona**, three miles northwest of downtown on US-180, rivals Phoenix's Heard Museum as the best museum in the state, and makes an essential first stop for any first-time visitor to the Colorado Plateau (daily 9am–5pm; $5, under-18s $4; ☏928/774-5213, ⓦmusnaz.org). Although it covers local geology, geography, flora and fauna – and can help you come to grips with the various attempts to explain the origins of the Grand Canyon – its main emphasis is on documenting **Native American** life. It starts with an excellent run-through of the Ancestral Puebloan past, featuring stone knife blades still set in their wooden handles, an intact ancient loom and a collection of pottery miniatures whose purpose remains unknown. Attention then turns to contemporary Navajo, Havasupai, Zuni and Hopi cultures, with rooms devoted to pots, rugs, *kachina* dolls, and silver and turquoise jewellery. There are also temporary shows of local (not always Native American) arts and crafts, a well-stocked bookstore and a **nature trail** that runs through the small pinon-fringed canyon outside.

Ever since it was established, in 1928, the museum has actively encouraged traditional and even new skills among Native American craftworkers. The exquisite inlaid silver jewellery now made by the Hopi, for example, resulted from a museum-backed programme to find work for Hopi servicemen returning from World War II. During its annual Native American Marketplaces, every item is for sale; the **Zuni** show is in late May, the **Hopi** show on the weekend closest to July 4 and the **Navajo** one at the start of August.

For details of **Museum of Northern Arizona Ventures**, an extensive programme of tours and expeditions, which include multi-day Grand Canyon trips, see p.26 or visit ⓦwww.mnaventures.org.

Pioneer Museum

Alongside US-180, a little closer to town than the Museum of Northern Arizona, an impressive steam train guards the **Pioneer Museum** (Mon–Sat 9am–5pm; $5; ⓦarizonahistoricalsociety.org). Run by the Arizona Historical Society, and housed in what was once the county hospital, the museum holds a random but reasonably entertaining assortment of objects and images from old Flagstaff.

Sharing the same grounds, the **Coconino Center for the Arts** combines a concert hall with a gallery specializing in works by local artists (Tues–Sat 11am–5pm; Ⓦculturalpartners.org).

Lowell Observatory

Flagstaff's **Lowell Observatory**, located in the pine forest atop Mars Hill, a mile west of downtown, is famous as the place where the existence of the dwarf planet Pluto was first confirmed. Many of the necessary calculations were performed by Dr Percival Lowell, who founded the observatory in 1894 and also deluded himself that he'd discovered canals on Mars. Lowell died in 1916 – he's buried in a small domed mausoleum of blue glass on the hilltop – and Pluto was eventually spotted in 1930 by Clyde Tombaugh. Regarded for many years thereafter as the ninth planet, it was finally demoted in status in 2006.

From the **visitor centre** (daily: March–Oct 9am–5.30pm; Nov–Feb noon–5pm; $8, under-18s $4; ℡928/774-3358, Ⓦwww.lowell.edu), where only very technically minded visitors are likely to get much joy from playing with computers or watching explanatory movies, the **Pluto Walk** footpath climbs up to the tiny original observatory. Signs tick off the relative positions of the planets; if it kept going on the same scale, it would have to extend over six hundred miles, beyond Boise, Idaho, to show the position of the nearest star, Alpha Centauri.

Astronomy remains a passion in Flagstaff, and the town has won awards for minimizing night-time light pollution. The observatory reopens most evenings for after-dark **stargazing sessions** (June–Aug Mon–Sat 5.30–10pm; Sept–May Mon, Wed, Fri & Sat till 9.30pm; no additional charge).

Eating

While surprisingly short of high-end **restaurants**, central Flagstaff holds a lively assortment of both old-style Western **diners** and eclectic **budget** options. Thanks to all those students, the area around San Francisco Street, both north and south of the tracks, is filled with vegetarian cafés and espresso bars.

Alpine Pizza 7 N Leroux St ℡928/779-4109. Raucous downtown student hangout, with decent pizzas and lots of different beers. Mon–Sat 11.30am–2pm & 5–11pm, Sun 5–11pm.

Black Bart's 2760 E Butler Ave ℡928/779-3142. Enjoyable Western-themed steakhouse, across from *Little America* on the east edge of town, with waiting staff who sing and dance onstage between servings of barbecued steak, ribs and chicken ($19–30). Daily 5–10pm.

Charly's Pub & Grill *Hotel Weatherford*, 23 N Leroux St ℡928/779-1919. Café-restaurant in a classy Western setting, serving good, inexpensive meals accompanied by live music (cocktail piano at lunch, bands at night). Daily 8am–10pm, bar stays open later.

Criollo 16 N San Francisco St ℡928/774-0541. Smart, spacious restaurant, serving Latin American food worth lingering over. The full menu includes tapas as well as substantial dishes like pork belly

tacos, vegetarian quinoa fritters or *ropa vieja* (braised beef); nothing costs over $20. Mon–Thurs 11am–10pm, Fri till midnight, Sat 9am–midnight, Sun till 10pm.

Dara Thai 14 S San Francisco St ℡928/774-0047. Large Thai place just south of the tracks, where the service is great and a plate of delicious pad thai noodles costs just $8 at lunch, $10 at dinner. Mon–Fri 11am–10pm, Sat noon–10pm, Sun 4–9pm.

Diablo Burger 120 N Leroux St ℡928/774-3274. Stylish joint in the centre of town, with outdoor seating on Heritage Square. The $8–10 burgers feature exclusively local ingredients, most obviously free-range hormone-free cattle. Mon–Wed 11am–9pm, Thurs–Sat till 11pm.

Downtown Diner 7 E Aspen Ave ℡928/774-3492. Classic Route 66 diner a block north of the main drag, featuring leatherette booths and hefty burgers and sandwiches. Nothing costs over $10. Mon–Sat 5.30am–9pm, Sun 7am–6pm.

Late for the Train 107 N San Francisco St ☏ 928/779-5975. Little coffee bar opposite the *Monte Vista* that serves excellent home-roasted coffee and pastries to a slightly older, literary crowd. Sun–Thurs 6am–6pm, Fri & Sat till 9pm.

Macy's European Coffee House & Bakery 14 S Beaver St ☏ 928/774-2243. Not merely superb coffee, but heavenly pastries to go with it, in a chaotic but friendly, student-oriented atmosphere. Substantial vegetarian dishes include black bean pizza and even couscous for breakfast. You'll also find free wi-fi and an adjacent coin laundry. Daily 6am–10pm.

Monsoon on the Rim 6 E Aspen Ave ☏ 928/226-8844. This pan-Asian, sushi-centred restaurant, with huge plate-glass windows, clearly has more to do with the new West than the Old West. While pretty good rather than wonderful, the food is surprisingly cheap, with most of the Thai and Chinese options priced around $8 at lunchtime, $10 in the evening and the people-watching is fun. Mon–Sat 11.30am–9pm.

Pasto 19 E Aspen Ave ☏ 928/779-1937. Large downtown Italian place, with pasta dishes at $9 or $17 depending on size, and chicken, shrimp and vegetarian dishes for $18–24. Daily 11am–2pm & 5–9.30pm.

Nightlife

Milling with international travellers in summer and students the rest of the year, Flagstaff is the liveliest **nightspot** between Las Vegas and Santa Fe. Wander a block or two to either side of San Francisco Street downtown, both north and south of the railroad tracks, and you can't go wrong. Besides the *Monte Vista Lounge*, hotel bars that feature live music include both the *Exchange Pub* and the upstairs *Zane Grey Ballroom* at the *Weatherford*.

Beaver Street Brewery 11 S Beaver St ☏ 928/779-0079. Popular microbrewery that also serves inventive and inexpensive food, with an outdoor BBQ in the beer garden on Wednesday nights in summer. Sun–Wed 11am–1am, Thurs–Sat until 2am.

Flagstaff Brewing Company 16 E I-40 ☏ 928/773-1442. Bustling downtown pub, with outdoor seating, big windows and live music Thurs–Sat, plus a morning espresso bar. Daily 11am–2am.

Lumberyard Brewing Company 5 S San Francisco St ☏ 928/779-2739. Flagstaff's newest brewpub, immediately south of the tracks and run by the same team as the *Beaver St Brewery*, serves a full menu of home-brewed beers, sandwiches and deli snacks. Sun–Tues 11am–10pm, Wed–Sat 11am–2am.

The Mad Italian 101 S San Francisco St ☏ 928/779-1820. Highly sociable downtown bar with several pool tables. Daily 2pm–2am.

Monte Vista Lounge *Monte Vista*, 100 N San Francisco St ☏ 928/779-6971. Hip little bar and dance club in the basement of a venerable old hotel, with frequent live music or DJs. Daily 4pm until late.

The Museum Club 3404 E Route 66 ☏ 928/526-9434, ⓦ www.myspace.com/themuseumclub. A real oddity, this log-cabin taxidermy museum, popularly known as "The Zoo", somehow trans-mogrified into a classic Route 66 roadhouse, saloon and country music venue that's a second home to hordes of dancing cowboys. Daily 11am–2am.

Around Flagstaff

Dominated by the striking **San Francisco Peaks**, the area around Flagstaff is extraordinarily rich in natural and archeological wonders. Three national monuments – **Sunset Crater**, **Wupatki** and **Walnut Canyon** – lie within 25 miles. All are generally seen as day-trips from Flagstaff; only Sunset Crater of the monuments has even a campground.

San Francisco Peaks

The **San Francisco Volcanic Field**, north of Flagstaff, consists of around four hundred distinct volcanic cones, which have formed over the past two million years. During that time, the region has also been covered by glacial ice on three separate occasions, shaving around 3000ft off the top of the volcanoes.

The serrated **SAN FRANCISCO PEAKS**, visible from downtown Flagstaff, are the remnants of a single mountain; their highest point today, at 12,643ft, is the summit of **Mount Humphreys**. They were named by Spanish missionaries in honour of St Francis of Assisi, though the Hopi already knew them as *Nuvatukya'ovi*, the home of the *kachina* spirits, and to the Navajo this was

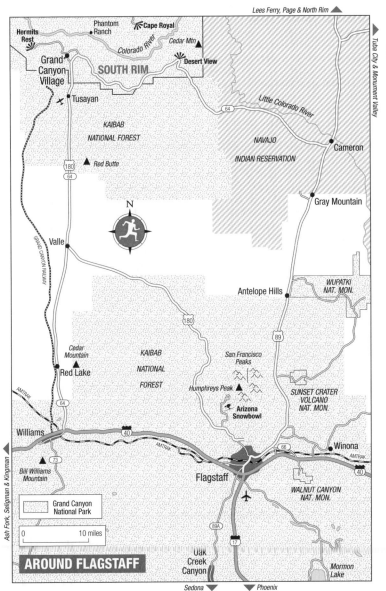

Dook'o'oosliid, one of the four sacred mountains. Seen from afar, topped by a semipermanent layer of clouds, it's obvious why the Hopi and Navajo regarded them as the source of life-giving rain. It's because they were sacred to both that they now belong to neither; federal law dictates that Native American reservations can only include lands of which a tribe can prove it has "exclusive use". The Hopi in particular still make annual pilgrimages on foot from their mesas, 65 miles east, to shrines hidden in the mountains.

Arizona Snowbowl

Considering that the San Francisco Mountain, which has not erupted for 220,000 years, is dormant rather than extinct, the time may come when the gods decide that Flagstaff's own **ski resort**, the **Arizona Snowbowl**, is a desecration no longer to be tolerated. For the moment, it survives, nestling between Mount Humphreys and Mount Agassiz at the end of a seven-mile spur road north of US-180, and featuring ski runs such as "Boo-Boo" and "Bambi". There's not enough water up here to make artificial snow – another early name for the peaks was the **Sierra Sin Agua**, or "waterless range" – so the season typically runs from mid-December to early April. The *Ski Lift Lodge* provides both food and cabin accommodation (☎928/774-0729; ➍), while lift tickets cost $49 for a full day (9am–4pm), or $41 for the afternoon. For more information, contact ☎928/779-1951 or ⓦarizonasnowbowl.com.

In summer, the longest of the Snowbowl's five chair lifts, which climbs to within a few hundred feet of the 12,350ft summit of Mount Agassiz, remains open as the **Scenic Skyride** (mid-May to mid-Sept daily 10am–4pm, mid-Sept to mid-Oct Fri–Sun same hours; $12, under-13s $8). To protect the fragile vegetation, you can't hike any further from there, but there are plenty of other **trails** in the mountains, all intended for day use only. One switchbacks right to the top of Mount Humphreys, giving seventy-mile views to the Grand Canyon and beyond.

Sunset Crater Volcano National Monument

The focus of **SUNSET CRATER VOLCANO NATIONAL MONUMENT**, three miles down a loop road that heads east off US-89 twelve miles north of Flagstaff, is the youngest of the San Francisco volcanoes. Its most recent eruption, around 1045 AD, had a profound impact on the local population and economy. Thick deposits of ash for miles around opened up previously infertile land to cultivation, accelerating – if not triggering – a land rush that threw different Native American cultures into contact and competition for the first time.

John Wesley Powell named Sunset Crater for its multicoloured cone, which swells from a black base through reds and oranges to a yellow-tinged crest. Unfortunately, its shifting cinders are too unstable to allow hikers to climb to the rim. Instead, the one-mile **Lava Flow Trail** at its base offers an up-close look at the jagged black lava that streamed out across the desert, while the steeper one-mile **Lenox Crater Trail** ascends a lesser cone nearby.

All is explained at the **visitor centre** just off the highway (daily: May–Oct 8am–5pm; Nov–April 9am–5pm; ☎928/526-0502, ⓦnps.gov/sucr), opposite the Forest Service's *Bonito* **campground** (late May to mid-Oct; $16; ☎928/527-0866). The monument admission fee ($5 per person) also covers entry to Wupatki.

Sunset Crater is just one of dozens of cones here, up some of which trees have been steadily climbing for a thousand years, while others remain all but untouched by vegetation. Artist James Turrell has spent over thirty years turning one such cone, **Roden Crater**, into a sculptural installation-cum-astronomical observatory, inside which it will one day be possible for paying guests to spend the night.

Wupatki National Monument

A dozen miles north of Sunset Crater along the same loop road, a cluster of several distinct and exceptionally well-preserved ancient ruins, dramatically poised between the volcanoes and the desert, jointly constitute **WUPATKI NATIONAL MONUMENT**. They appear to testify to a period in which different tribal groups lived side by side in harmony. At some time after the Sunset Crater eruption – though not necessarily because of it, as archeologists formerly believed – the Sinagua people already present here, who surely witnessed the explosion, were joined by many others, including the Ancestral Puebloans and the Hohokam. When the rich new soil had been exhausted, around 150 years later, they all moved on once more.

To get the most out of your visit, it's best to start at the monument's excellent **visitor centre** (daily 9am–5pm; $5 per person, including Sunset Crater; ☎928/679-2365, ⓦnps.gov/wupa). If you're arriving from Sunset Crater, it's just past the turn-off for the Wukoki pueblo. Here you'll find informative displays on the history and culture of the Sinagua and their neighbours, placing them firmly within the context of the traditional migration story of their modern descendants, the Hopi.

A paved loop trail leads down from the visitor centre to the main three-storey, hundred-room pueblo block of **Wupatki** ("long cut house") itself, moulded to a sandstone hillock that conceals a number of natural caves. The site's most intriguing features, however, lie a little further along. First comes what seems to be an amphitheatre, a walled circular plaza of unknown purpose. Beyond it is an oval **ball court**, the northernmost such court ever found. Similar arenas throughout central America were used for a game – part ritual, part sport – in which players tried to propel a rubber ball through a stone hoop high on a wall, using their knees and elbows alone, much like modern basketball (except that the losers were sacrificed at the end). Alongside the ball court, cracks in the ground have created a natural **blowhole**, through which air is either sucked or blown depending on pressure and temperature. The audible "breathing" of the earth made this a sacred shrine for Wupatki's ancient inhabitants.

Wukoki, at the end of its own 2.5-mile spur road, takes its name from a modern Hopi word meaning "big house". Reminiscent of the castle-like structures at Hovenweep in southern Utah, it's located within sight of a procession of rounded cinder cones, but was probably positioned for its commanding prospect of the Painted Desert to the north and east. Windows in its central tower – again moulded to the contours of a red-rock outcrop, and built with bricks of the same material – look out in all directions. Archeologists believe some are precisely aligned to monitor the sunrise at significant moments. With the Little Colorado River a full five miles distant, the pueblo's inhabitants must have been desperately short of water.

The loop road past Sunset Crater and Wupatki rejoins US-89 twenty miles south of Cameron (see p.117). Outcrops along its final few miles hold more pueblos, such as one known for obvious reasons as **The Citadel**, perched on and fully occupying a hilltop. While its interior, which appears to contain a large circular *kiva*, remains unexcavated, much of its outer wall is still standing, incorporating striped bands of black lava boulders. It too is dotted with tiny "windows" that may have served defensive or astronomical purposes.

Walnut Canyon National Monument

WALNUT CANYON NATIONAL MONUMENT is another Sinagua site, as spectacular in its own way as Wupatki. It lies just south of I-40, ten miles east of Flagstaff, or eight miles from downtown via Route 66. Between 1125 and 1250 AD, this shallow canyon was home to a thriving Sinagua community, who lived in small family groups rather than in communal pueblos. Literally hundreds of their **cliff dwellings** still nestle beneath overhangs in the canyon walls. They simply walled off alcoves where softer strata of rock had eroded away, and put up partitions to make separate rooms. No single dwelling is on the same scale as at Wupatki, and only a handful are accessible to visitors, but cumulatively they make an impressive spectacle.

A large scenic window in the **visitor centre** (daily: May–Oct 8am–5pm; Nov–April 9am–5pm; $5 per person; ☎928/526-3367, ⓦnps.gov/waca) gives an excellent overall view. **Walnut Creek** itself, long since diverted to provide Flagstaff's drinking water, now runs dry, but you can see how fertile this valley must have been when the Sinagua first arrived. Trees cling to the porous rock to shade the ancient dwellings, and the vegetation thickens down to a valley floor dense with black walnut and oak.

Only visitors who arrive an hour or more before closing time are allowed to set off down the mile-long **Island Trail**; as the dwellings are at their most photogenic in late afternoon, that calls for careful timing. Having dropped steeply down from the visitor centre, the trail crosses a narrow causeway to an isthmus of rock high above a gooseneck of the creek. Once there, you can go inside a few Sinagua homes; note the T-shaped doorways, which could only be entered headfirst, and the ceilings blackened by the smoke of generations of fires. Petroglyphs have been found in the other ruins visible on all sides, but none remain on the trail.

Rangers also lead **guided hikes** to lesser-known and otherwise inaccessible sites within the monument; check the website for current details. No accommodation, and only minimal snack food, is available at the canyon.

Williams

Although Flagstaff is generally regarded as the obvious base for visitors to the Grand Canyon's South Rim, **WILLIAMS**, 32 miles west, is in fact the closest interstate town to the national park. While it can't boast half the charm or pizzazz of its neighbour, it's a nice enough little place, filled with Route 66-era motels and diners and retaining a certain individuality despite the stream of tourists. Its setting helps, cupped in a high grassy valley amid pine-covered hills; the largest peak, the 9264ft **Bill Williams Mountain** to the south, was named after pioneer trapper and "mountain man" Bill Williams (1787–1849), and gave its name in turn to the town, founded thirty years after his death.

Like Flagstaff, Williams originally based both its architecture and its economy on the ponderosas of the surrounding forests. Since 1901, however, when the Santa Fe Railroad first linked it with the canyon rim, sixty miles due north, Williams has lived off tourism. Though the railroad went out of business in 1968, it reopened in 1989 as the **Grand Canyon Railway**, promoted as a fun ride rather than a serious means of transport. Most people who spend the night in Williams are here to take the morning train up to the canyon.

Arrival and information

Amtrak's *Southwest Chief* **trains** call in twice daily at **Williams Junction**, three miles east of town, heading east at 4.30am and west at 9.33pm. The *Grand Canyon Railway Hotel* (see below) runs free connecting shuttle buses into town.

See p.40 for schedules and prices for the **Grand Canyon Railway** (T928/773-1976 or 1-800/843-8724, Wthetrain.com), which sets off daily, usually at 9.30am, from the **Williams Depot** in the centre of town.

Williams' **visitor centre**, near the railroad depot at 200 W Railroad Ave (daily: summer 8am–6.30pm; winter till 5pm; T928/635-4061 or 1-800/863-0546, Wwilliamschamber.com), hands out brochures, and doubles as an entertaining **museum** of neighbourhood history.

Marvelous Marv's Tours run daily **guided van tours** of the South Rim from Williams, with the $85 adult rate including park admission (T928/707-0291, Wmarvelousmarv.com).

Accommodation

Although the *Grand Canyon Railway Hotel* is Williams' leading **accommodation** option, plenty of alternatives exist. The downtown streets are lined with vintage motels as well as the odd B&B, while national chains congregate near the interstate exits at either end of town.

If you're **camping**, you can choose between two year-round *KOA* campgrounds – the *Circle Pines*, three miles east (T928/635-2626 or 1-800/562-9379, Wkoa.com), and the *Grand Canyon*, five miles north (T928/635-2307 or 1-800/562-5771, Wkoa.com) – or ask at the Chalender Ranger Station, 501 W Route 66 (T928/635-2676), for details of secluded summer-only mountain sites in the Kaibab National Forest.

Best Western Inn of Williams 2600 W Route 66 T928/635-4400 or 1-800/635-4445, Wbestwesternwilliams.com. Spacious, well-equipped motel-resort, with a pool and hot tub, perched near I-40 exit 161 at the west end of town. **4**

Grand Canyon Hotel 145 W Route 66 T928/635-1419. Not to be confused with the much larger *Railway Hotel* (see below), this attractively restored downtown "boutique hotel" offers individual beds in a clean, crisp dorm for $25, plus themed private doubles with and without en-suite facilities. **4**

Grand Canyon Railway Hotel 1 Fray Marcos Blvd T928/635-4010 or 1-800/843-8724, Wthetrain.com/hotel. The Grand Canyon Railway's flagship hotel opened in 1908 as the *Fray Marcos*; rebuilt and renamed, it lacks character, though the large open lobby is pleasant enough, and there's also an indoor pool, spa and saloon. All rooms provide two queen beds. **7**

The Lodge on Route 66 200 E Route 66 T928/635-4534, Wthelodgeonroute66.com. Restored Route 66 motor-court motel in the heart of town, with spotless and very comfortable rooms and friendly management. **4**

Mountain Side Inn 642 E Route 66 T928/635-4431 or 1-800/462-9381. Large, comfortable motel, set back from the road at the east end of town, with an outdoor pool and a horse and wagon parked outside. **4**

Red Garter Bed & Bakery 137 W Railroad Ave T928/635-1484 or 1-800/328-1484, Wredgarter.com. Plush four-room B&B in a former downtown bordello, serving fresh-baked breakfasts from its own downstairs bakery. Look for discounted rates online. Closed mid-Dec to mid-Feb. **5**

Red Lake Hostel AZ-64 T928/635-4753 or 1-800/581-4753, Eredlake@azaccess.com. Adjoining a Mustang gas station at a lonely curve on AZ-64 nine miles north of town, this bright red converted motel offers rudimentary accommodation; $15 for a dorm bed in a double room, or $30 for a room with either twin singles or a double bed. Also offers tent and RV camping. **1**

Rodeway Inn Downtowner 201 E Route 66 T928/635-4041 or 1-877/424-6423, Wwww.rodewayinn.com. Though from outside this small and very central chain motel looks much like any other, the actual rooms have been well renovated and are very comfortable and good value. **5**

The Town

Williams holds a definite romantic appeal as the very last town on the old **Route 66** to have been bypassed by the I-40 interstate. Until October 13, 1984, when Bobby Troup of (*Get Your Kicks On*) *Route 66* fame fronted a closing ceremony, the only trafficlight encountered by cross-country travellers between Chicago and Los Angeles stood outside the Williams visitor centre. To this day, the centre of town remains a major rendezvous for **bikers**, and on summer Saturdays especially it's usually thronging with Harley Davidsons.

Much of the former Route 66 frontage remains barely changed, with quirky antiques stores selling vintage memorabilia alongside Native American crafts and jewellery. However, while it's fun to explore the central blocks along the two main one-way streets – Route 66, running west to east, is paralleled by the east–west **Railroad Avenue** – an hour's evening or morning stroll is enough; Williams is not really a place to spend the day.

For rail enthusiasts, the Williams Depot holds the slowly expanding **Grand Canyon Railway Museum** (daily 7.30am–5.30pm; free). As well as great hand-tinted old photos, it's bursting with vintage tools and implements, with cases of ancient arm-rests and window catches.

Highlights on Williams' annual events calendar include the Labor Day **rodeo** and **Rendezvous Days**, on Memorial Day weekend, when locals dress up as buckskinned pioneers.

Eating

Williams' restaurant selection is generally disappointing. A few places conjure up the feel of its Route 66 heyday, but no place serves anything out of the ordinary.

American Flyer 326 W Route 66 ☎928/635-1255. Funky, friendly café that serves espressos, juices and pastries, with a couple of outdoor tables and free wi-fi. Daily 6am–9pm.

Dara Thai *Grand Canyon Hotel*, 145 W Route 66 ☎928/635-2201. Dependable outpost of Flagstaff's long-standing Thai restaurant, serving good Thai dishes for $8 at lunch, $10 at dinner. Mon–Sat 11am–2pm & 5–9pm.

Grand Depot Café Williams Depot ☎928/635-8970. Adequate but dull family restaurant aimed at speedily satisfying hungry tour groups. All-you-can-eat buffets are available at every meal, and you can also order predictable à la carte options. Daily 6.30am–9pm.

Pancho McGillicuddy's 141 W Railroad Ave ☎928/635-4150. Popular but very average Mexican cantina, housed in an attractive tin-ceilinged building downtown, with its own authentic-looking saloon. South-of-the-border standards like flautas, tostadas, tamales or carnitas, cost just over $10, while mixed platters go for $16, and you can also get steaks and grills. Daily 11am–10pm.

Pine Country Restaurant 107 N Grand Canyon Blvd ☎928/635-9718. Traditional central diner with friendly staff, where the food is actually pretty good and the home-made pies are irresistible. Daily 6am–9pm.

Ash Fork

The ranching community of **ASH FORK**, stretched along a brief curving fragment of Route 66 north of the interstate another twenty miles west of Williams, is smaller, less picturesque and far less involved in catering to travellers. By this point I-40 has pulled clear of the forests, so downtown Ash Fork is constructed from yellowish local sandstone rather than timber.

The major **motel** chains haven't bothered to set up shop, but if you're really desperate to spend the night Ash Fork holds a few run-down homespun alternatives, including the large, pink *Ash Fork Inn*, at the west end of town near I-40 exit 144 (☎928/637-2514; ❷). There are also a couple of basic diners in the thick of what few things Ash Fork has to its name.

Seligman

Starting a few miles west of Ash Fork, the old Route 66 parallels its modern replacement at a discreet distance for the twenty or so miles to **SELIGMAN**. This flyblown desert outpost now feels more than a little stranded, a mile or two north of the interstate, but if you're in the mood to be seduced by its kitsch diners and drive-ins, it makes a mildly diverting stop in a long day's drive. Every business strives to outdo the others with eye-catching displays – mannequins of Elvis and Marilyn waving from oddball parked vehicles and the like – and the passing traffic is worth watching too, with all kinds of vintage roadsters making pilgrimages along the "Mother Road".

You might even choose to follow Route 66's original course as it curves northwards, through a dozen fading villages and part of the **Hualapai reservation** (see Chapter 8), and back south to Kingman. That's a total drive of 88 miles, as opposed to the dreary 65-mile run west on I-40. It also provides access to **Havasu Canyon**, in the depths of the Grand Canyon, which as described in Chapter 7 is one of the Southwest's least-known marvels.

Seligman offers I-40's only **accommodation** between Ash Fork and Kingman, with nicely restored and very clean vintage properties like the *Canyon Lodge*, 114 E Route 66 (☎928/422-3255 or 1-800/700-5054, ⊛route66canyonlodge .com; ❸), and the *Historic Route 66*, 500 W Route 66 (☎928/422-3204; ❸), as the pick of its motels.

The wackiest local **diner** has to be *Delgadillo's Snow Cap* at 301 E Route 66 (☎928/422-3291; closed Dec–Feb), where every malt or burger comes with a side order of outrageous puns and put-ons. If you're just looking for a square meal, the *Copper Cart*, in the former railroad station (☎928/422-3241), serves a standard all-American menu.

Kingman

With a population of over thirty thousand, **KINGMAN**, 65 miles on from Seligman and thirty miles short of California, ranks second to Flagstaff among Arizona's I-40 towns. As all traffic between Phoenix or the Grand Canyon and **Las Vegas** – a mere hundred miles northwest on US-93 – is obliged to pass this way, Kingman's thirty-plus motels stay busy year round. The best that can be said for it, however, is that it's not particularly ugly – apart from the long sprawl beside the railroad tracks north of the interstate – and it's not lifeless. Apart from that, it's a humdrum pit stop with a slight tinge of Route-66 quaintness.

Curving alongside the tracks, Kingman's main street is named in honour of native son **Andy Devine**, the actor who drove the eponymous *Stagecoach* in John Ford's 1939 movie. As the town's promotional brochure puts it, "There must be somebody who hasn't heard of Andy Devine, but that person sure doesn't live in Kingman." His career, the culture and basketwork of the Hualapai, and other unlikely components of Mohave County's heritage, are explored in the **Mohave Museum of History & Arts**, 400 W Beale St (Mon–Fri 9am–5pm, Sat 1–5pm; $4; ⊛mohavemuseum.org). 1939 was clearly a big year for Kingman: Carole Lombard and Clark Gable were married here on March 29.

Arrival and information

Kingman's large **Powerhouse Visitor Center**, on the western edge of downtown at 120 W Andy Devine Ave (daily: March–Oct 9am–6pm, Nov–Feb 8am–5pm; ☎928/753-6106 or 1-866/427-7866, ⊛kingmantourism.org), displays and sells Route 66 memorabilia and is a wi-fi hotspot.

The old station in the midst of town welcomes Amtrak **trains** on the run between Flagstaff and LA, though at unearthly hours of the night, while Greyhound **buses** travelling between Phoenix and Las Vegas, as well as east–west routes, use a terminal up near the interstate at 3264 E Andy Devine Ave (☎928/757-8400).

Accommodation

Granted that you're unlikely to spend more than one night in Kingman – or linger in the morning, either – its ordinary but inexpensive **motels** should easily meet your needs. There's beautiful **camping** in the hills five miles southeast of town, in the county-run **Hualapai Mountain Park** (☎928/681-5700, ⊛mcparks.com), which also holds the *Hualapai Mountain Lodge Resort* (☎928/757-3545; closed Mon; ❹).

Best Western A Wayfarer's Inn 2815 E Andy Devine Ave ☎928/753-6271 or 1-800/548-5695, ⊛bestwesternarizona.com. Hundred-room chain property, a couple of miles northeast of town near I-40 exit 53, charging reasonable rates for its smart if anonymous rooms, and offering a pool and indoor spa. ❹
Quality Inn Kingman 1400 E Andy Devine Ave ☎928/753-4747 or 1-800/228-5151, ⊛qualityinn.com. Standard motel half a mile from downtown, with small but adequate rooms, which offers a bit

of character via a strong Route 66 theme, including a retro breakfast room and outdoor vintage gas pumps. ❹
Ramblin' Rose 1001 E Andy Devine Ave ☎928/753-5541. Simple, spruced-up independent motel just east of downtown that provides some of Kingman's best budget rooms. ❷
Super 8 3401 E Andy Devine Ave ☎928/757-4808 or 1-800/800-8000, ⊛super8.com. Reliable, inexpensive chain motel well east of town, just north of I-40 exit 53. ❸

Eating

Most Kingman **restaurants** play on the Route 66 angle. It's all too spread out to wander around comparing menus, but hop in your car and you'll find something.

Dambar & Steakhouse 1960 E Andy Devine Ave ☎928/753-3523. Classic Western steakhouse atop the hill, all sawdust and bare timber, serving grilled and barbecued ribs and chicken, as well as massive steaks. Main dishes around $20 at dinner, more like $10 at lunch. Daily 11am–10pm.
Mr D'z Route 66 Diner 105 E Andy Devine Ave ☎928/718-0066. Loving recreation of a classic Route 66 roadhouse, across from the visitor centre

and bursting with memorabilia, neon and lurid moulded trimmings. Good burgers and shakes, malts and floats, and fries with everything. Daily 7am–9pm.
Redneck's Southern Pit BBQ 420 E Beale St ☎928/757-8227. Large portions of tangy Southern BBQ, ordered cafeteria style and enjoyed in a family atmosphere. Mon–Sat 11am–9pm.

The Havasupai Indian Reservation

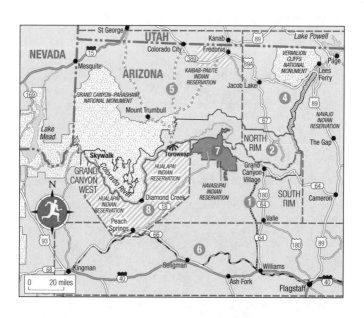

CHAPTER 7

Highlights

✳ **Hualapai Trail** Busy with hikers and Havasupai alike, not to mention mules and horses, the sandy Hualapai Trail is the only way to reach the heart of the reservation. See p.172

✳ **Guided hiking** Join one of the Grand Canyon Field Institute's expert-led backpacking trips to Havasupai. See p.172

✳ **The new falls** Interrupting the new, amazingly green streambed of Havasu Creek, these newly carved falls represent nature at its rawest. See p.174

✳ **Havasu Falls** These astonishing, lush, turquoise waterfalls, buried deep within Havasu Canyon, are the main reason visitors flock to the reservation. See p.175

✳ **Mooney Falls** The hair-raising hike to the foot of these falls, named after a prospector who died in the attempt, is rewarded with magnificent views. See p.175

▲ New Navajo Falls

The Havasupai Indian Reservation

Nestled deep within the Grand Canyon, at the heart of the **Havasupai Indian Reservation**, **Havasu Canyon** is one of the most spellbindingly beautiful places in the entire Southwest. Though just 35 miles west of the national park's headquarters at the South Rim, it can only be accessed via the I-40 interstate, making a road trip of almost two hundred miles. The last ninety miles of that, once you leave I-40, crosses the endless Coconino Plateau.

Those visitors who brave the eight-mile desert hike down the **Hualapai Trail** from road's end – the only route into the canyon itself – are rewarded by a stunning oasis of **turquoise waterfalls** and lush vegetation, a Shangri-La that has been home for centuries beyond record to the same small group of Native Americans. The five hundred or so **Havasupai** owe their existence here to a geological fluke. Although the canyon receives only nine inches of rain each year, all the water that falls in the surrounding three thousand square miles funnels down into this one narrow gorge, creating the year-round torrent of **Havasu Creek**. The down side of that is that the canyon is prone to repeated, devastating **flash floods**. The major flood in 2008, which caused immense damage and carved out a new set of waterfalls, was the fifth such in twenty years.

One 1930s anthropologist described Havasu Canyon as "the only spot in the United States where native culture has remained in anything like its pristine condition". Since then, tourism has become the mainstay of the tribal economy, but visitor numbers are kept deliberately low, at around 35,000 per year. The Havasupai have rejected all suggestions of building a road – or even a tramway – down into the canyon, to minimize the impact on their traditional way of life. Instead, tribal members earn their keep by ferrying non-hikers up and down the trail on pack mules and horses, and operating a creekside **campground** as well as a comfortable lodge in the village of **Supai**. While visitors should not expect sweeping views of the Grand Canyon itself – or to have much interaction with residents – for spectacular desert scenery, and sheer romance, the Havasupai reservation is beyond compare. The one crucial factor to bear in mind if you're planning a trip is that you **must** have an advance reservation for either the lodge or campground. That's easier said than done; between May and October, the lodge is almost invariably booked months in advance, and the campground is usually full at weekends. On top of that, the telephone line down to Supai can fail for weeks at a time.

Unless you travel by **helicopter**, as detailed on p.172, it's impossible to visit Havasu Canyon as a **day-trip**; quite apart from the drive to the trailhead, the twenty-mile round trip hike to the falls, which lie two miles beyond the village, would take well over ten hours.

A history of the Havasupai

Archeologists have identified the earliest inhabitants of Havasu Canyon as the **Cohonina**. Like the Ancestral Puebloans, their neighbours to the east, they are thought to have occupied the region between around 700 and 1100 AD. At some point during that period, a Yuman-speaking group who call themselves the "**Pai**" – a word that simply means "people" – made their first appearance in the Southwest. So little is known about the Cohonina that no one knows whether the Pai were their cousins, their descendants or an entirely new group.

What is certain, however, is that by 1300 AD, a couple of hundred years after the Cohonina abandoned the canyon, a band of Pai had taken their place. The Pai as a whole had by this time quarrelled, splitting to form the **Hualapai** ("People of the Tall Pines") of northwest Arizona, and the **Yavapai** ("Almost-People", who apparently no longer quite deserved to be regarded as people), who settled along the Colorado further south. It was a group of Hualapai families who moved into the canyon, and became the **Havasupai** – the "people of the blue-green water". Although not related to any of the many different Pueblo peoples, the Hualapai established close links with the Hopi and the Zuni, from whom they eventually acquired the art of raising sheep, horses and crops such as peaches.

Despite taking their name from the turquoise river that watered the fields here, the Havasupai only lived on the floor of the Grand Canyon, here and elsewhere, during the summer, building houses of hide-covered branches. In winter, the canyon made a cold, miserable home, lacking big game and firewood and receiving as little as five hours of sunlight per day. Instead the Havasupai would move up onto the plateau to hunt deer, elk and antelope, using artificial water holes to lure them closer. Their territory covered perhaps 2.3 million acres, extending far beyond the region now occupied by Grand Canyon Village to the San Francisco Peaks near modern Flagstaff, and as far north as what's now Tuba City, Arizona.

The outsiders arrive

In June 1776, shortly before the Declaration of Independence was signed in Phila-delphia, the Havasupai welcomed their first white visitor. **Father Francisco Tomás Garcés**, a missionary from San Xavier del Bac near Tucson who made several pioneering expeditions into the unknown West, was greeted with five days of feasting. Describing the Grand Canyon as a "calaboose of cliffs and canyons", he dubbed it the Puerto de Bucareli in honour of the viceroy who had despatched him; more enduringly, he was the first to name the **Río Colorado**. Garcés himself travelled eastwards along the South Rim to meet the Hopi, while the rest of his expedition blazed a trail to California, where they founded San Francisco.

The Havasupai then remained undisturbed for another eighty years, until Anglo prospectors and surveyors began to enter the region. Conflict arose in 1866, when, to encourage the spread of the railroads, Congress granted the Atlantic and Pacific Railroad company ownership of swathes of land adjoining its tracks across northern Arizona. Native resistance soon escalated into a disastrous **war**, after which the defeated Hualapai spent several years confined to a reservation near Ehrenberg, 150 miles downstream along the Colorado. Because the Havasupai did not participate in the fighting, they were allowed to remain in their traditional territory, then known to the US authorities as **Cataract Canyon**. Only now did

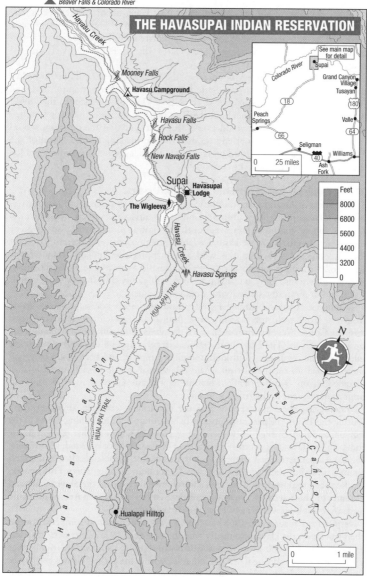

THE HAVASUPAI INDIAN RESERVATION

See main map for detail

Colorado River

Supai

Grand Canyon Village

Tusayan

18

Peach Springs

Valle

66

180

64

Seligman

Williams

40

Ash Fork

0   25 miles

Mooney Falls

✕ Havasu Campground

Havasu Falls

Rock Falls

New Navajo Falls

Supai

Havasupai Lodge

The Wigleeva

Havasu Creek

Havasu Springs

HUALAPAI TRAIL

Hualapai Canyon

HUALAPAI TRAIL

Havasu Canyon

Hualapai Hilltop

Feet
8000
6800
5600
4400
3200
0

N

0   1 mile

they begin to regard themselves as a separate "tribe" rather than just another band of Hualapai.

In negotiations over the extent of a permanent Havasupai reservation, the government was as usual only prepared to acknowledge Native American "ownership" of land that held permanent settlements and cultivated fields. Areas used for hunting, gathering or even grazing, especially if use was shared by more than one band, were not recognized. Fearful of being deported themselves, the Havasupai settled in 1882 for a tiny plot at the bottom of Havasu Canyon – at a mere 518 acres, it amounted to less than one square mile. Restricted to a fraction of their former range, they were obliged to farm what little land they were granted as intensively as possible.

During the ensuing century of hardship, the Havasupai repeatedly petitioned to have their reservation enlarged. Suffering great spiritual uncertainty, both the Havasupai and Hualapai took part in the **Ghost Dance** movement in the 1890s, when Native Americans throughout the West joined in trance-like rituals designed to ensure that white men would vanish from the land and the old ways would return. The Havasupai also briefly adopted the rain-making *kachina* dances of the Hopi, until a catastrophic **flood** on January 1, 1910 destroyed their village, which then stood half a mile from its current site.

The Havasupai and the national park

The creation of **Grand Canyon National Park** in 1919 placed yet more restrictions on Havasupai use of traditional lands. One early supervisor avowed that the Grand Canyon "should be preserved for the everlasting pleasure and instruction of our intelligent citizens as well as those from foreign countries; I therefore deem it just and necessary to keep the wild and inappreciable Indians from off the Reserve". Park proposals during the 1920s to build a direct road along the South Rim and down into Havasu Canyon were probably only thwarted by the Crash of 1929, and re surfaced repeatedly for decades to come.

Although Coconino National Forest, south of the reservation, takes its name from the Hopi word for the Havasupai (which also, anachronistically, explains how the Cohonina got their name), tribal members could only graze animals there by annual permit. The Havasupai survived largely through disobeying whatever unenforceable regulations outsiders sought to impose, and continuing to spend their winters up on the plateau. Many Havasupai in due course found jobs in Grand Canyon Village, while tourism to Havasu Canyon itself became an important element in the tribal economy.

Nonetheless, the Park Service and the Havasupai remained at loggerheads. During the 1950s, the park surreptitiously bought up defunct mining claims in the canyon, and then opened its own campground – the same one that remains in use today under Havasupai control – on a former Havasupai burial ground. Meanwhile, the Havasupai petitioned tirelessly for the return of their lands. It might sound strange now, but their greatest ally was Republican senator **Barry Goldwater**, while ranged against them were such environmental groups as the **Sierra Club** and **Friends of the Earth**, who had yet to be convinced that Native Americans could look after wilderness lands as well as the Park Service.

Despite having agreed in 1968 to accept $1.24 million as final compensation for their lost lands, the Havasupai finally won their battle in 1975. The reservation was expanded by 185,000 acres, and the Havasupai were also awarded rights over 95,300 acres of "traditional use" land that lay within the park. This was the largest tract of land ever returned to Native Americans, but came with the proviso that it must remain "forever wild". No mining, logging or manufacturing was to be permitted on the traditional use lands, and no dams or railroads could be built.

The settlement came only just in time. Almost immediately, the Grand Canyon region experienced a boom in **uranium** mining, with over 3500 claims filed in the Arizona Strip during the ensuing decade. In 1988, Energy Fuels Nuclear was granted rights to develop a uranium mine known as **Canyon Mine**, at a site outside the reservation, close to **Red Butte** in the Kaibab National Forest, which is sacred to the Havasupai as *Mat Taav Tijundva*. Despite fears that the mine might contaminate Havasu Creek, Havasu Canyon and ultimately the Colorado itself, federal courts blocked Havasupai attempts to stop it. The mine was built, but did not go into operation at the time, thanks to a drop in world uranium prices. It now belongs to the Denison Corporation, which in 2009 recommenced uranium mining in the Arizona Strip, and as this book went to press was pushing hard to be granted the water rights that would enable it to open Canyon Mine itself.

The other major threat facing the Havasupai is that any future tourist development at the South Rim – along the lines of the abortive "Canyon Forest Village" scheme (see p.203) – would be liable to deplete the water table for hundreds of miles around. That could mean that Havasu Creek would finally run dry.

Getting to the reservation

Since the enlargement of their reservation in 1975, the Havasupai have closed all except one of the possible access routes into their land. Now the only way to get here by road is from **I-40**, turning off at **Seligman** if you're coming from Flagstaff or Grand Canyon Village, or at **Kingman** from Las Vegas or California. In total, it takes between three and four hours to drive from Flagstaff, more like five from Las Vegas. Stock up with food, water and gas when you leave the interstate, then follow **AZ-66** – the only surviving segment of Route 66 not to have been super-seded by newer roads, and still closely parallel to the main east–west railroad – to the poorly marked intersection with **Arrowhead Hwy-18**, six miles east of **Peach Springs**. From Seligman, that's a straight run of around 29 miles; from Kingman it's more like sixty miles, but there is at least the option of an overnight stop in the *Hualapai Lodge* in Peach Springs (see p.185).

Hwy-18 runs for its entire sixty-mile length with hardly a building in sight, across bare sagebrush desert interrupted by patches of thick ponderosa forest. Despite maps to the contrary, it's paved throughout, and there's no possibility of losing your way. Eventually it starts to wind down through burgeoning canyon-lands, coming to an end at the large plateau known as **Hualapai Hilltop**.

At an elevation of 5200ft, the plateau commands a long view of the white-walled **Hualapai Canyon**, cutting into the tablelands as it stretches north towards its meeting with Havasu Canyon. Although the hilltop holds no more than a small cluster of dilapidated shacks, with no accommodation, food or gas available, there are usually far more vehicles parked here than you might anticipate for such a remote spot. Do yourself a favour and drive to the end of the road before you choose a parking spot; the first parked cars you see may well be several hundred yards from the end.

Hikers are free to set off from Hualapai Hilltop whenever they choose. From the end of the car park, the **Hualapai Trail** to Supai village zigzags steeply down the hillside to the right, and can then be seen threading its way across the valley floor below. As stressed above, do not attempt to go down unless you have already reserved accommodation.

Horse rides

If you prefer to **ride** down on either horse or mule, make a reservation when you book your accommodation. The mule train leaves the hilltop at some point between 10am and noon; if you arrive any later than noon, you won't be able to ride down, and you'll lose both your reservation and your deposit. To ride as far as the **village** costs $70 per person one-way and $120 return, and should be arranged with the management of the lodge (☎928/448-2111); riding to the

campground costs $93.50 each way, $187 return, and is arranged by the **Havasupai Tourist Enterprise** (☎928/448-2121 or 2141, ⓦhavasupaitribe .com). Riders' baggage weighing over ten pounds has to be carried separately – one animal can carry up to four packs, again for $70 one-way, $120 return – and many hikers also arrange to have their bags carried.

Helicopters

Airwest operate a **helicopter shuttle** service between Hualapai Hilltop and Supai. Current schedules are posted on ⓦhavasupaitribe.com; flights are available between 10am and 1pm on Thurs, Fri, Sun and Mon between mid-March and mid-October and on Fri & Sun only from mid-October until mid-March. The service operates on a first-come, first-served basis, with a one-way fare of $85.

The Hualapai Trail

Apart from its initial switchbacks down the Coconino Sandstone hillside, the **Hualapai Trail** is not especially difficult. It is, however, a long eight-mile walk to the village, with no shade for the first three miles and no reliable water source until near the end. Allow a little over three hours to reach the village (and more like four or more to come back up again, when the final switchbacks are a real killer), and be sure to carry all the food and water you'll need for a day in the desert.

The route is very obvious, and kept busy throughout the day with small supply trains of mules and horses. Once you reach the valley floor, after perhaps 45 minutes, you follow the bed of a dry wash as it drops ever deeper between red-rock cliffs that slowly but inexorably climb to form the two walls of the deep, narrow Hualapai Canyon. The sand underfoot is so thick in summer that it splashes at every step, but the potential for flash floods is clear from the much-scoured rocks to either side. Mighty boulders occasionally all but block the path, or poise precariously overhead, while solitary cottonwoods reach up towards the thin strip of sky. Atop the Esplanade Plateau straight ahead, the pale, stark butte of **Mount Sinyala** repeatedly looms into view.

Guided tours and excursions

Various organizations offer guided expeditions to the Havasupai Reservation. Especially recommended is the Grand Canyon Field Institute (see p.92), which typically runs two or three four-day hiking and camping tours each summer, costing around $665 (☎928/638-2485 or 1-866/471-4435, ⓦgrandcanyon.org/fieldinstitute).

Some commercial operators promise a more luxurious experience. Arizona Outback Adventures (☎480/945-2881 or 1-866/455-1601, ⓦaoa-adventures.com) offers three-, four- and five-day trips with accommodation at their own "Base Camp". Assorted options including hiking and/or helicopter transport cost from $848 up to $1918. Discovery Treks (☎520/404-1151 or 1-888/256-8731, ⓦdiscoverytreks.com) arranges three-day trips with a choice of hiking, horseback riding and helicopter rides, and camping or staying in the lodge. Prices range from $975 upwards.

It's not currently possible to take a helicopter trip to Havasu Canyon from anywhere other than Hualapai Hilltop (see above). However, Papillon Helicopters offered $500 day-trips from the South Rim prior to the 2008 floods, and may re-start the service at some point; check ⓦpapillon.com for updates.

After almost seven miles, the trail reaches its intersection with Havasu Canyon; until the disastrous flood of 1910 (see p.170), this was the site of Supai village. All of Havasu Canyon was formerly known as **Cataract Canyon**, but now that old name only applies to its dry segment, to the right of the junction. Whatever you do, don't turn right – it took three weeks to rescue a dehydrated camper who did so in 1975. That said, however, what little tourist traffic the Havasupai received a century ago would arrive this way, along the **Topocoba Trail**, which reaches Cataract Canyon by means of Lee Canyon, at the end of a thirty-mile dirt-road drive from Grand Canyon Village. Although the Havasupai continue to make occasional use of that trail, recreational hikers are not permitted to do so.

Bear left at the trail junction instead, at a dense cluster of small trees. The sound of rushing water soon signals the emergence of **Havasu Creek** from hidden crevices in the rock. Before long it's flowing through the parched landscape in all its blue-green splendour, at an average capacity of an amazing 38 million gallons per day.

Not far beyond a new footbridge across the creek, you cross a low rise to be confronted by the meadow that holds the modern village, and the two red-rock pillars that watch over Supai from the high canyon wall on the far side. Known as the **Wigleeva**, these twin sentinels, of which one is considered to be male and the other female, are regarded as the guardian spirits of the Havasupai.

Supai

Though located in a superb natural setting – a wide, flat clearing surrounded on all sides by forbidding walls of red sandstone – the village of **SUPAI** is not in itself attractive. The Havasupai were only obliged to build a year-round settlement down in the canyon by the loss of their lands on the plateau above (see p.170), and this site was their second choice after the first proved prone to flooding. It too has suffered repeated damage from floods. It therefore consists of just a scattering of basic timber-frame houses and prefabricated cabins, interspersed with large bare yards where horses graze. Even the name itself is a flimsy fabrication: "Supai" is a meaningless abbreviation of "Havasupai", invented by the US Postal Service.

Once the Hualapai Trail, running alongside a line of irrigation ditches, has become what's jokingly called "Main Street" and shepherded you into the village, the first building you come to holds the tribal **registration office**. Only campers are obliged to pay the $35 reservation **entrance fee** here; for lodge guests, it's added to their bill. A back room holds a small **museum** (daily 7am–7pm; donations welcome), with a random but reasonably interesting assortment of century-old photographs and newspaper cuttings. The Havasupai are famous for crafts such as basket-making, so there's a case of assorted baskets, one of which has been coated with pine pitch to make it waterproof. On the whole, however, ancient artefacts have become too expensive for the museum to afford.

Fifty yards farther, you reach Supai's dusty, flyblown **plaza**. To the right, attached to the only post office in the US that still receives its mail by pack mule, the village's lone **grocery store** is its main social centre, where older Havasupai gather each evening on benches outside. The younger set, together with a vast population of dogs, are more likely to be found on the terrace of the **café**, opposite. Once past that, the trail skirts the edge of the village school, then branches left and descends towards the campground. Visitors are forbidden to wander away from the main trail into the farmlands around the village.

Havasupai Lodge

Havasupai Lodge (☎928/448-2111 or 448-2201, ⓦhavasupaitribe.com; ⑥) is located deliberately away from things, at the edge of the village, close to the canyon wall behind the school. It's a simple two-storey structure, built in the style of a functional motel rather than an atmospheric park lodge, and arranged around a central lawn. Each plain but comfortable air-conditioned room holds almost nothing beyond a bed and a dresser; there aren't even any pictures on the walls, let alone phones or TVs. All sleep up to four people. Lobby hours vary, but are usually 8am–5pm, meaning no on-site assistance is available in the evenings. Advance bookings are essential, and very hard to get between May and October.

Note that the $35 reservation entrance fee is added to all bills at the lodge, which like all prices on the reservation are also subject to an additional ten percent **tribal sales tax**.

Eating

The only place to get a **meal** in Supai is at the **Tribal Cafe** (daily: hours vary from 6am–7pm in summer down to 8am–5pm in winter; ☎928/448-2981). The food is far from exciting, with fried breakfasts, and a lunch or dinner of beef stew, fry bread or burritos; pretty much everything seems to cost around $7, or more if you want grated cheese on top. All transactions are cash only. As usual, no **alcohol** is available, here or anywhere on the reservation.

The **grocery store** across the plaza sells a limited selection of processed items, all carried in by mule and priced accordingly.

Below Supai: the falls

All the **waterfalls** for which the Havasupai reservation is famous lie further down the canyon beyond Supai. To get there, follow the footpath out of the village from near the lodge; it takes several minutes to get clear of the straggle of farms and homes.

New Navajo Falls and Rock Falls

The riverbed immediately below the village is forever being reshaped by flash floods and fresh erosion. The flood of August 2008 scoured out a great new chasm, well over a hundred feet deep. Obliterating the former Navajo Falls, it created two spectacular new cascades, neither of which has yet been officially named by the tribe. The first you come to, known for the moment as **New Navajo Falls**, is a short walk left of the trail roughly a mile down. Tumbling over a wide cliff face in countless separate strands, it shrouds a regrowth of young ferns and saplings in a mist of white spray.

From the foot of the falls, Havasu Creek has carved a new course through a churned-up landscape of bare mud. The riverbed itself is extraordinarily green and verdant, but scores of dead aspens, whose roots no longer reach the water table, look down forlornly from the high cliffs on its far side. The main trail continues well above the river level, though the Havasupai have been working to lay new trails closer to the flow.

Another quarter-mile along, the second of the new falls, temporarily named **Rock Falls**, usually consists of a single expansive cascade. The full width of the river roars over a 20ft drop, immediately before making a sharp turn.

Havasu Falls

When the trail appears to divide, around half a mile beyond Rock Falls, take the left fork and follow it down to a footbridge over the creek (the right fork climbs briefly to an unimportant overlook). You're now approaching the stupendous **Havasu Falls**. If you choose, you can veer off to the right here and scramble through the rocks to where the stream starts to drop through a succession of steep gullies.

For a first glimpse of the actual falls, however, continue on the path and you'll swiftly reach an overlook more or less level with the top. Here you're confronted by an absolutely breathtaking sight. The creek foams white as it hurtles over a 150ft cliff, to crash into shallow terraces filled with limpid turquoise water. The rock formations all around are formed from water-deposited limestone known as **travertine** – the same stuff that clogs the inside of domestic kettles. It's the light travertine coating on the riverbed that gives the water its astonishing blue-green glow. It may look incredibly unreal, like the sort of pink cement they make grottoes out of at Disneyland, but be sure not to walk onto it in bare feet; travertine is horrendously sharp stuff.

In the days when it was known to the Park Service as **Bridal Veil Falls**, Havasu was a broad cascade, which explains the solidified sheets and curtains of travertine that run right across its wide brim. Then a flash flood punched out a deep notch right in the centre, through which the falls now gush.

Side trails off the main path lead down to an idyllic shaded "beach" beside the largest, deepest pool, where the ceaseless roar makes conversation difficult, but **swimming** is all but irresistible. Cross to the far side of the river, traversing the travertine dams that divide the various terraces, to reach a group of picnic tables standing in a cottonwood grove at the mouth of a side canyon.

A short **horseback excursion** from Supai to Havasu Falls costs $60; for reservations, contact Havasupai Tourist Enterprise (see p.172).

Havasu Campground

A short distance beyond Havasu Falls, two miles down from Supai village, you finally reach the Havasu **campground**, set in an especially narrow and high-walled segment of the canyon. Once the tribal cremation and burial ground, this site was excluded from the original reservation on account of its rich deposits of lead, silver and zinc. After mining activities ceased, but before the Havasupai managed to claim it back in 1975, it fell into the hands of the national park, which turned it into a campground in 1957. As one Havasupai bitterly complained during hearings before the US Senate in 1973, "dead people's things have long since walked off with hikers".

Today, the campground stretches for around three quarters of a mile, and is capable of holding around three hundred campers. Sadly, this entire area sustained major damage in the 2008 flood, and was heavily denuded of its formerly luxuriant cottonwood trees. Facilities are primitive in the extreme, though at least safe drinking water is provided by fresh springs in the canyon wall. Tents can be pitched to either side of the creek, which is usually shallow and is in any case crossed by makeshift footbridges. There are no showers or phones, and fires are not permitted. Reservations are required (☎928/448-2121, 448-2141 or 448-2174, ⓦhavasupaitribe.com), and there's a fee of $17 plus tax per person, per night. Although villagers are barred from the area in summer by tribal edict, groups of horses stand tethered at the entrance, waiting to carry campers back up the hill.

Mooney Falls and the Colorado River

Havasu campground is brought to an abrupt end by the precipitous, and once again luridly turquoise, 196ft **Mooney Falls**. This natural barrier was long regarded, even by the Havasupai, as impassable. Its modern name comes from an unfortunate prospector who fell to his death here in 1880, after a rope snagged as he was being lowered to the bottom. Colourful stories that he dangled for three days before the rope broke are untrue, but it did take several months before his companions managed to bore through the travertine to retrieve his body, which lay by then beneath a fresh coating of limestone.

Though Mooney Falls was barely affected by the 2008 flood, the trail to the bottom remains little better today. Having scrambled down the travertine ledges to reach the two successive tunnels made by Mooney's cohorts that drop through the cliff face, you come to a sheer section that was blasted away in a 1993 flood, and now consists of a vertical series of footholds aided by an iron chain fixed into the rock. The prospect of having to climb back up is terrifying enough to make many hikers turn back at this point; if you press on, there are also two steep ladders to contend with. Assuming you do make it to the bottom, the pools and swimming holes at the foot of the falls are once again gorgeous.

A long day hike from the campground continues on for three miles to **Beaver Falls**, a quick-fire set of rapids that's as far as the Havasupai recommend any visitors should try to go. Negotiating an onwards route involves climbing up to and along a high ledge, after which it takes four more miles before you eventually reach the Colorado itself. Quite possibly, you'd be greeted by river runners who preferred to get here the easy way, shooting the 157 miles of whitewater from Lees Ferry (see p.126).

8

The Hualapai Indian Reservation

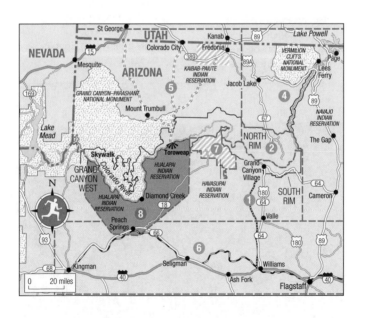

CHAPTER 8

Highlights

✴ **Skywalk** While it may not quite live up to the hype, the Skywalk is a stunning feat of engineering. See p.182

✴ **Indian Village** Featuring authentic Native American dwellings, cultural performances and crafts, Indian Village strives to lend Grand Canyon West a genuine Hualapai identity. See p.183

✴ **Guano Point** The one true Colorado overlook at Grand Canyon West, Guano Point features fascinating historical relics and commands a superb prospect of the canyon. See p.183

✴ **Flying to the river** Only at Grand Canyon West is it possible to ride a helicopter on a fearsome plummet to the Colorado River. See p.184

✴ **Rafting day trip** The only one-day rafting trip available in the Grand Canyon proper starts daily from Peach Springs. See p.186

▲ The Skywalk

8

The Hualapai Indian
Reservation

T he **Hualapai Indian Reservation** spreads across almost a million acres of northwest Arizona. From its northern border, defined by a 108-mile stretch of the Colorado at the extreme western end of the Grand Canyon, the reservation extends south on average between twenty and thirty miles – just far enough to include curving thirteen-mile sections of both the original **Route 66** and parallel transcontinental **railroad**. Straddling the highway, the reservation's only town, **Peach Springs**, is home to just under a thousand of the total Hualapai population of around 1500.

The tribe's main business these days is **tourism** – specifically, promoting a cluster of overlooks above their river frontage, far northwest of Peach Springs and not connected to it by road, as **Grand Canyon West**, or the **"West Rim"** of the Grand Canyon. This canny piece of marketing is aimed squarely at the 35 million tourists who flock to **Las Vegas** each year. The Hualapai reservation is the closest spot to the city from which it's possible to see the Grand Canyon, and most of its visitors are first-time day-trippers who don't realize that they're not seeing the canyon at its best. This far west, the canyon is starting to peter out; it lacks the colossal depth and width of its central section, and holds none of the towering mesas, buttes and temples so conspicuous from the South or North rim viewpoints. Neither, unfortunately for the Hualapai, is there anything to match the sumptuous waterfalls of the neighbouring Havasupai reservation. That said, for anyone new to the canyonlands of the Southwest, the so-called West Rim makes an impressive spectacle.

The Hualapai take full advantage of their most crucial asset – their independent status, outside the national park and free from federal regulations. The most dramatic result has been the construction of the glass-bottomed, U-shaped **Skywalk**, officially unveiled by astronaut Buzz Aldrin in 2007. A joint venture between the tribe and entrepreneur David Jin, it's been widely promoted as the greatest Grand Canyon viewpoint of them all, but that claim is very far from the truth; it's not even the best viewpoint at Grand Canyon West, a distinction that belongs to the superior **Guano Point**. For a start, the Skywalk is not above the inner gorge of the canyon, let alone the Colorado River; it simply sticks out from the rim of a lesser side canyon, with a drop below of less than a thousand feet.

The Hualapai also offer two further unique enticements for visitors: **helicopter flights** that drop below the rim and land by the river, and **one-day whitewater**

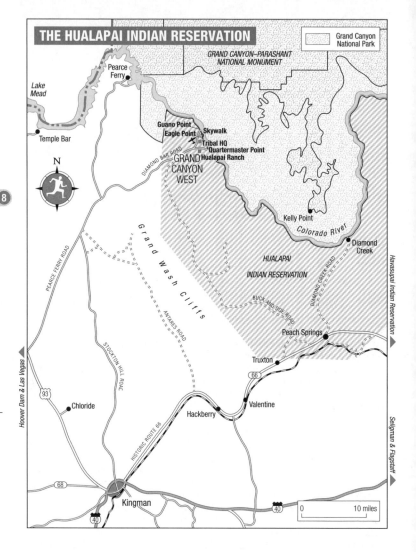

THE HUALAPAI INDIAN RESERVATION

Grand Canyon National Park

GRAND CANYON–PARASHANT NATIONAL MONUMENT

Lake Mead

Pearce Ferry

Temple Bar

Guano Point
Eagle Point
Skywalk
Tribal HQ
Quartermaster Point
GRAND CANYON WEST
Hualapai Ranch

N

Kelly Point

Colorado River

Diamond Creek

HUALAPAI INDIAN RESERVATION

Grand Wash Cliffs

DIAMOND BAR ROAD

PEARCE FERRY ROAD

ANTARES ROAD

STOCKTON HILL ROAD

BUCK AND DOE ROAD

DIAMOND CREEK ROAD

Peach Springs

Truxton
66

Chloride

Hackberry

Valentine

HISTORIC ROUTE 66

93

68

Kingman

40

0   10 miles

Hoover Dam & Las Vegas

Havasupai Indian Reservation

Seligman & Flagstaff

rafting trips on the Colorado. Ultimately, they hope to develop a high-end resort close to the Skywalk and make Grand Canyon West more than just a day-trip destination. For the moment, however, virtually all of its roughly 300,000 annual visitors fly in from Las Vegas for just a few hours. If you're among the very few who drive here, the long, empty route evokes a sense of penetrating unexplored wilderness that you certainly *don't* get from driving to the South Rim.

A history of the Hualapai

Though the Hualapai – whose name is pronounced *Wa-la-pie* – are now less known than the Havasupai, the latter were originally a minor offshoot of the

Hualapai tribe. As detailed on p.168, both were descended from a group known as the **Pai** – "The People" – who make their first appearance in the archeological record shortly after 700 AD. Also called the **Cerbat**, the Pai trace their tribal origin to Spirit Mountain, further down the Colorado near modern-day Bullhead City, Arizona. The Hualapai lived in the forests of the South Rim from around 1100 – hence their name, "People of the Tall Pines" (rather belied by the pine-free lands they occupy today). While their initial base was **Meriwhitica Canyon**, a side canyon towards the western end of the current reservation, the Hualapai seem eventually to have supplanted Ancestral Puebloans throughout most of the Grand Canyon proper, in many cases inheriting their craft skills, survival techniques and even their homes.

The Hualapai were traditionally a very mobile people, who planted crops and collected wild plants deep in the canyon in summer, then spent the winter hunting on the plateaus and up into the mountains farther south. Significant contact with outsiders only came in the 1860s, when prospectors established a wagon route deep into Hualapai territory to pursue the copper, lead, silver and gold deposits in the Cerbat Mountains to the west. Conflict soon escalated into the **Hualapai War**, a guerrilla struggle that lasted from 1865 to 1869. With a quarter of all Hualapai men killed in the fighting, and the tribe further decimated by disease, the survivors were rounded up and force-marched into internment at La Paz, near modern-day Parker, Arizona. They soon escaped and returned to their ancestral lands, a situation that was formalized in 1883 – two years after the railroad reached Peach Springs – by the creation of their own reservation.

Between the 1950s and the 1970s, Hualapai leaders vociferously supported plans to construct the **Bridge Canyon Dam** on their reservation, to block the Grand Canyon at its narrowest point. The Hualapai stood to gain not only in terms of construction jobs, but also in long-term royalties and increased visitation. When environmentalists, appalled at the notion of damming the canyon, campaigned against the project, the Hualapai accused them of "condemning our families to lifelong poverty by forcing us to keep our homeland a wilderness". The proposals were nevertheless defeated, and the Hualapai turned their attention exclusively to promoting tourism. Development of Grand Canyon West started in 1988, and the current generation of leaders now speaks of preserving the canyon, even if that goal can at times seem to be undermined by their development programme.

Grand Canyon West

Grand Canyon West, also known as the **West Rim**, is a remote group of inner canyon viewpoints roughly fifty miles northwest of Peach Springs and 120 miles east of Las Vegas. If you're touring the canyon region, the West Rim is perhaps the least essential stop to include on your itinerary; its sole *raison d'être* is to generate income for the Hualapai by granting tourists from Vegas a glimpse of the canyon on an easy day trip. That said, it's only easy if you come by air; by car, it's a long detour down barren desert roads.

While **Guano Point** offers an undeniably great prospect of the inner gorge, the canyon as a whole here is simply not as majestic as in its better-known segments. Come expecting natural wonders and you may well end up feeling short-changed. Although the glass-floored **Skywalk** has been tremendously hyped in the last few years, it's more of an expensive novelty than a must-see attraction. If you're an outdoors type, with a passion for the desert wildernesses of the Southwest, the Skywalk is probably not for you.

Driving to Grand Canyon West

In terms of road conditions, the best routes to Grand Canyon West approach not from the east via Peach Springs, but from the west and south. In recent years the Hualapai have paved two separate approach roads to the West Rim. The busiest of the pair, **Pearce Ferry Road**, heads northeast from **US-93** (the main highway between Arizona and Las Vegas), thirty miles north of Kingman and forty miles south of the Hoover Dam. Twenty-eight miles along, you'll turn east on **Diamond Bar Road**. The other paved route to this same spot, the forty-mile **Stockton Hill Road**, runs due north from central Kingman to meet Pearce Ferry Road around twelve miles short of **Diamond Bar Road**.

Diamond Bar Road itself climbs for fourteen rocky miles, through foothills scattered with Joshua trees, and up the Grand Wash Cliffs, to reach the Hualapai reservation, where the airstrip and Grand Canyon West headquarters lie five miles farther up the road. The nine miles of this route that remain unpaved are graded, and normally suitable for all vehicles other than RVs. If you'd rather not drive your own vehicle on this stretch, a Park'n'Ride **bus** will take you the rest of the way (departures daily 8.30am, 9.30am & 1.30am; return $15 per person; check schedules on Ⓦwww.grandcanyonskywalk.com).

Two further routes remain unpaved, but may be improved by the time you read this; ask locally before taking either of them. The more likely of the two is **Antares Road**, which runs north from Route 66, eighteen miles northeast of Kingman, and meets Pearce Ferry Road at much the same juncture as Stockton Hill Road. The fifty-mile **Buck and Doe Road**, which heads north from Route 66, four miles west of Peach Springs, and meets Diamond Bar Road three miles short of the end, will probably remain unpaved and impassable to standard vehicles indefinitely.

Flying to Grand Canyon West

Several companies fly day-trip **air tours from Las Vegas** to the airstrip alongside the West Rim headquarters. Papillon Grand Canyon Helicopters (Ⓣ702/736-7243 or 1-888/635-7272, Ⓦwww.papillon.com), Maverick Helicopter Tours (Ⓣ702/261-0007 or 1-888/261-4414, Ⓦwww.maverickhelicopter.com) and Sundance Helicopters (Ⓣ702/736-0606 or 1-800/653-1881, Ⓦwww.helicoptour.com) provide **helicopter** tours at $250–500, while **fixed-wing** operators, using small airplanes, include Scenic Airlines (Ⓣ702/638-3200 or 1-800/634-6801, Ⓦwww.scenic.com), whose cheapest Skywalk package costs $194.

Exploring Grand Canyon West

Your initial impression of Grand Canyon West is likely to be of the featureless grey desert plateau that leads to the edge of the abyss. All visitors report to a small, single-storey building to the right of the highway, a few hundred yards short of the rim, which serves as the **tribal headquarters** for tours and permits, and as the **terminal** for both the helicopter pad and the airstrip across the road.

The only way to reach the two main viewpoints, farther down the road, is by riding the Hualapai-run "Hop On Hop Off" **buses** from the terminal. If you've flown in, some form of package tour will already be included in the overall price you've paid; otherwise, the various permutations and possibilities are outlined in the box below.

Eagle Point and the Skywalk

Eagle Point, a mile down the road from the terminal, is not located right on the main canyon rim, but facing across a narrow, unnamed side canyon. In the right light – especially in the morning – the central portion of the long knife-edged

The sheer cost of visiting Grand Canyon West

Any independent traveller planning to visit Grand Canyon West needs to be aware that it's much, much more **expensive** than any other outdoors destination covered in this book. The following charges apply to all independent visitors to Grand Canyon West; if you buy a flight-seeing or other tour from Las Vegas, check exactly what the quoted price includes.

All visitors have to buy the $43 **Hualapai Legacy** package; the price includes tribal taxes and an $8 "impact fee", and covers use of the shuttle-buses to reach Eagle Point, Guano Point and Hualapai Ranch, but *not* the Skywalk or any food. Note that, in theory at least, you are not permitted to bring your own food or drink onto the reservation.

The $56 **Legacy Silver** package includes a meal at any of the viewpoints, which would otherwise cost $16 if bought separately, while the $87 **Legacy Gold** package additionally includes a ticket for the **Skywalk**, which costs $32 if bought separately. Having your photo taken on the Skywalk – you can't take your own camera – costs another $30.

Further optional extras include **horseback** rides ($11 for 10min in the arena; rim rides $38 for 30min, $82 for 90min); a sightseeing **helicopter** flight ($138 for 15min); and a **helicopter** flight down to the river, where you take a pontoon **boat** ride ($171).

Thus two adults who drive to the West Rim, and walk on the Skywalk, will pay a minimum of $174 for the day. With no reductions for children, families can expect to pay double that.

Full details can be found on Ⓦ www.grandcanyonwest.com.

sandstone spur that forms the canyon's opposite wall bears an uncanny resemblance to a massive eagle with its wings outstretched.

You can see the **Skywalk** itself (Ⓦ www.grandcanyonskywalk.com), jutting from the rim at the tip of Eagle Point, from a perfunctorily roped-off viewing area alongside the bus stop. To set foot on this horseshoe-shaped, glass-bottomed walkway, however, you have first to shuffle through an empty, incomplete building scheduled at some point to hold a restaurant. As you can't carry anything out onto the Skywalk, all bags and cameras have to be left in lockers, and you also have to wear disposable booties over your shoes.

Whatever impression the publicity may give, when you step out onto the Skywalk, you're not poised 4000ft above the Colorado River, but at most 800ft above the talus slope of the side canyon, with the river visible away to the left. The floor of the walkway consists of scuffed glass plates separated by tiny chinks, so you can indeed look straight down an open drop, but it's really not very scary. You're free to spend as long as you like on the Skywalk; it's a self-guided tour.

A short trail from Eagle Point leads to the **Indian Village**, which consists of various authentic dwellings built by the Hualapai and other local Native American tribes, including the Navajo, Hopi and Apache. Tribal representatives are on hand to explain their history and symbolism, there are regular dance performances and crafts are sold in the **Hualapai Market**.

Guano Point

At the dead end of the road, two miles beyond the terminal, the buses reach the appetizingly named **Guano Point**. This windswept rounded headland, poised atop sheer 3000ft cliffs at an intersection with an enormous side canyon, surveys long stretches of the Colorado in both directions. Though the Grand Canyon looks as if it could go on forever, in fact it comes to an end not far beyond the next bend in the river to the west, where it bisects the Grand Wash Cliffs.

The views from Guano Point are actually far more impressive than from Eagle Point, providing some consolation for those visitors disappointed with the Skywalk. Originally, in fact, it was planned to build the Skywalk here, until surveys showed that the rock was too unstable to support its weight.

Follow the short trail that loops just below the tip of the point, and you'll find large pylons and chunks of abandoned machinery littering the landscape. Dating from the 1940s and 1950s, these are relics of the days when guano – bat dung, an excellent fertilizer – was commercially mined from the so-called **Bat Cave**, still visible on the far side of the river. A cable car carried the congealed dung across the canyon. The mine was eventually shut down after a rabies scare, but it's said that the actual cables were cut by USAF fighter planes flying illegally low during a training mission; unlike the National Park Service, the Hualapai allow the Air Force to conduct flight training within the canyon.

An ugly, rather futuristic shelter on the point serves all-you-can-eat **buffet lunches** – chicken, ribs and the like – included in certain tour packages.

Hualapai Ranch

Roughly two miles from the terminal in the opposite direction from Eagle and Guano points, **Hualapai Ranch** is perhaps the strangest of the attractions the Hualapai have built at Grand Canyon West. Bearing little relevance to either the tribe or the canyon, it's basically a themed Wild West stockade atop the empty plateau, set well back from the rim. In addition to serving as the headquarters for horseback rides, it stages such Western-style events as country music performances and professional bison riding, and also offers cookout lunches – a fancy way of saying that an outdoor café ladles out plates of beans and BBQ chicken.

Part of the ranch, centring on the so-called Telegraph Office, holds well-equipped rental cabins, which offer the only **overnight accommodation** at Grand Canyon West (☎1-888/868-9378 or 928/769-2230, ⊛www.grandcanyonwest.com/ranch .php; $150 per person, including Legacy Silver package but not Skywalk).

Quartermaster Point

A third viewpoint, **Quartermaster Point**, lies beyond Hualapai Ranch. Perched just west of deep Quartermaster Canyon, the overlook commands views straight up Burnt Canyon, across the Colorado, towards the long promontory of Kelly Point on the North Rim.

The Colorado River

No hiking trails connect Grand Canyon West with the **Colorado River** below, but a high proportion of visitors take the four-minute **helicopter** ride down from the terminal (for prices, see box on p.183). The flight in itself is a major adventure, and it's also a real thrill to find yourself strolling along beside the river in the depths of the inner gorge. You'll land close to the south bank, which is not only much broader than its northern counterpart but also, crucially, belongs to the Hualapai. There's little here in the way of amenities, apart from a basic arbour for shade, but with its flowering cacti and dense thickets of tamarisk, it's an attractive and fascinating spot.

A short footpath leads down from the landing site to the river's edge, where wooden jetties serve as a base for the pontoons and jet boats that sweep visitors out for a quick swirl on the river. The adjoining beach is the terminus for the Huala-pai's one-day rafting trips (see p.186); participants fly out from here.

Note that if you take one of the one-day helicopter tours from Las Vegas to Grand Canyon West that land within the canyon but do *not* include a river trip, your landing will probably be at a different vantage point, a mile or so upriver, which arguably enjoys better views but does not offer access to the river itself.

Peach Springs and around

The lone sizable Hualapai community, **PEACH SPRINGS**, stands at the northern extremity of Route 66's sweeping curve away from I-40, 53 miles northeast of Kingman and 35 miles northwest of Seligman. Entirely distinct from, and not conveniently connected with, Grand Canyon West, it lies just six miles west of the turn-off for Arrowhead Hwy 18, the one road into the Havasupai Indian Reservation. Aside from Seligman itself, there's a disappointing lack of kitsch Americana along Route 66, but driving the much-mythologized "**Mother Road**", crossing vast desert expanses with only the railroad for company, remains an evocative experience.

With the purchase of a backcountry sightseeing permit in Peach Springs you can also drive north to **Diamond Creek** from here – the only spot within the Grand Canyon where you can drive all the way to the **river**, and also the starting point for the Canyon's only **one-day rafting trip**.

Practicalities

Peach Springs is no more than a straggle of buildings along the highway, of which the most prominent by far is the shiny, modern **Hualapai Lodge** (℡1-888/868-9378 or 928/769-2230, ⊛grandcanyonwest.com/lodge.php; April–Oct ❺, Nov–March ❹). Its sixty good-sized bedrooms are broadly equivalent to what you'd expect to find in one of the slightly smarter hotel chains, and the building has free wi-fi. Its **dining room**, the Diamond Creek Restaurant, is open all day every day (daily: April–Sept daily 6.30am–9pm; Oct–March Mon–Thurs till 8.30pm, Fri–Sun till 8pm). "West Rim dinners", with soup or salad bar plus a main meal, cost $20, or you can get Hualapai frybread or a pizza for $8–12.

A desk in the lobby serves as the headquarters of the **Hualapai River Runners** (Mon–Fri 9am–5pm; same phone and website; see p.186 for details). As well as organizing the rafting trips described below, this office sells **tickets** for visits to Grand Canyon West (though very few of the drivers heading there come via Peach Springs; see p.182), and permits for **backcountry sightseeing** ($15 per day) and **camping** on Diamond Creek Road ($20, including sightseeing fee; see below). The tribe's separate **Wildlife Office** (Mon–Fri 8am–4.30pm; ℡928/769-2227), a short way west across the highway, issues similar permits for exploration elsewhere on the reservation, as well as permits to fish and hunt (up to $20,000 for a trophy bighorn sheep).

Diamond Creek

The unpaved twenty-mile road that leads due north of Peach Springs to the river at **Diamond Creek** is used almost exclusively by rafters, either leaving the Colorado after a multi-day expedition or taking one of the Hualapai's day trips. However, with the appropriate **backcountry sightseeing permit** from *Hualapai Lodge*, you can simply drive down for a look.

Thanks to deep **Peach Springs Canyon**, Diamond Creek is the only place within the Grand Canyon where a road runs all the way to the river, dropping 3000ft en route. Not much of a road, though: the views of soaring canyon walls on either side are great, but the surface is terrible and liable to be rendered impassable to standard cars by the slightest rain. The final two miles are often washed out altogether by summer flash floods.

Despite the difficult terrain, there was a hotel down here between 1884 and 1889, before access improved to what's now called the South Rim. These days, there's just a rather rudimentary tribal **campground**, set back from the river amid the sand dunes ($20 per night, including sightseeing fee).

One-day rafting trip

Operating under the name **Hualapai River Runners** (☎1-888/868-9378 or 928/769-2230, ⓦgrandcanyonwest.com/rafting.php), the Hualapai run the Grand Canyon's only **one-day rafting trip** – a 35-mile float from **Diamond Creek** to **Quartermaster Canyon** that includes significant stretches of whitewater. No rowing or paddling is involved; instead they use motorized pontoons, capable of carrying up to ten passengers aged 8 or over. The price is a hefty $328 per person. At a potential cost of more than $1300 for a family of four, it makes a very expensive day out and simply getting here in the first place takes quite a commitment, but the trips are nonetheless popular with those who lack the time for a longer river trip.

Daily between mid-March and mid-October, the trips set off from *Hualapai Lodge* by van at 8am. After a ninety-minute drive down to the river at Diamond Creek, you'll board the rafts and immediately confront whitewater. The first ten miles shoot the canyon's final ten rapids, with a maximum difficulty rating of 7 (see p.193). Following a riverside picnic lunch and optional short hike, the trip winds down with a tranquil 25-mile float to Quartermaster Canyon, where a **helicopter** awaits to fly you up to the canyon rim. It's a two-hour drive back to Peach Springs, with a typical return time of around 7pm. Many passengers stay overnight at the lodge before or after the trip.

Rafting the Colorado River

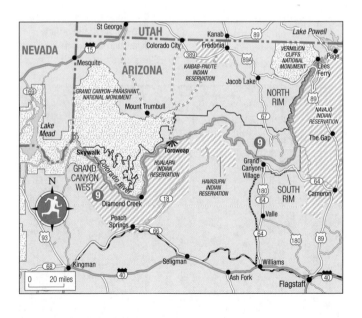

CHAPTER 9

Highlights

* **Dory trips** Follow in the wake of John Wesley Powell by tackling the Colorado in a genuine wooden dory. See p.192

* **The sound of strings** Remarkably, Canyon Explorations offers an annual rafting trip during which participants are serenaded by a string quartet. See p.194

* **Specialist trips** Arizona Raft Adventures' many rafting expeditions include trips designed for hikers, natural historians and even geologists. See p.194

* **Marble Canyon float trip** Floating the Colorado from Glen Canyon Dam to Lees Ferry gives you a spectacular taste of river rafting in just half a day. See p.196

* **Hualapai River Runners** At the far western end of the Grand Canyon, the Hualapai tribe offers a one-day rafting trip that culminates in an exhilarating helicopter ride. See p.196

▲ Rafting in the Inner Gorge

Rafting the Colorado River

I conclude the Colorado is not a very easy stream to navigate.

– Diary entry of George Bradley, member of the first Powell expedition,
at the end of the first-ever day's boating on the Colorado

Part white-knuckle ride, part leisurely scenic cruise, **rafting** the **Colorado River** through the Grand Canyon ranks unquestionably among the greatest outdoor adventures our planet has to offer. Yes, you can admire the canyon from the safety of the rim, but only when you've raced its every rapid, drenched to the skin and deafened by its thundering roar, can you truly claim to know it inside out. And there's much more to a river trip than pure adrenaline: you can also picnic on sandy riverside beaches; camp beneath the stars; hike up little-known side canyons to hidden waterfalls, mysterious caves and narrow sandstone slots; swim in streams and water holes; and generally escape from the modern world into a remote, timeless wilderness.

When **John Wesley Powell**'s crew set out in 1869 to become the first party to travel down the Colorado by boat (see p.201), they had no way of knowing whether such a voyage was possible. All the way, they were haunted by the fear that a mighty waterfall might lie around the next bend, or that some fearsome rapid might fill the canyon wall to wall at a point where there was no way to climb out. As it turned out, there were no waterfalls, and it *is* possible to float the full length of the Colorado. It's still far from easy, of course, and not something you should even dream of attempting without the most expert guidance and advice. Nevertheless, river craft and techniques have become so refined that professional rafting companies carry thousands of inexperienced passengers through the canyon each year in safety. Yet as weather and water levels fluctuate and flash floods reshape the canyon's contours, the thrill of uncertainty remains, and every trip presents a new challenge.

The prime reason why rafting the Grand Canyon is so exciting is the fact that there are an estimated 161 sets of **rapids** along the way. The Colorado here is what's known as a **"pool and drop"** river, meaning that it consists of tranquil lake-like sections, where it meanders along at an average speed of around six miles per hour, that alternate with hectic rapids, when it's constricted into a narrower, debris-strewn channel. These occur where rocks washed down the side canyon by a tributary stream have tumbled into the riverbed. The resultant **whitewater** flows at perhaps twenty or thirty miles per hour, creating an obstacle course of

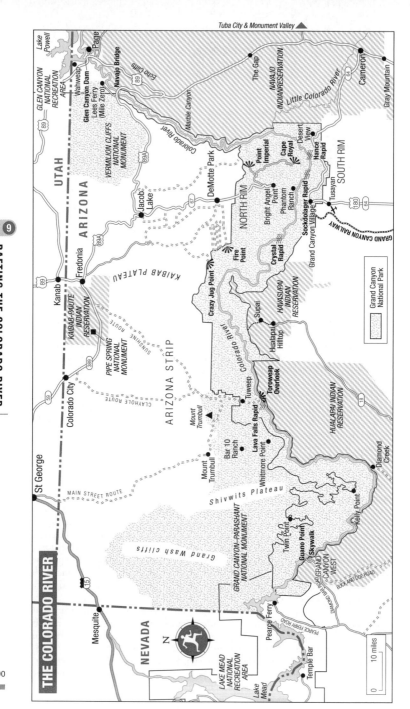

Tuba City & Monument Valley ▲

THE COLORADO RIVER

9

RAFTING THE COLORADO RIVER

190

concealed boulders and treacherous whirlpools that canyon boatmen learn to navigate by both instinct and experience.

The **rafting season** begins in mid-April, and runs until mid-September for motorized trips, and as late as early November for oar-powered expeditions. The busiest period is **summer**, between June and August, despite daytime temperatures that often exceed 100°F and a high likelihood of thunderstorms from late July into September. In **spring** and **autumn**, when temperatures are cooler and the canyon quieter, many operators offer longer trips to allow for extra hiking, while spring also sees the canyon flora at its most colorful. Typical daytime highs are in the 60–80°F range in April and November, and more like 70–100°F in May, September and October. Nightly lows vary from as low as 40°F in April up to a muggy 90°F in July. Whenever you come, however, you must be prepared for extremes of both heat and cold, and also potential rain. Although the Colorado itself remains consistently cool year-round, barely straying from 48°F – which is cold enough to cause hypothermia – streams and pools in the side canyons allow for great swimming in summer.

Both the two basic types of rafting trip are strictly regulated by the Park Service – you certainly can't just turn up at the Colorado with your own raft and set off. You can either join a **commercial** trip with one of the accredited concessionaires listed on pp.194–195, or, if you have a great deal of whitewater experience and an even greater amount of patience, put together your own **non-commercial** party and join the waiting list for a time slot. As it currently takes around nine years to reach the top of the list, the commercial option is much more realistic.

Commercial rafting trips

Anyone planning to take a commercial rafting trip down the Grand Canyon faces a fundamental choice between joining a **motorized** or an **oar-powered** expedition. Both typically cost between **$250 and $350 per person, per day**, though oar-powered trips tend to cost a little more per day, and take longer overall. On a motorized trip, the professional guides are entirely responsible for the actual work of running the river; on an oar-powered one, you don't necessarily have to do any rowing, but guides often allow passengers to paddle some or even all of the way. As a rule, the **minimum age** for participants on motorized trips is 8, while on oar-powered trips it's 12.

Although purists insist that the comparative silence and sense of physical involvement of an oar-powered trip provides a far more "authentic" river-running experience than a motorized trip, the day-to-day routine is quite similar whichever type you choose. Even the fastest trips of either type spend little more than five hours actually on the river each day; it's taken for granted that everyone wants to stop for picnics and hikes.

The boats

For the most part, commercial operators use different kinds of **inflatable rubberized rafts**. Powell's wooden boats were built for speed, very hard to manoeuvre and rowed by two men, seated in traditional rowboat style with their backs to what lay ahead. Modern rafts are flat-bottomed, extremely manoeuvrable and capable of bouncing undamaged off obstacles; the single boatman faces forward and often slows down by paddling against the current, jockeying for position until a route opens up.

Motorized trips, not surprisingly, travel significantly faster. Each raft can be up to 30ft long, equipped with outriggers for extra stability, and carry up to ten passengers. The Park Service has long considered banning motorized craft altogether, arguing that they increase both noise and environmental pollution. Industry lobbyists have so far managed to stymie a complete ban, but motorized expeditions remain restricted in terms of both the total passengers permitted each year and the season they can operate (mid-April to mid-September).

Nonmotorized, or **oar-powered**, rafts average around eighteen feet long and are usually rowed and steered by a single guide with the only oar while the four or five passengers simply enjoy the ride. Some outfitters also offer **paddle rafts**, however, of a similar size and passenger capacity, on which everyone has their own paddle, and the guide is only responsible for steering. Adventure sports enthusiasts tend to prefer **paddle-only** trips, during which paying customers are expected to paddle all the way; it's also possible to take a **hybrid** trip, which incorporates both vessel types and allows passengers to choose each day whether to ride in a paddle boat or be rowed by a guide.

For those determined to echo the conditions experienced by the early river pioneers, two operators, **Grand Canyon Expeditions** and **O.A.R.S.** (under the name Grand Canyon Dories), offer significantly more expensive rowing trips in hard-bodied **dories**. These are the closest modern approximation to Powell's boats, albeit extensively adapted for Grand Canyon use. Because dories require such skilled handling, only the crew may row, making the trips significantly more expensive.

Choosing a trip

The Grand Canyon is officially 277 miles long, with each river mile being numbered downstream from Mile 0 at **Lees Ferry** (see p.126). Itself just under sixteen miles downstream from Glen Canyon Dam, Lees Ferry is the only spot from which it's possible to **launch** a rafting expedition. Boats and/or passengers can, however, **leave** at various different junctures.

The canyon ends at Mile 277, where the Colorado emerges onto the open waters of **Lake Mead**; three miles on, at Mile 280, a paved road accesses the lake at **Pearce Ferry** (also spelled Pierce Ferry). However, over the final 43 miles of the canyon, the true river channel lies submerged beneath the calmer waters of Lake Mead. Many river trips, therefore, end at **Diamond Creek**, on Hualapai land at Mile 226, where boats and passengers can be driven out of the canyon along a gravel road. Some operators curtail their trips even sooner, at **Whitmore Wash** (Mile 187), scooping up customers from river level by helicopter and whisking them to the **Bar 10 Ranch** on the North Rim, where an airstrip facilitates onward flights to Las Vegas or elsewhere. There's also one other potential stopping place en route: **Phantom Ranch**, at Mile 87, from where passengers can hike out to either the South or the North Rim. It's also possible for passengers to join an existing trip at Phantom Ranch, though there's no way to get a boat down to the Colorado at that point.

The permutations for possible trips are endless. What are advertised as full-length Grand Canyon expeditions may be 187, 226 or 280 miles long and take anything from six motorized days to 22 oar-powered days (the record, incidentally, for the full 277 miles is just under 37 hours, by an unauthorized expedition undertaken in 1983 during dangerous flooding, when the canyon was closed to all craft). Most operators also offer an **Upper Canyon** option, starting at Lees Ferry and ending with a hike out from Phantom Ranch, which typically takes three nights, four days, and a **Lower Canyon** trip, starting by hiking down to Phantom Ranch, and taking out somewhere downstream after four or five nights.

You can also take a **one-night**, two-day river trip if you fly down into the canyon at Whitmore Wash with Arizona River Runners (see p.194), or a **one-day** trip from Diamond Creek with Hualapai River Runners (see p.186).

Neither an Upper nor a Lower Canyon trip is "better" than the other. If you take the Upper Canyon trip, you'll know that all your fellow passengers are starting at the same time as you, as opposed to joining an established group, and you'll also get a gentler, more progressive introduction to the canyon and its rapids. On the other hand, there's less placid water overall, and you'll have to hike out at the end. A Lower Canyon trip will give you a slightly longer ride, but also plunge you straight away into some really major rapids.

Although whitewater experts traditionally grade the difficulty of rapids on the world's rivers on a scale of one to six, on the Colorado they're ranked from one to ten, so a "4" here won't be the same as one elsewhere. Both the Grand Canyon's two unquestioned tens lie downstream from Phantom Ranch – **Crystal Rapid** at Mile 98, created by a flash flood in 1966, and **Lava Falls Rapid** further west at Mile 179, which is visible from Toroweap Point (see p.145). There are, however, a couple of almost-as-intense rapids in the Upper Canyon: **Hance Rapid** at Mile 76, and **Sockdolager Rapid** – named by Powell after a contemporary word meaning "knockout punch" – just past the start of the Granite Gorge at Mile 78.

Other highlights in the Upper Canyon include **Vasey's Paradise**, a flower-filled natural garden at Mile 31; the **Redwall Cavern** at mile 33, a vast sand-floored alcove which Powell overeagerly estimated could hold fifty thousand people; and the confluence with the **Little Colorado** at Mile 61, where, thanks to a rich concentration of salts from springs not far upstream, the tributary flows in from the east as a resplendent turquoise stream.

The biggest treats for **hikers** come in the Lower Canyon, with the successive **Olo**, **Matkatamiba** and **Havasu** canyons between miles 145 and 156. Both the first two are narrow "slot canyons", interspersed with hidden pools and waterfalls and boasting rock walls sculpted by flash floods into beautiful swirling patterns; the splendours of Havasu Canyon are described in full in Chapter 6, though rafters seldom hike any further up the canyon than to Beaver Falls, four miles up, but two miles below Mooney Falls.

Commercial rafting operators

A complete list of all operators authorized to conduct commercial river trips within the Grand Canyon appears below; you can also find the current list online, with active links, at ⓦ www.nps.gov/grca/planyourvisit/river-concessioners.htm. For an overview of what's available at any one time, contact **Rivers and Oceans** (ⓣ 1-800/473-4576 or 928/526-4575, ⓦ rivers-oceans.com), a travel broker that specializes in making bookings with them all.

In choosing which company to go with, be clear whether their published rates include any **transport** and/or overnight **accommodation** that may be required before or after your trip. While you might be tempted to cut costs by driving yourself to Lees Ferry, that can leave you with a serious logistic problem. Also, if you're a long way from home, taking a trip that includes return transport from and to Flagstaff or Las Vegas can spare you from having to pay for a **rental car** you won't be using for several days.

All rates include unlimited **food** and **beverages** for the duration, though you have to supply any alcoholic drinks yourself. You should, however, check exactly what **equipment** is included in the price. Some operators charge rental fees to passengers who don't bring their own sleeping bags and mats, others provide everything.

Individual companies also provide checklists of what you should and shouldn't bring. Recommended **clothing** includes a full set of raingear, long insulating underclothes, a fleece jacket and hat, a swimsuit and sandals with soft rubber soles. Among items not to carry are mobile or satellite phones, radios and other electrical devices.

Finally, bear in mind that it's customary to **tip** your river guides between five and ten percent of the total cost at the end of your trip.

Arizona Raft Adventures Flagstaff, AZ
℡1-800/786-7238 or 928/526-8200, ⊛azraft
.com. ARA's motorized voyages operate between May and mid-August, costing around $2420 for the 8-day standard trip, and $2930 for the 10-day Natural History Discovery in April. Paddling trips, for riders who want to paddle all the time, leave once monthly between May and mid-September, at around $2040 for 6 days, $2800 for 9 days and $3600 for 14 days. For slightly cheaper rates, you can also join one of their 24 hybrid trips between late April and October, on which passengers choose each day between riding in an oar-powered raft, or actively crewing a paddle boat.

Arizona River Runners Phoenix, AZ ℡1-800/477-7238 or 602/867-4866, ⊛raftarizona.com.
Motorized trips down the full length of the canyon, available between May and September, cost $2250 for 6 days, $2395 for 7 days or $2450 for 8 days; a "Hiker's Special" trip in early April is significantly cheaper. Oar-powered expeditions run monthly between April and October, and are $1750 for the 6-day Upper Canyon voyage; $2295 for the 8-day trip from Phantom Ranch to Diamond Creek; and $3295 for the full 13-day voyage from Lees Ferry to Diamond Creek. Every few days between May and September, they also do a 3-day "Grand Canyon Escape" from Las Vegas, in which you fly to the Bar 10 Ranch and spend a night there, then take a helicopter down to the river for a 1.5-day trip and return to Las Vegas from Lake Mead, all for $1350.

Canyon Explorations/Canyon Expeditions Flagstaff, AZ ℡1-800/654-0723 or 928/774-4559, ⊛canyonexplorations.com. An extensive programme of river trips of differing lengths is available between April and October. All begin and end with transport to and from Flagstaff, and several are extended to allow for extra hiking. Whether you take a hybrid trip, which includes not only oar boats and a paddle boat but also inflatable kayaks, or an all-paddling expedition, the cost is the same, depending solely on the length. Rates vary from $1790 for 6 days, via $2710 for 9 days up to $4135 for 17 days; bizarrely enough, one of their 15-day trips, costing $3735, carries a string quartet along with it. Kayakers can join any trip, for a $200 additional fee.

Canyoneers Flagstaff, AZ ℡1-800/525-0924 or 928/526-0924, ⊛canyoneers.com. Canyoneers

specialize in sending massive powered pontoons down the Grand Canyon. Weekly between mid-April and mid-September, they run its entire length in 7 days (6 nights) for $2295 ($2195 in April only). Some but not all trips offer the option of a $995 3-day, 2-night sprint through the Upper Canyon or a $1750 5-day, 4-night trip through the Lower Canyon, which costs $1950 if you choose to spend a night at Phantom Ranch first. Once each in June, July and August, they also offer oar-powered trips, costing $1795 for the 5-night Upper Canyon segment, $2350 for the 8-night Lower Canyon stretch, or $3250 for the full 13- or 14-day trip. All trips start and end in Flagstaff.

Colorado River & Trail Expeditions Salt Lake City, UT ℡1-800/253-7328 or 801/261-1789, ⊛crateinc.com. Weekly motorized expeditions between mid-May and the end of August, at $1400 for the 4-day Upper Canyon; $2085 for the 6-day Lower Canyon run; and $2700 for the whole thing, in either 8 or 9 days. Between late July and late September, they also offer three hybrid trips, and one exclusively paddling trip, both of which cost $1800 for the 5 days from Lees Ferry to Phantom Ranch; $2800 for the 7 days from Phantom Ranch to Whitmore Wash; and $3450 for the 11 days from Lees Ferry to Whitmore Wash.

Diamond River Adventures Page, AZ
℡1-800/343-3121 or 928/645-8866, ⊛diamondriver.com. Female owned and managed rafting company, which offers Grand Canyon expeditions of between 4 and 13 days by either oar or motorboat. The season runs from early April to early October, with motorized trips setting off more or less weekly, and seven oar-powered ones in total. Four-day Upper Canyon motorized trips start at around $990, while to run the full length with a motor takes 7 days and costs $2290. By oar, it takes from 10 to 13 days, for around $3250.

Grand Canyon Expeditions Company Kanab, UT ℡1-800/544-2691 or 435/644-2691, ⊛gcex.com.
A huge number of motorized expeditions, with dozens of departures between mid-April and mid-September each year. Some are devoted to special interests like ecology, archeology and photography, and thereby offer longer pauses at, and extra hikes to, sites of particular significance, with guidance from experts in the relevant field. The 8-day run from Lees Ferry to Lake Mead costs

$2550. They also offer four rowing trips each summer, in May, June, July and September, using modern dories, which take either 14 days, costing $3700, or 16 days for $3900.

Hatch River Expeditions Marble Canyon, AZ ☎1-800/856-8966 or 928/355-2241, ⊛hatchriverexpeditions.com. Regular seven-day, 188-mile motorized trips between Lees Ferry and Whitmore Wash; passengers leave the canyon well before the end, via helicopter, for connecting flights to Las Vegas or Marble Canyon. Taking the whole cruise costs $2310, or you can take a 4-day version, which costs $1200 for the Upper Canyon, exiting at Phantom Ranch, or $1250 for the Lower Canyon, entering at Phantom Ranch. In April they offer longer trips for hikers. They also run a similar programme of oar-powered trips, with the full-length 12-day trip costing $3625.

Moki Mac River Expeditions Salt Lake City, UT ☎1-877/394-9897 or 801/512-2088, ⊛www.mokimac.com. Between April and late October, Moki Mac run twelve 14-day oar-powered trips between Lees Ferry and Lake Mead – priced at $3800 for the whole thing, $1950 for the Upper Canyon and $2900 for the Lower Canyon – and nine 8-day motorized trips on the same route, only sold as the entire trip and costing $2600. All rates cover return transport to and from Las Vegas.

O.A.R.S. Angels Camp, CA ☎1-800/346-6277 or 209/736-4677, ⊛oars.com. Adventure-tour operator, active throughout the West, who offer two separate kinds of Grand Canyon trips, on a very flexible programme that runs from mid-April into early November. Of their conventional paddled raft trips, the full canyon voyage from Lees Ferry to Lake Mead takes either 15 or 17 days and costs around $4350 or $4800 respectively, while the many shorter stretches on offer include the usual Lees Ferry to Phantom Ranch stretch in 5–7 days ($1900–2500), and Phantom Ranch to Diamond Creek takes 7–12 days ($3000–3800). As Grand Canyon Dories, they also offer trips in flat-bottomed wooden dories (rowboats), with the full canyon length taking up to 19 days at $5500, the Upper Canyon taking 6–8 days ($2250–2900) and the Lower Canyon taking 9–12 days ($3450–4300).

Outdoors Unlimited Flagstaff, AZ ☎1-800/637-7238 or 928/526-4511, ⊛outdoorsunlimited.com. Oar-powered trips between May and August, all of which take at least one paddle boat along, and

some of which are all-paddling. The standard trip from Lees Ferry to Lake Mead costs $3295 for the full 13 days, or you can take a 5- or 6-day Upper Canyon run for $1665/$1855 respectively, or the 8- or 9-day Lower Canyon segment for $2415/$2620. An all-paddling trip is slightly more expensive, while in April and September you can pay a little more again to join an extended trip that offers more opportunities for hiking.

Tour West Orem, UT ☎1-800/453-9107 or 801/225-0755, ⊛twriver.com. Between April and mid-September, Tour West send 21 motorized expeditions down the canyon. A 6-night trip from Lees Ferry to the Bar 10 Ranch costs $2360, an 8-night trip from Lees Ferry to Lake Mead costs $2530,and you can also take a 3-night jaunt from the Bar 10 Ranch to Lake Mead for $12950. They also offer ten 12-night rowing trips, five of which are in September, for $3530.

Western River Expeditions Salt Lake City, UT ☎1-866/904-1160 or 801/942-6669, ⊛westernriver.com. Western River runs a very slick programme of brisk, motorized Grand Canyon expeditions, offering two basic choices on just over fifty separate expeditions between mid-April and September each year. You can either take a 6- or 7-day run from Lees Ferry to the Bar 10 Ranch, which involves being helicoptered out of the canyon 187 miles along, just after Lava Falls; or be choppered in at that point, for a 3-day float down to Lake Mead (with an optional extra first night at the ranch). The former costs $2500–2700, the latter more like $1300; both are ten percent cheaper in April.

Wilderness River Adventures Page, AZ ☎1-800/992-8022 or 928/645-3296, ⊛riveradventures.com. Oar-powered and motorized trips. The oar-powered ones, using six boats each capable of carrying up to five passengers, set off every 2–3 weeks between mid-May and mid-September. They cost around $1885 for the 5-day Upper Canyon ride; $2640 for the Lower Canyon, from Phantom Ranch to the Bar 10 Ranch, with a flight out to Las Vegas or Page; and $3165–5175 for the 12–16 days of the full-length Grand Tradition. Motorized expeditions, using two 15-passenger boats, run regularly between late April and mid-September, taking 3.5 days for the Upper Canyon ($1150); 4.5 days for the Lower Canyon ($2150); and 6–8 days for the whole thing ($2500–2800).

One-day trips

No one-day rafting trips are available within Grand Canyon National Park. There are, however, two alternatives if you only have a day to spare, one at either end of the canyon.

As described on p.124, Colorado River Discovery (☎928/645-9175 or 1-888/522-6644, ⓦraftthecanyon.com) offer half-day **float trips** that start immediately below **Glen Canyon Dam** and take out at **Lees Ferry**. Participants rendezvous at 130 Sixth Ave in the centre of Page, Arizona, not far from the dam; there are two trips daily between May and September, with participants setting off from Page at 7am and 12.30pm, and one daily in March, April, October and November, leaving Page at 10.30am. The cost is $84 for adults, $74 for children aged 4 to 11. Simple snacks are available for purchase at the end of the trips, but otherwise you have to bring your own food and drink.

Between March and May, and September and November, the same company also offers full-day oar-powered **rowing trips** (Mon, Wed & Sun only, leaving Page at 8.30am; adults $161, children $151).

At the far western end of the canyon, the Hualapai River Runners run daily 35-mile motorized trips along the Colorado, including several rapids. You'll find full details in the **Hualapai reservation** chapter on p.186.

Non-commercial trips

Between two and three hundred **private rafting expeditions** are allowed onto the Colorado River each year, with a maximum of sixteen participants each. Every participant must have a permit, issued by the Park Service; full details can be found on ⓦwww.nps.gov/grca/planyourvisit.

As far more people want to go than places are available, who gets the permits is decided by means of a "**weighted lottery**", conducted for each calendar year. To apply, you have to create an online profile at ⓦhttps://npspermits.us. All members of a potential expedition must be listed, and each member can appear on only one application per year, but only the designated leader has to pay the $25 fee to participate in the lottery, naming five specific dates in the coming year.

The precise details of how the lottery is conducted are fiendishly complicated, but basically your chances vary according to how long it is since you last rafted the river; if you never have, your chances are five times better than someone who did so last year. No one is permitted to make two river trips, whether private or commercial, in the same year. Very broadly speaking, applications for dates in May or June have less than one chance in a hundred of succeeding, while winter launches are much less in demand. The main draw takes place in February, though further lotteries are held to cover dates that fail to fill or have cancellations.

Contexts

Contexts

History

T he Grand Canyon might seem a supremely inhospitable, pristine environment, but it has been home to humans for around twelve thousand years. Native Americans once farmed along the canyon floor, across its plateaus, and up on the rims, while Spanish adventurers arrived eighty years before the *Mayflower* set sail. Only within the last hundred years, however, has it occurred to anyone to come here for fun.

Native peoples

The oldest traces of a human presence at the Grand Canyon are a handful of flaked-stone spear-points that date back to around 10,000 BC. They were produced by the so-called **Clovis** culture, which spread throughout North and South America until around 8000 BC. Living in small groups, constantly on the move, Clovis hunters pursued their prey over long distances. Their weapons have been found poking from the ribs of dead mammoths, and they seem to have been such successful killers that they drove the indigenous fauna – which included giant sloths, camels and even horses – to extinction.

As the large animals died out, the inhabitants of the Grand Canyon adapted to become **hunter-gatherers**, who migrated seasonally between the canyons and plateaus in search of food. Judging by the small figurines that have been found in caves in Marble Canyon and elsewhere – made from split willow twigs to represent deer and bighorn sheep and often run through by little "spears" – they developed shamanistic rituals to encourage hunting success.

The so-called **Archaic Era** was brought to an end by the infiltration of influences from Mexico, especially **agriculture**. The skill of growing **corn**, passed northwards from group to group and accompanied by the prayers and rituals necessary to ensure a good harvest, reached the canyon around 1000 BC. At first, low-level farming merely supplemented the traditional diet; large-scale cultivation of corn and also **squash** probably began around 100 BC. The people responsible, known as the **Basketmakers**, lived in extended family groups in shallow **pithouses** – rectangular pits, 2–6ft deep, with earthen roofs that rose above ground level. They hunted using the *atlatl* – a spear-throwing device – and cooked by dropping hot rocks into yucca-leaf baskets lined with waterproof pitch. They also domesticated **dogs**, for hunting, and **turkeys**, used for feathers rather than food.

Pottery arrived a few centuries later, and with it the ability to boil **beans**, the third great staple Southwestern food. By around 500 AD, the Basketmakers were also growing **cotton** and using **bows and arrows**. Sizable **villages** (what the Spanish later called **pueblos**) started to appear. Each focused around one pithouse, larger than the rest, which was set aside for public or ritual use. These were the first **kivas** – the ceremonial underground chambers still at the heart of Pueblo religion. By 700 AD, the Grand Canyon was populated by the ancestors of the modern Pueblo Indians, a people now known as **Ancestral Puebloans**, in preference to the previously common term **Anasazi**, which comes from a Navajo word meaning "enemy ancestors".

The heyday of agriculture in the Grand Canyon came roughly one thousand years ago, when increased levels of precipitation meant that corn, beans and squash could be planted throughout the canyon. Deltas at the mouths of major side canyons, such as **Unkar Creek** and **Chuar Creek**, made prized living spots.

Modern visitors can see typical Puebloan dwellings both down in the canyon, close to Phantom Ranch (see p.98), and up on the plateaus, most notably at the **Tusayan Ruin** on the South Rim (see p.62) and **Walhalla Glades** on the North Rim (see p.78). Ancestral Puebloans seem to have roamed readily between rim and river; their ladders and even footbridges still survive in certain well-hidden places, while their trails form the basis of almost all the park's hiking routes.

By around 1150, rainfall had again diminished, the soil was becoming depleted and an exodus from the region began. There are also indications of conflict for scant resources between competing groups. The Ancestral Puebloans of the canyon can be subdivided into the **Kayenta** peoples of its eastern and central reaches and the **Cohonina** further west, who with less fertile farmland depended to a greater extent on roasting wild agave plants. Fortified watchtower-like structures along the rim suggest that these previously amicable neighbours may have fallen out, or that perhaps the Cohonina left the canyon earlier than the Kayenta and were supplanted by the less friendly **Cerbat** people. The **Paiute** also made their appearance around this time, along the western end of the North Rim.

Although only a minimal population remained in the canyon proper by 1250, Puebloan groups have maintained close spiritual links ever since. The many distinct Pueblo peoples that survive today came into being when groups of migrants coalesced in various locations well to the east of the canyon between around 1100 and 1300. Geographically the closest are the **Hopi**, whose mesas lie sixty miles east. They regard a dome-shaped hot spring known as the *sipapu*, not far up the Little Colorado from its confluence with the Colorado, as the hole through which they entered the world, and still make pilgrimages to it along the **Salt Trail**. Some **Zuni**, who now live in New Mexico, also trace their origins back to the canyon, and particularly to Rainbow Falls below the North Rim.

Further west, the Cerbat never left the vicinity of the canyon. Their descendants became the **Hualapai**, and also the **Havasupai**, whose continued existence deep in Havasu Canyon represents the closest modern approximation to the ancient way of life.

The coming of the Spanish

In 1540 – less than twenty years after Cortés conquered the Aztecs of Mexico and before any European settlements had been established anywhere in what's now the United States – the first **Spaniards** reached the Southwest. An expedition led by **Francisco Vásquez de Coronado**, hoping to find cities of gold and consisting of more than three hundred Spanish soldiers plus hundreds more Native American "allies" and servants, marched up through Arizona and reached the Zuni pueblos on July 7. After a bloody battle – the first ever fought between Europeans and Native Americans – secured the area as a temporary base, exploring parties were sent out in all directions.

At the Hopi mesas, one such group was told of a great river not far to the west, inhabited by people with very large bodies (presumably the Havasupai, who tend to be significantly bigger than the Hopi). Four men, under **García López de Cárdenas**, were dispatched to investigate. They reached the Grand Canyon after twenty days, a puzzlingly long march that suggests their Hopi guides were deliberately leading them astray. The Spaniards were assured that no trails descended all the way to the river, and were taken to a spot where none was visible; no one knows exactly where, but it's generally reckoned to have been somewhere near Moran or Grandview points.

Cárdenas' men spent three days on the South Rim, searching for a route to the bottom. Three eventually made an abortive attempt, only to discover that "some huge rocks on the sides of the cliffs [that] seemed to be about as tall as a man…were bigger than the great tower of Seville". They turned back a third of the way down, concluding that "it was impossible to descend".

The Spanish hoped to find a river route to the so-called "South Sea", the Gulf of California, and identified the Colorado as being the *Río Tíson*, or Firebrand River, up which a simultaneous naval expedition was attempting to sail; it managed 225 miles, reaching the modern site of the Hoover Dam. Cárdenas himself, who seems to have been an unsavoury character, rejoined Coronado and was later responsible for burning two hundred Native American hostages alive at the pueblo of Tiguex.

Although Coronado's expedition ultimately failed, the Spaniards returned in force in 1598 to establish the colony of **New Mexico**, the boundaries of which nominally included the Grand Canyon. However, no further Spanish visits to the canyon are recorded before **1776**, when a group of explorers from Santa Fe, led by the Franciscan friars **Domínguez** and **Escalante** (see p.130), set out to map what later became the Old Spanish Trail to California. On their return they wandered extensively across the Arizona Strip and failed to cross the river at the site of Lees Ferry. That same year, **Father Garcés** from Tucson penetrated what he called a "calaboose of cliffs and canyons" to visit the Havasupai in the western canyon.

John Wesley Powell

One or two "mountain men" and trappers may have seen the Grand Canyon during the first half of the nineteenth century, but by the time jurisdiction over the region passed from Mexico to the United States, in 1848, it had never been surveyed and did not even have a fixed **name**. To the Havasupai it was *Wikatata* ("Rough Rim"); Spanish maps showed it as the *Río Muy Grande* ("Very Big River"); and Yankee prospectors knew it as the Big Cañon.

The first serious attempt to explore it came in 1857, when the US War Department despatched **Lieutenant Joseph Christmas Ives** to find out whether the Colorado River was navigable by **steamboat**. Like his Spanish predecessors, Ives got little further than the future site of Hoover Dam, but he then continued on foot all the way to the Little Colorado River. An accompanying geologist made the first accurate scientific observations of the canyon, but the expedition is best remembered for Ives' own very negative assessment: "The region is, of course, altogether valueless…Ours has been the first, and will doubtless be the last, party of whites to visit this profitless locality."

The name **Grand Canyon**, first used on a map in 1868, was popularized by the one-armed Civil War veteran **John Wesley Powell**, whose dramatic 1869 boat trip along the fearsome and uncharted Colorado captured public imagination. Such a trip had long been mooted, but in the words of John Frémont, the legendary "Pathfinder" of the West, "no trappers have been found bold enough to undertake a voyage which has so certain a prospect of a fatal termination".

Powell's ten-man **Colorado River Exploring Expedition** set off from Green River, Wyoming, on May 24, 1869. This was just two weeks after the completion of the transcontinental railroad, which carried his four heavy Whitehall oak rowing boats here from Chicago. Another expedition, led by Thomas Hook, set off a few days later, but was abandoned almost immediately, after Hook drowned in a rapid. Powell himself soon lost one of his boats, but he reached what would become Green River, Utah, on July 13; then the previously unseen confluence of the Green and (larger) Grand rivers, which marks the start of the Colorado, on July 16; and the mouth of the San Juan on July 31. From what's now Lees Ferry, he launched himself into the Grand Canyon on August 5.

It was a gruelling, even nightmarish trip, for which Powell's boats were wholly unsuitable. His crew counted a total of 476 rapids, 62 of which they had to portage – that is, physically carry their boats over the riverside rocks. Eventually, however, the bedraggled, ravenous crew emerged from the canyon on August 29. In a dreadful irony, three members of the party, terrified by the interminable prospect of yet more rapids, had abandoned the river the day before, only to be murdered as they hiked out of Separation Canyon. Their deaths have traditionally been blamed on Native Americans, but compelling recent evidence suggests that they were in fact killed by Mormon settlers.

Powell was both a genuine hero and a consummate self-publicist, who, thanks in part to the acclaim he received for his journals – an unacknowledged amalgam of both this voyage and a second two years later – later became director of both the Bureau of American Ethnology and the US Geological Survey. He returned repeatedly to the canyon with scientific teams, one of which, in 1875, included the artist **Thomas Moran**. Moran's paintings and engravings, and the detailed geological report prepared by **Clarence Dutton** in 1880–81 – which first gave quasi-religious names to the various "temples" and monuments below the rim – did much to place the canyon firmly in the American consciousness.

The growth of tourism

As the Grand Canyon was being recognized as the most extraordinary natural wonder in the US, settlers moved to the vicinity in ever greater numbers. Isolated Mormon communities sprang up across the Arizona Strip, on the plateaus of the North Rim, while pioneers from the east began to stake claims close to the South Rim. There has been tension ever since between this new permanent population, determined to survive in such an unforgiving environment, and visitors hoping to find unspoiled wilderness. Broadly speaking, **logging** and **grazing** interests long retained control of the plateau forests, while in the canyon itself most attempts at **mining** were defeated by the difficult terrain; **tourism** soon proved a far more lucrative proposition.

When the **railroad** first crossed northern Arizona in 1882, visitors were taken by stagecoach from **Peach Springs**, the nearest station to the Grand Canyon, to stay at the *Diamond Creek Hotel* by the river. With the growth of the timber towns to the east, that locality soon declined; by the 1890s, **Flagstaff** was the main terminus, connected to the canyon by three weekly stagecoaches. The railroad reached the canyon itself, via a branch line from **Williams**, in September 1901. That triggered the growth of **Grand Canyon Village**, built under the auspices of the Fred Harvey Company, a subsidiary of the Santa Fe Railroad, and dependent on water carried by rail from Del Rio, 120 miles away. The company's grand *El Tovar* hotel – still the showpiece canyon-edge lodging – opened in January 1905, and its early marketing strategies influence the experience of canyon visitors to this day. Following an internal memo to "get some Indians to the Canyon at once", the company built the Hopi House souvenir store, modelled on the Hopi village of Old Oraibi, and staffed it with Hopi craftspeople. Similarly, the company exhorted Navajo weavers to produce rugs to suit tourist tastes, using previously unfavoured "earth" colours such as brown. Pseudo-Pueblo architecture became the dominant theme, in line with the vision of architect Mary Jane Colter (see p.54).

Late nineteenth-century proposals to create a **Grand Canyon National Park** aroused vigorous local opposition. In due course, however, naturalist **John Muir** – who had earlier championed Yosemite Valley in California and declared the Grand Canyon to be "unearthly…as if you had found it after death, on some other star" – found a powerful ally in **Theodore Roosevelt**. Presidential authority only entitled Roosevelt to protect sites of historical, rather than geological, interest, so he used the pretext of preserving Ancestral Puebloan ruins to proclaim **Grand Canyon National Monument** in 1908. Having failed to persuade the Supreme Court to overrule the president, Arizonan politicians finally came around to the idea of a national park after Arizona achieved statehood in 1912. Even so, by the time the boundaries of the new **Grand Canyon National Park** were fixed in 1919, they had trimmed away large tracts of grazing land. The park encompassed only about 1000 square miles and included just 56 miles of the actual canyon.

Meanwhile, tourism to the South Rim had not stood still. **Ralph Cameron** had been accumulating bogus mining claims along the South Rim since 1890, which enabled him to charge a toll of $1 to riders using the Bright Angel Trail. In 1905, he built his own hotel alongside the railroad terminal, forcing the Fred Harvey Company to relocate the station out of sight of its upstart rival. When the national park came into being, Cameron continued to be a thorn in its side. Elected to the US Senate in 1920, he spent a few years hacking at the park's budget before his mining claims were eventually invalidated. His control of the Bright Angel Trail had by then spurred development of the competing **Kaibab Trail**, which stretches from rim to rim by way of the Kaibab Suspension Bridge. Plans to pave that route never materialized, but a slight enlargement of the park in 1927 permitted the construction of a road east to Desert View, which, with the completion in 1928 of the **Navajo Bridge** across Marble Canyon, reduced what had been a 600-mile drive between the rims to a more feasible 215 miles.

The first **car** showed up at the canyon in 1902, despite running out of gas twenty miles short. By 1926, more visitors were coming by car than by train, and Flagstaff was once again the major point of access, and by 1938, the throngs of visitors necessitated advance reservations for both mule rides and lodging. Annual visitor numbers first exceeded a million in 1956 and ran at over five million through most of the 1990s. Anticipating that visitation would continue to increase at an exponential rate, the Park Service drew up plans around the turn of the millennium to build a **light rail** network and a huge new tourism complex close to the South Rim, to be known as **Canyon Forest Village**. However, visitor numbers have now dropped back below five million – no one really knows why, though the downward trend has continued since the attacks of September 11, 2001 – and the political will to make major changes has disappeared.

Environmental issues

The biggest issues to face the Grand Canyon during the twentieth century centred on the **environment**. The 1935 damming of Black Canyon, just west of the Grand Canyon, by the **Hoover Dam**, inspired a spree of dam-building in the western US. Bureau of Reclamation proposals included damming the Green River in northwest Colorado, the San Juan in New Mexico and the Colorado itself in both Arizona's Bridge Canyon and Utah's Glen Canyon. The axe eventually fell on **Glen Canyon**, which although it had enchanted John Wesley Powell remained almost completely unknown.

The story of the construction of Glen Canyon Dam and creation of Lake Powell is told in full on pp.122–123. Most environmentalists regard it as a disaster, and it's easy to forget that although the Grand Canyon itself has not been dammed, the dam at Glen Canyon has utterly changed the character of the Colorado River and thus the ecology of the inner Grand Canyon. At least no further dams have been built; green activists, for example, halted plans to construct the **Bridge Canyon Dam** on the Hualapai reservation in the 1970s, despite the eagerness of the Hualapai themselves (see p.181).

Commercial **logging** and **mining** were finally banned from the Grand Canyon when the park boundaries were redrawn and enlarged in 1975. President Clinton followed Roosevelt's example in 2000 by using his presidential prerogative to protect two vast enclaves within the overall Grand Canyon ecosystem, proclaiming the 294,000-acre **Vermilion Cliffs National Monument** (see p.128) and the million-acre **Grand Canyon–Parashant National Monument** (see p.144). Fears persist, however, that **uranium mining** may return to areas just outside the park along the South Rim, as evidenced by Havasupai concern over the prospective **Canyon Mine** (see p.170).

Geology

The merest glance at the Grand Canyon reveals that this vast landscape is composed of layer upon layer of different kinds of rock, each with its own distinct colour and texture. Some layers form thin stripes, some sheer cliffs hundreds of feet tall; others vary in width and in places may disappear altogether. Taken as a whole, however, the consistency of these horizontal bands, identifiable throughout the canyon, acts as a reassuring counterpoint to the bewildering complexity of the terrain, with its tangle of buttes, mesas and side canyons.

Geologists often talk of "reading" the various strata like a book, which tells the story not only of the canyon but also of the earth itself. What makes the Grand Canyon such a good read is that it's very rare for such an even, undisturbed set of rock layers to exist so high above sea level, and unique for them to be exposed to view to such an amazing depth. Common sense tells us that the deepest layers are the oldest, and the saga does indeed start at the bottom, almost **two billion** years ago. What's less obvious, however, is that in geological terms the canyon is not old, but very **new**. The processes that put all those buried strata into place were entirely separate from those that created the canyon itself.

At various times, the spot that now holds the Grand Canyon has lain underwater, or at the edge of a very different continent, or even embedded in the planet's one massive supercontinent. As it swirled around the globe, it also spent long periods at the equator. Until less than six million years ago, there was no canyon here. Then the **Colorado Plateau** started to rise, somehow climbing several thousand feet without greatly deforming its thick layers of sedimentary rock, and its many rivers began to cut deeper and deeper.

While scientists still can't decide quite how it happened, the canyon took shape quickly. It had acquired essentially its present form a million years ago, and since then has only burrowed a further fifty feet. Finally, a new phase began in 1963, when completion of the **Glen Canyon Dam** rendered the Colorado River barely capable of maintaining the canyon, let alone enlarging it.

The story in the stone

Almost every rock layer visible from the rim of the Grand Canyon is **sedimentary**, and was originally deposited on the bed or along the shoreline of some shallow primeval sea. Such rocks can be further subdivided into **sandstone**, which consists mostly of sand, perhaps mixed with a little silt or clay, and cemented with silica or calcite; **limestone**, which is largely biological, made up of dead sea creatures and, especially, their shells; and **mudstone** such as shale and siltstone, carried down to the sea by rivers as mountain ranges rise and fall.

There are two other types of rock in the canyon. **Igneous** – fire-formed – rocks well up from the depths of the earth, both in the ocean along the edges of the lithospheric plates that hold the separate continents, and via volcanic action on the surface. **Metamorphic** rocks are those that have been altered by heat and pressure over time, which happens especially when continents collide.

The oldest rocks of all are both igneous and metamorphic. The gnarled, dense tangle of dark rock that's not only exposed at river level, but forms the entire 1000ft-deep **Granite Gorge**, originated with lava flows 1.84 billion years ago (while that makes it old by any standard, the oldest visible rocks on the planet, dating back almost four billion years, lie along the shore of the Great Slave Lake in Canada's Northwest Territories). Around 1.7 billion years ago, when the seabed on which they rested collided with what became the North American continent, those deposits were metamorphosed into what's now known as **Vishnu Schist**, and also became threaded with lighter veins of pink Zoroaster Granite. Life had already established its first tentative foothold on earth during this **Precambrian** era, but no fossils could hope to survive such an inferno of molten rock.

In parts but not all of the canyon, a further medley of both igneous and sedimentary Precambrian rocks lies immediately above the Vishnu Schist. Where it exists, as for example in the vicinity of Desert View, this **Grand Canyon Supergroup** is immediately recognizable, because, unusually for the canyon, the normally horizontal strata are tilted at a twenty-degree angle.

If we think of each layer as being a "page" of the canyon's great geologic textbook, then we have to bear in mind that many pages are missing altogether. Just as there are eras when new strata are being added, there are also periods, like our own, when not only is nothing new being deposited, but pre-existing layers lie exposed to the elements and erode away. Such gaps in the record are known as **unconformities**. The most obvious, dubbed the **Great Unconformity** by John Wesley Powell, is the line that separates the Precambrian rocks of the Inner Gorge from the sedimentary strata of the **Paleozoic** era above. It's especially striking when the Grand Canyon Supergroup is absent, in which case it represents an interlude of a billion years. Far from being unique to this region, the Great Unconformity is a global phenomenon, but nowhere is it more conspicuous than here. From inner-canyon viewpoints such as Ooh Aah Point on the South Kaibab Trail (see p.101), for example, it's readily apparent as an abrupt line close to the top of the Inner Gorge.

During the **Paleozoic epoch**, which lasted from 550 million until 250 million years ago, much of what's now North America was covered by water. The oldest Paleozoic groups consist of three consecutive strata – **Tapeats Sandstone**, **Bright Angel Shale** and **Muav Limestone** – which collectively form the **Tonto Group**, as seen in the broad Tonto Platform at the 4000ft elevation. Each seems to have been deposited in progressively deeper water, which may reflect shifting shorelines, or perhaps higher water levels caused by melting polar ice caps.

Next comes another unconformity, followed by the **Temple Butte Formation** from the **Devonian** era and the distinctive **Redwall Limestone** layer, responsible for the 500ft cliffs that pose such a problem on many inner-canyon trails. Despite its namesake colour, the Redwall is not naturally red, but dyed by leaching from the iron-rich rocks of the thick **Supai Group** above. These mingle limestone, sandstone, shale and siltstone, testifying to an era when the coastline repeatedly rose and fell.

The Paleozoic era ends with a final four-part sequence: the **Hermit Shale**, left by rivers on a coastal plain; the pale **Coconino Sandstone**, the solidified dunes from a windswept ancient desert; the **Toroweap Formation**, a mixture of limestone and shale that once more lay beneath the waves; and the **Kaibab Formation**, a similar but harder blend that tops the canyon rim all the way from Lees Ferry to the heart of the national park.

And there the story stops, roughly 250 million years ago, at which point all the world's landmasses were jammed together to form a giant supercontinent now known as **Pangaea**. Although only the tiniest traces of anything newer survive at the Grand Canyon, it's thought that another four or five thousand feet of rock was deposited on top, during the **Mesozoic** era. Those are the rocks that form the **Navajo Sandstone** of Arizona's spectacular Canyon de Chelly, and the multicoloured shales of the nearby **Painted Desert**. The canyon is rich in marine fossils, but it holds nothing from the age of the dinosaurs, which ended a mere 65 million years ago.

Those final blank pages do hold one last footnote, however. A series of **lava cascades** inundated the western canyon during the last three million years, culminating around 1.2 million years ago when the largest flow created the **Prospect Dam**. That backed up the Colorado into a lake that stretched even further upstream than modern-day Lake Powell, and took around twenty thousand years to erode away. Volcanoes remain active in the vicinity; **Sunset Crater**, near Flagstaff (see p.158), last erupted in 1065.

The power of erosion

The physical mechanisms that have sculpted the Grand Canyon are well understood, not least because they can still be observed in action. All fall under the broad heading of **erosion**, with **water** as the dominant force. Whatever intuition might suggest, however, the Colorado River alone did not carve the canyon. The river only operates at river level, so while it's responsible for the **depth** of the canyon – and continues to scour its way deeper – it did little to create its **width**. The fantastic pyramids and mesas that tower above the central gorge are the result of the interplay of water, wind, gravity, and extreme cycles of heat and cold.

Erosion is often pictured as a gradual process, under which grains of sand tumble one by one from the rim. In fact, the canyon has been shaped to a much greater extent by cataclysmic events, and none more so than **flash floods**. The very fact that the Grand Canyon is located in a desert means that what rain does fall can have a disproportionate impact. There's little soil cover to absorb the monsoon-like thunderstorms that hit the region each year, especially in late July and August. Instead they pour onto bare stone and quickly gather into storm channels that feed in turn into side canyons and the main canyon. Vast quantities of mud and rock are picked up and swept along in these violent upheavals, widening the old routes down to the river and battering out new ones.

An even more fearsome phenomenon is **debris flow**, in which a morass of gravel, stone and sand becomes sufficiently sodden after rains that it begins to flow like concrete. Such flows occur somewhere in the canyon roughly twice every year. One created Crystal Rapid in 1966; another, in Monument Creek in 1984, threw boulders weighing as much 37 tons each into the Colorado.

Subtler activity can produce equally spectacular results. Some of the water that falls as rain or snow finds its way into cracks in the earth. As it subsequently freezes and expands, the water chisels vast slabs of stone away from their moorings, unseen and unsuspected until one day a mighty rockfall shatters the peace of the canyon.

Many of the **side canyons** in which so much of this activity takes place follow courses that were originally created by **earthquakes**, and only later widened by water; seismic action, including the occasional earthquake, still continues. Major cracks include the **Bright Angel Fault**, which made possible the "Corridor" hiking trails between the South and North rims, and the **Toroweap Fault** downstream. The side canyons tend to be so barren and dry that visitors are inclined to think of them as somehow peripheral to the Grand Canyon proper; see them roar into life after a storm, and you'll be in no doubt as to the important part they've played in its creation.

The effects of erosion vary according to the different rock strata. **Cliffs** are usually composed of sandstone or limestone that has been deposited in broad bands and erodes only slowly, whereas **slopes** form from constantly crumbling shales. Assorted combinations of rock, piled up like a layer cake and then eroding at differing speeds, have resulted in the bizarre monuments so conspicuous toward the eastern end of the canyon. Broad, flat, hard-capped **mesas** erode to form smaller **buttes**, taller than they are wide, or potentially the pyramids known at the Grand Canyon as **temples**. It was Clarence Dutton, a student of comparative religion who wrote the first Geological Survey report on the canyon in 1881, who started the custom of naming prominent canyon features – **Brahma Temple**, **Shiva Temple**, **Vishnu Temple**, and so on – for religious architecture. His tradition was followed by later cartographers such as François Matthes, who named **Krishna Shrine** and **Walhalla Plateau**.

To return finally to the Colorado River, even if it hasn't been so very instrumental as an erosive force, the crucial role it *has* played is to carry all the debris away. It would take around a thousand cubic miles of rock to fill in the Grand Canyon as we see it today, and that's how much the Colorado has taken away. Originally, all the debris was deposited towards the river mouth in the Gulf of California, thus renewing the cycle of sedimentation. After 1935, the Colorado set about filling in **Lake Mead**, behind the Hoover Dam. What now worries scientists is that the Colorado simply isn't itself anymore. Flash floods still sweep the side canyons and hurl debris into the river, but the cold steady stream that's allowed through the Glen Canyon Dam no longer experiences surges of its own, and it no longer has the brute strength necessary to clear away the obstacles thrown into its path. Any year now, some new debris flow may create a monster rapid that the river can't remove.

The creation of the canyon

Despite their success in explaining how its building blocks were put in place, and even how they subsequently eroded away again, geologists have yet to agree how the canyon itself came into being. At least they know what set the ball rolling: the **Laramide Orogeny**, which began at the end of the Mesozoic era, 65 million years ago. An "orogeny" is an ongoing period of upheaval and mountain-building; this one, caused when the Pacific plate collided with, and slipped beneath, the North American plate, was primarily responsible for creating the Rocky Mountains, but also had the effect of partially defining the **Colorado Plateau.** Later on, within the last five or six million years, the plateau has been rapidly lifted several thousand feet higher, while its rivers, the Colorado among them, have become incised ever more deeply into the earth.

The crucial mystery, however, is that the Colorado Plateau in the Grand Canyon region is not flat. It's an enormous hill, known as the **Kaibab Plateau** from a Paiute word meaning "mountain with no peak", which slopes southwards from a ridge that runs roughly a dozen miles north of the North Rim, more or less along the national park boundary. Thus the Colorado has eaten away a chunk of the hillside, about a third of the way up the southern slope – which explains why the North Rim is a thousand feet higher than the South. The pivotal point in the course of the modern Colorado comes when it hits the Kaibab Plateau, close to Desert View, and rather than veering away, perhaps to the southeast, turns west instead and cuts directly into the plateau.

Why, or how, the Colorado River slices straight through that hill has long taxed the scientific imagination. The oldest serious theory proposed that the Colorado was what's called an "antecedent" river, which has always followed its modern course, and simply remained in place as the plateau rose around it. A more subtle refinement describes a process of "superposition", suggesting that the river previously ran atop new, even layers of sediment that had smothered the hills and uplifts we see today, and that when the plateau rose, it wore away those upper layers to reveal the hills, including the Kaibab Plateau, that we find so puzzling today. The trouble with both theories is that the Colorado does not predate either the recent uplift, or the canyon; they have all grown up together.

All the hypotheses currently in favour argue for some form of "**stream piracy**", in which the Colorado originally followed some other course, but was later "captured" by another river and began to flow in that direction instead. Such a capture might have occurred when a powerful stream, at the head of its own canyon, eventually cut so far back that it breached the stone barrier that separated it from the Colorado. The Colorado would then rush through, abandoning its own course and usurping this alternative channel.

While it has been shown that until five million years ago, the ancestral Colorado River did indeed skirt the Kaibab Plateau, it's not known in which direction its ultimate destination lay. Suggestions that it used to flow down the gorge of the Little Colorado to meet the Rio Grande have largely been discounted due to lack of evidence, as has the idea that all of northern Arizona's rivers may once have flowed in the opposite direction. It's now thought most likely that the Colorado circled the southern edge of the Kaibab and then continued northwest. As ground levels to the southwest subsided, in tandem with the uplift of the Colorado Plateau, new rivers began to flow down to the Gulf of California. In some long-disappeared spot, one such river eventually captured, and thus became, the Colorado. The Grand Canyon was born.

Flora and fauna

Considering that the Grand Canyon measures almost 300 miles in length, and ranges 8000ft in depth from the highest point on the North Rim to the lowest elevation at Lake Mead, it's hardly surprising that it's home to a tremendous assortment of plant and animal life. Naturally, all share one basic trait: they've adapted to survive in a **desert**, where the low rainfall, of around fifteen inches per year on the South Rim and twice that on the North, ensures that the soil cover is poor where it exists at all. Within these parameters, however, the range of life forms and environments is breathtaking, with such treats in store for visitors as the spectacle of an amazing **California condor** soaring above the rim, and the lush hidden oases that punctuate the cactus-studded plateaus of the inner canyon.

It was at the Grand Canyon, with its clearly stratified layers, that scientists first realized that just as different groups of plants and animals inhabit different latitudes between the equator and the poles, so too are different collections of species found at the various levels of a mountainside or canyon. The crucial factor is, of course, **temperature**. In the canyon, altitude substitutes for latitude; the higher the elevation, the cooler the temperature.

The first scientist to describe and name the distinct **life zones** was Clinton Merriam of the US Biological Survey. After visiting the Grand Canyon in 1889, he announced that its range of habitats corresponded to those encountered in a trip from the deserts of Mexico to the forests of the Canadian mountains. His work remains the basis for accounts of the canyon's wildlife to this day, though, as he pointed out, much more than just elevation determines what will survive where. The temperature at any one spot also varies according to how much direct **sunlight** it receives, which itself depends on the angle of the slope and the direction in which it faces; localized **moisture**, from springs or streams; and how exposed it is to the currents of hot and cold air that rise and fall within the canyon.

Early explorers imagined that miraculous creatures might lurk in the canyon's recesses. Sadly, twentieth-century expeditions disproved tales of tiny horses – finding only some rather stunted and very thirsty ones – and of "lost worlds" atop such lone, isolated summits as Shiva Temple. The canyon does, however, offer some fascinating cases of **divergent evolution**, such as the distinct species of squirrel that inhabits the North and South rims.

The North Rim

At between 8000 and 9000ft above sea level, the highest portions of Grand Canyon National Park, along and just back from the **North Rim**, belong to the **Boreal Zone**. As in the forests of Canada, the tree population here consists largely of **aspen**, **spruce** and **fir**, though higher elevations also hold **Douglas fir** – which is not a true fir but is capable of growing 130ft tall – while **ponderosa pines** appear closer to the rim. Relatively high precipitation has resulted in richer soil, and the dense woodlands of the plateau are interspersed with Alpine **meadows**. These support wildflowers such as asters and sunflowers and also hold burrowing creatures like weasels and voles, which in turn attract their own predators.

In the hundred years since Theodore Roosevelt first protected it within a national monument, the ecology of the North Rim has been particularly affected by Park Service attempts at management. The long-standing policy of suppressing

wildfires has had an adverse effect on the ponderosas. Without the natural fires that should sweep through regularly to eliminate needles and brush from the forest floor, debris accumulates to levels where it can fuel a major conflagration that burns long enough to kill the pines. In recent years, the park has moved towards allowing natural fires to blaze away – even though the charred landscape spoils the look of the place for visitors – and also setting its own "controlled burns".

A notorious example of early **wildlife management** techniques centres on the **mule deer** of the North Rim. Roosevelt's priority in "protecting" the deer was to preserve them for the sport of hunters such as himself. Natural predators like mountain lions, wolves and coyotes were therefore to be eliminated; a single warden, James Owens, shot 532 lions in twelve years. History has long recorded that the deer population then mushroomed from four thousand to a hundred thousand and stripped the Kaibab Plateau bare before starving to death en masse during the winter of 1924–25. Although those figures are now being questioned, with scientists suggesting that such boom-and-bust cycles may be a normal feature of wild deer herds, the Park Service has abandoned the idea of culling predators, and hunting is no longer permitted. The wolves never returned – and as yet, there's been no move to reintroduce them, as at Yellowstone – but there are now thought to be around a hundred lions on the North Rim, as well as plentiful coyote.

The South Rim

A thousand feet lower than the North Rim, the **South Rim** is in what's called the **Transitional Zone**. Here spruce and fir give way to **ponderosa pines**, interspersed with such species as **Gambel oak**, the only tree to lose its leaves in winter amid all the canyon's evergreens.

The largest inhabitants of the ponderosa forest are **elk**, for which the only pure ponderosa stand on the South Rim itself, near Grandview Point, is a favoured haunt. Among smaller species, which include skunks, chipmunks, rabbits and porcupines, perhaps the most ubiquitous is the **Abert's squirrel**, which exists in mutual dependence with the ponderosa, eating its bark, pollen and seeds; by failing to find all the seeds it buries, the squirrel unwittingly plants new generations of trees. In the best-known instance of how distinct species have evolved on opposite sides of the canyon, the corresponding **Kaibab squirrel** is only found on the North Rim. Once the river separated these two populations, no further interbreeding could take place. Both species have tasselled ears, but the Abert's squirrel has a reddish back and a dark tail with a white underbelly, while the Kaibab squirrel is dark grey with a white bushy tail.

Below the ponderosas comes the stunted **"pygmy forest"** of **piñon** (also spelled pinyon) pine and Utah **juniper** that's characteristic of the **Upper Sonoran Zone**, which starts above the rim on the South Rim but beneath it on the North Rim. Each of these gnarled, desiccated trees, which grow to between 20 and 30ft and live for hundreds of years, depends for survival on its own attendant **bird** species. The piñon jay harvests and buries nuts from the piñon, while the Townsend's solitaire eats juniper berries and then excretes the seeds they contain.

Just to illustrate that the demarcation lines between these various zones seldom strictly follow map contours, small groups of Douglas firs, normally found at much higher elevations, can be seen in north-facing alcoves below the South Rim, while if you hike down from the North Rim, you'll find that ponderosa reappear at cooler spots below the piñon-juniper level.

The inner canyon

As the piñon-juniper forest thrives at elevations between approximately 7500ft and 4000ft, it extends far below the rim on both sides of the canyon. While the plant and animal life of the inner canyon remains within the broad category of the Upper Sonoran Zone as far down as the Tonto Platform, the piñon and juniper are progressively replaced by even drier species as conditions become hotter.

First come the **prickly pear** cacti so noticeable on the Bright Angel Trail and flowering shrubs such as cliff rose and Apache plume. Soon the landscape is dominated by desert scrub, particularly **blackbrush**, so named because its stems turn a deep black when wet. The Tonto Platform is also scattered with agave, yucca and mesquite. Small **mammals** like mice and shrews are abundant, though as most are nocturnal, visitors rarely spot them. Snakes, too, come out at night, most notably the pink-hued and poisonous **Grand Canyon rattlesnake**, which is endemic to the inner canyon (two distinct but related species are to be found along either rim: the Hopi rattlesnake atop the South Rim and the Great Basin rattlesnake on the north side).

Around five hundred **desert bighorn sheep**, which grow up to 6ft in length, inhabit remote side canyons. Because no domestic sheep have ever been introduced into the region, this remains a remarkably pristine population, free from the imported diseases that have decimated bighorn numbers elsewhere in the West. For many years, they shared their range with wild descendants of **donkeys** released by prospectors around 1900, but few donkeys remain. To protect grazing for the bighorn, the Park Service killed thousands of burros, and eventually, after protests from wildlife campaigners, airlifted the rest out by helicopter in 1980.

Wherever **water** is present in the inner canyon, the picture becomes very different. Majestic **willows** and **cottonwoods** line natural springs and tributary streams such as Bright Angel Creek; **hummingbirds** and **canyon wrens** dart through the air; mosses and maidenhair ferns cling to damp crevices; and there are even **tree frogs**, preyed upon by skunks and raccoons.

The **Lower Sonoran Zone**, which starts below the Tonto Platform, is home to the very hardiest of desert survivors. Hikers along the central Corridor Trails experience little of this world, as where the sheer walls of the Inner Gorge are breached at all, it's usually by watercourses that have their own microenvironments. Towards the western end of the canyon, however, where elevations are lower and broad, dry side canyons reach right to the river, the flora and fauna are significantly different. Sadly, you won't encounter anything as distinctive as the multi-armed saguaro cacti found in the Sonoran Desert of southern Arizona, but many characteristic species are present, including **scorpions**, **king snakes**, large brown lizards known as **chuckwallas** and **kangaroo rats**, which are so finely adapted to the desert that they never need to drink.

The Colorado River

The banks of the Colorado form a **riparian** environment of the kind described above, lined with rich vegetation, alive with insects and amphibians and a magnet for whole echelons of predators. However, the river is now the least natural part of the canyon; nowhere in the Grand Canyon has human impact had a more dramatic effect.

The Colorado today is a very different creature to the river that flowed through the canyon before the completion of the **Glen Canyon Dam** in 1963. It used to range in temperature from close to freezing in winter up to as much as 80°F (27°C) in summer. Now it remains a chilly, unvarying 48°F (9°C) year round. What's more, where formerly the river was charged with colossal quantities of silt and subject to massive floods, it now runs almost crystal-clear at flow rates that fluctuate within a much more limited spectrum, according to the demand for electricity from the dam.

The effect of those changes has been to eliminate four of the canyon's eight native **fish** species, including the 6ft **squawfish**, and leave the remainder barely clinging to life. The once ubiquitous **humpback chub** can now only find the murky waters it requires for spawning by swimming up the Little Colorado River. It has been supplanted, and often literally eaten, by species introduced for sport, such as **rainbow trout**, **carp** and **striped bass**. **Crayfish** too, introduced as food for the trout, are now thriving, while **bald eagles** have turned up to prey on the trout in turn.

Before the dam went up, regular flooding ensured that the banks of the Colorado were unable to sustain growth below the high-water mark. Now they've become lined by coyote willow trees and almost taken over by alien **tamarisk**. Many riverside beaches have disappeared altogether, as sand that's swept away by the river can't be replaced by the silt that now settles instead to the bottom of Lake Powell. Since 1966, three **artificial floods** have been engineered in the canyon by simply turning up the valves at the dam for short periods. They have succeeded in briefly regenerating several beaches, and disrupting non-native species, but such effects have so far failed to last more than six months.

Books

The books listed below proved useful, interesting, or entertaining during the writing of this guide. Many are only available in the US, and most you'd be lucky to find in bookstores anywhere outside the immediate vicinity of the Grand Canyon.

Richard Abanes *One Nation Under Gods*. Polemic but fascinating account of Mormon history from an unyielding Christian perspective, which documents some very murky goings-on during the nineteenth century.

Donald L. Baars *A Traveler's Guide to the Geology of the Colorado Plateau*. Among the more readily comprehensible explanations of the geology of the Grand Canyon and Four Corners region.

Bruce Babbitt (ed) *Grand Canyon: An Anthology*. A collection of classic canyon writing, put together in 1978, which includes first-hand exploration accounts from centuries past, as well as entertaining, seldom-seen pieces by the likes of Theodore Roosevelt and J.B. Priestley. Well worth seeking out.

Elias Butler and Tom Myers *Grand Obsession: Harvey Butchart and the Exploration of Grand Canyon*. The fascinating story of the maths professor whose lifelong passion for the canyon blazed the trail for every modern hiker.

Pedro de Castañeda *The Journey of Coronado*. An invaluable historic document; the journals of a Spaniard who accompanied Coronado into the Southwest in 1540, including the first written report of the Grand Canyon.

Richard O. Clemmer *Roads in the Sky*. A history of the Hopi, with an emphasis on the twentieth century and the role of prophecy.

Christopher M. Coder *An Introduction to Grand Canyon Prehistory*; **Rose Houk** *An Introduction to Grand Canyon Ecology*; **L. Greer Price** *An Introduction to Grand Canyon Geology*. These three slim, very readable and beautifully illustrated volumes, sold individually or as a discounted set in the national park bookstores, jointly form an ideal introduction to the canyon.

Edward Dolnick *Down The Great Unknown*. Deft retelling of the saga of John Wesley Powell's first canyon voyage that takes great pains to make it all intelligible to modern readers, with a thick and fast flow of analogies.

Colin Fletcher *The Man Who Walked Through Time*. Enjoyable account by the first man to hike the full length of the Grand Canyon.

Richard Flint *No Settlement, No Conquest*. Published in 2008, a satisfying and accessible overview of current knowledge about Coronado's epochal expedition, from an author who's written and edited several more academic volumes.

Philip L. Fradkin *A River No More*. The story of the Colorado River, from John Wesley Powell to the water-management issues of today.

Michael P. Ghiglieri *Canyon*. A highly experienced river guide reveals the lore of the Colorado River, mile by mile; an enjoyable read, even if he tells a bit more about his personal life than many might prefer.

Michael P. Ghiglieri and Thomas M. Myers *Over The Edge: Death in Grand Canyon*. In their bid to account for the demise of every single person known to have died within the Grand Canyon, the authors transcend the merely morbid to throw fascinating light on every aspect of the canyon's history, and provide masses of useful advice on how to avoid becoming another fatality. The morbid stuff's good too.

J. Donald Hughes *In The House of Stone and Light*. A comprehensive human history of the Grand Canyon in words and pictures, filled with fascinating yarns about the early days of tourism.

Robert H. Keller and Michael F. Turek *American Indians and National Parks*. What happens when the federal park system appropriates land from its former indigenous inhabitants; the Grand Canyon and Pipe Spring National Monument are among examples considered in great detail.

John D. Lee *Mormonism Unveiled*. In his "Life and Confession", John Lee, of Lees Ferry fame, doesn't quite tell all he knows – like where he buried the gold – but there's a lot of eye-opening material in here.

Raymond Friday Locke *The Book of the Navajo*. Comprehensive history of the Navajo, from their mythic origins to the present day.

Russell Martin *A Story That Stands Like A Dam*. Meticulously chronicled indictment of the West's last great dam, which inundated Glen Canyon in the 1960s.

Lisa Michaels *Grand Ambition*. Gripping novelistic reconstruction of a true-life romantic mystery: just what did happen to honeymooners Glen and Bessie Hyde in the winter of 1928, when they tried to become the first couple to row down the Grand Canyon?

Barbara J. Morehouse *A Place Called Grand Canyon*. Fascinating academic analysis of how the canyon has been defined and exploited.

Stephen Plog *Ancient Peoples of the Southwest*. Probably the best single-volume history of the pre-Hispanic

Southwest, packed with diagrams and colour photographs.

James Lawrence Powell *Dead Pool*. This latterday Powell (no relation) brings the story of his namesake lake bang up to date, and explores the future of water in the West.

John Wesley Powell *The Exploration of the Colorado River and Its Canyons*. Major Powell certainly embellished his original journals in adapting the details of his first epic journey down the Colorado for public consumption, but they still make exhilarating reading.

Stephen J. Pyne *How the Canyon Became Grand*. Historical analysis of how the canyon has been perceived over the centuries, with particular reference to the artists of the late Victorian era. Some of the ideas are intriguing, even if the prose style isn't.

Wayne Ranney *Carving Grand Canyon*. An up-to-the-minute, well-illustrated overview of how geologists have attempted to explain the formation of the canyon.

Marc Reisner *Cadillac Desert*. The definitive, damning saga of the twentieth-century damming of the West.

Jeremy Schmidt *Grand Canyon National Park: A Natural History Guide*. A superb single-volume account of the canyon's environment, ecology and geologic origins.

Stephen Trimble *The People*. Excellent introduction to all the Native American groups of the Southwest, bringing the history up to date with contemporary interviews.

Stewart L. Udall *Majestic Journey*. Lively, well-illustrated chronicle of Francisco Coronado's 1540–42 *entrada* into the Southwest, written by a former US Secretary of the Interior.

John C. Van Dyke *The Grand Canyon of the Colorado*. First published in 1920,

Van Dyke's work represents a determined attempt to apply academic rigour to developing a new aesthetic for appreciating the canyon; it's more interesting than it sounds.

Ted J. Warner (ed) *The Domínguez-Escalante Journal*. The extraordinary diary of the two Franciscan friars who crossed Utah in 1776 in search of a new route to California and came back via the Grand Canyon (see p.130).

Frank Waters *The Book of the Hopi*. As authoritative an account of Hopi religion as it's possible to find, though it's said that Waters' informants were not themselves initiated into all the secrets of the *kiva*.

Richard White *It's Your Misfortune and None of My Own*. Dense, authoritative and all-embracing history of the American West that debunks the notion of the rugged pioneer by stressing the role of the federal government.

Charles Wilkinson *Fire on the Plateau*. This authoritative examination of the recent history of the Colorado Plateau is good on environmental and legal issues, but a bit heavy on personal reminiscence. *Between Sacred Mountains* is a superb overview of Navajo history, culture and politics, written by Navajo teachers and parents as a sourcebook for Navajo students.

Travel store

Travel

Andorra The Pyrenees, Pyrenees & Andorra Map, Spain
Antigua The Caribbean
Argentina Argentina, Argentina Map, Buenos Aires, South America on a Budget
Aruba The Caribbean
Australia Australia, Australia Map, East Coast Australia, Melbourne, Sydney, Tasmania
Austria Austria, Europe on a Budget, Vienna
Bahamas The Bahamas, The Caribbean
Barbados Barbados DIR, The Caribbean
Belgium Belgium & Luxembourg, Bruges DIR, Brussels, Brussels Map, Europe on a Budget
Belize Belize, Central America on a Budget, Guatemala & Belize Map
Benin West Africa
Bolivia Bolivia, South America on a Budget
Brazil Brazil, Rio, South America on a Budget
British Virgin Islands The Caribbean
Brunei Malaysia, Singapore & Brunei [1 title], Southeast Asia on a Budget
Bulgaria Bulgaria, Europe on a Budget
Burkina Faso West Africa
Cambodia Cambodia, Southeast Asia on a Budget, Vietnam, Laos & Cambodia Map [1 Map]
Cameroon West Africa
Canada Canada, Pacific Northwest, Toronto, Toronto Map, Vancouver
Cape Verde West Africa
Cayman Islands The Caribbean
Chile Chile, Chile Map, South America on a Budget
China Beijing, China,

Hong Kong & Macau, Hong Kong & Macau DIR, Shanghai
Colombia South America on a Budget
Costa Rica Central America on a Budget, Costa Rica, Costa Rica & Panama Map
Croatia Croatia, Croatia Map, Europe on a Budget
Cuba Cuba, Cuba Map, The Caribbean, Havana
Cyprus Cyprus, Cyprus Map
Czech Republic The Czech Republic, Czech & Slovak Republics, Europe on a Budget, Prague, Prague DIR, Prague Map
Denmark Copenhagen, Denmark, Europe on a Budget, Scandinavia
Dominica The Caribbean
Dominican Republic Dominican Republic, The Caribbean
Ecuador Ecuador, South America on a Budget
Egypt Egypt, Egypt Map
El Salvador Central America on a Budget
England Britain, Camping in Britain, Devon & Cornwall, Dorset, Hampshire and The Isle of Wight [1 title], England, Europe on a Budget, The Lake District, London, London DIR, London Map, London Mini Guide, Walks In London & Southeast England
Estonia The Baltic States, Europe on a Budget
Fiji Fiji
Finland Europe on a Budget, Finland, Scandinavia
France Brittany & Normandy, Corsica, Corsica Map, The Dordogne & the Lot, Europe on a Budget, France, France Map, Languedoc & Roussillon, The Loire, Paris, Paris DIR,

Paris Map, Paris Mini Guide, Provence & the Côte d'Azur, The Pyrenees, Pyrenees & Andorra Map
French Guiana South America on a Budget
Gambia The Gambia, West Africa
Germany Berlin, Berlin Map, Europe on a Budget, Germany, Germany Map
Ghana West Africa
Gibraltar Spain
Greece Athens Map, Crete, Crete Map, Europe on a Budget, Greece, Greece Map, Greek Islands, Ionian Islands
Guadeloupe The Caribbean
Guatemala Central America on a Budget, Guatemala, Guatemala & Belize Map
Guinea West Africa
Guinea-Bissau West Africa
Guyana South America on a Budget
Holland see The Netherlands
Honduras Central America on a Budget
Hungary Budapest, Europe on a Budget, Hungary
Iceland Iceland, Iceland Map
India Goa, India, India Map, Kerala, Rajasthan, Delhi & Agra [1 title], South India, South India Map
Indonesia Bali & Lombok, Southeast Asia on a Budget
Ireland Dublin DIR, Dublin Map, Europe on a Budget, Ireland, Ireland Map
Israel Jerusalem
Italy Europe on a Budget, Florence DIR, Florence & Siena Map, Florence & the best of Tuscany, Italy, The Italian Lakes, Naples & the Amalfi Coast, Rome, Rome DIR, Rome Map, Sardinia, Sicily, Sicily Map, Tuscany & Umbria, Tuscany Map,

Venice, Venice DIR, Venice Map
Jamaica Jamaica, The Caribbean
Japan Japan, Tokyo
Jordan Jordan
Kenya Kenya, Kenya Map
Korea Korea
Laos Laos, Southeast Asia on a Budget, Vietnam, Laos & Cambodia Map [1 Map]
Latvia The Baltic States, Europe on a Budget
Lithuania The Baltic States, Europe on a Budget
Luxembourg Belgium & Luxembourg, Europe on a Budget
Malaysia Malaysia Map, Malaysia, Singapore & Brunei [1 title], Southeast Asia on a Budget
Mali West Africa
Malta Malta & Gozo DIR
Martinique The Caribbean
Mauritania West Africa
Mexico Baja California, Baja California, Cancún & Cozumel DIR, Mexico, Mexico Map, Yucatán, Yucatán Peninsula Map
Monaco France, Provence & the Côte d'Azur
Montenegro Montenegro
Morocco Europe on a Budget, Marrakesh DIR, Marrakesh Map, Morocco, Morocco Map,
Nepal Nepal
Netherlands Amsterdam, Amsterdam DIR, Amsterdam Map, Europe on a Budget, The Netherlands
Netherlands Antilles The Caribbean
New Zealand New Zealand, New Zealand Map

DIR: Rough Guide **DIRECTIONS** for short breaks

Available from all good bookstores

For more information go to www.roughguides.com

Visit us online

www.roughguides.com

Information on over 25,000 destinations around the world

- **Read** Rough Guides' trusted travel info
- **Access** exclusive articles from Rough Guides authors
- **Update** yourself on new books, maps, CDs and other products
- **Enter** our competitions and win travel prizes
- **Share** ideas, journals, photos & travel advice with other users
- **Earn** points every time you contribute to the Rough Guide
  community and get rewards

BROADEN YOUR HORIZONS

Small print and

Index

A Rough Guide to Rough Guides

Published in 1982, the first Rough Guide – to Greece – was a student scheme that became a publishing phenomenon. Mark Ellingham, a recent graduate in English from Bristol University, had been travelling in Greece the previous summer and couldn't find the right guidebook. With a small group of friends he wrote his own guide, combining a highly contemporary, journalistic style with a thoroughly practical approach to travellers' needs.

The immediate success of the book spawned a series that rapidly covered dozens of destinations. And, in addition to impecunious backpackers, Rough Guides soon acquired a much broader and older readership that relished the guides' wit and inquisitiveness as much as their enthusiastic, critical approach and value-for-money ethos.

These days, Rough Guides include recommendations from shoestring to luxury and cover more than 200 destinations around the globe, including almost every country in the Americas and Europe, more than half of Africa and most of Asia and Australasia. Our ever-growing team of authors and photographers is spread all over the world, particularly in Europe, the US and Australia.

In the early 1990s, Rough Guides branched out of travel, with the publication of Rough Guides to World Music, Classical Music and the Internet. All three have become benchmark titles in their fields, spearheading the publication of a wide range of books under the Rough Guide name.

Including the travel series, Rough Guides now number more than 350 titles, covering: phrasebooks, waterproof maps, music guides from Opera to Heavy Metal, reference works as diverse as Conspiracy Theories and Shakespeare, and popular culture books from iPods to Poker. Rough Guides also produce a series of more than 120 World Music CDs in partnership with World Music Network.

Visit www.roughguides.com to see our latest publications.

Rough Guide credits

Text editor: Alison Roberts
Layout: Ajay Verma
Cartography: Animesh Pathak
Picture editor: Natascha Sturny
Production: Louise Daly
Proofreader: Amanda Jones
Cover design: Nicole Newman, Dan May
Photographer: Greg Ward
Editorial: London Andy Turner, Keith Drew, Edward Aves, Alice Park, Lucy White, Jo Kirby, James Smart, Natasha Foges, James Rice, Emma Beatson, Emma Gibbs, Kathryn Lane, Monica Woods, Mani Ramaswamy, Harry Wilson, Lucy Cowie, Lara Kavanagh, Eleanor Aldridge, Ian Blenkinsop, Joe Staines, Matthew Milton, Tracy Hopkins; **Delhi** Madhavi Singh, Jalpreen Kaur Chhatwal, Jubbi Francis
Design & Pictures: London Scott Stickland, Dan May, Diana Jarvis, Mark Thomas, Nicole Newman,

Sarah Cummins; **Delhi** Umesh Aggarwal, Jessica Subramanian, Ankur Guha, Pradeep Thapliyal, Sachin Tanwar, Anita Singh, Nikhil Agarwal, Sachin Gupta
Production: Rebecca Short, Liz Cherry, Erika Pepe
Cartography: London Ed Wright, Katie Lloyd-Jones; **Delhi** Rajesh Chhibber, Ashutosh Bharti, Rajesh Mishra, Jasbir Sandhu, Swati Handoo, Deshpal Dabas, Lokamata Sahu
Marketing, Publicity & roughguides.com: Liz Statham
Digital Travel Publisher: Peter Buckley
Reference Director: Andrew Lockett
Operations Coordinator: Becky Doyle
Operations Assistant: Johanna Wurm
Publishing Director (Travel): Clare Currie
Commercial Manager: Gino Magnotta
Managing Director: John Duhigg

Publishing information

This third edition published May 2011 by
Rough Guides Ltd,
80 Strand, London WC2R 0RL
11, Community Centre, Panchsheel Park, New Delhi 110017, India

Distributed by the Penguin Group

Penguin Books Ltd,
80 Strand, London WC2R 0RL

Penguin Group (USA)
375 Hudson Street, NY 10014, USA

Penguin Group (Australia)
250 Camberwell Road, Camberwell, Victoria 3124, Australia

Penguin Group (NZ)
67 Apollo Drive, Mairangi Bay, Auckland 1310, New Zealand

Rough Guides is represented in Canada by Tourmaline Editions Inc. 662 King Street West, Suite 304, Toronto, Ontario M5V 1M7

Cover concept by Peter Dyer.

Typeset in Bembo and Helvetica to an original design by Henry Iles.

Printed in Singapore
© Greg Ward 2011
Maps © Rough Guides
No part of this book may be reproduced in any form without permission from the publisher except for the quotation of brief passages in reviews.
232pp includes index
A catalogue record for this book is available from the British Library
ISBN: 978-1-84836-744-9
The publishers and authors have done their best to ensure the accuracy and currency of all the information in **The Rough Guide to the Grand Canyon**, however, they can accept no responsibility for any loss, injury, or inconvenience sustained by any traveller as a result of information or advice contained in the guide.

1   3   5   7   9   8   6   4   2

MIX
Paper from responsible sources
FSC™ C018179

Help us update

We've gone to a lot of effort to ensure that the third edition of **The Rough Guide to the Grand Canyon** is accurate and up-to-date. However, things change – places get "discovered", opening hours are notoriously fickle, restaurants and rooms raise prices or lower standards. If you feel we've got it wrong or left something out, we'd like to know, and if you can remember the address, the price, the hours, the phone number, so much the better.

Please send your comments with the subject line "**Rough Guide to the Grand Canyon Update**" to ✉ mail@uk.roughguides.com. We'll credit all contributions and send a copy of the next edition (or any other Rough Guide if you prefer) for the very best emails.

Find more travel information, connect with fellow travellers and book your trip on ⊛ www.roughguides.com

Acknowledgements

Greg Ward would like to thank Sam for the whole caboodle with no kerfuffle, and everyone at Rough Guides, especially Alison Roberts for her dedication to producing the best guide possible. And thanks to everyone in Arizona who helped this time around, especially Allan Affeldt, Darla Cook, Robert Graff, Daisy Hobbs, Mona Mesereau, Marina Nicola and Mandi Walsh.

Readers' letters

Thanks to all the readers who have taken the time to write in with comments and suggestions (and apologies if we've inadvertently omitted or misspelt anyone's name):

Jon Cope and Marc Norton.

Photo credits

Index

Map entries are in colour.

X

Y